Also available by these authors

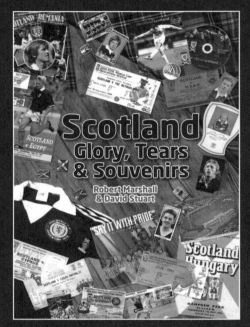

9781785313318

Scotland – Glory, Tears & Souvenirs is an offbeat collection of memories, mementos, rants and aspirations relating to Scotland's national football team. A 'look back in hunger' on the post-war era, with emphasis on the 1970s to date. A reminder of the way football was, the way it is now and the way we'd like it to be!

Scotland
Club, Country
& Collectables

This book is dedicated to the dedicated
— past, present and future...
and anywhere in between.

Scotland
Club, Country
& Collectables

David Stuart
& Robert Marshall

ANDY GRAY
Scotland

Glasgow born striker who made 62 League appearances for Dundee United and scored 36 goals, before transferring to First Division Aston Villa. In 1977 he was voted Player of the Year and Young Player of the Year, and he scored 54 goals in 113 League matches for his club. This outstanding 26 year old forward went into the record books when he was involved in a £1,500,000 transfer to First Division Wolverhampton Wanderers for whom he scored the winning goal in the 1980 League Cup Final against Nottingham Forest. He has now scored 4 goals in 14 international appearances for Scotland.

LIPTON

Pitch Publishing Ltd
A2 Yeoman Gate
Yeoman Way
Durrington
BN13 3QZ

Email: info@pitchpublishing.co.uk
Web: www.pitchpublishing.co.uk

First published by Pitch Publishing 2019
Text © 2019 Robert Marshall and David Stuart

A CIP catalogue record for this book is available from the British Library.

13-digit ISBN: 9781785315459
Design and typesetting by Olner Pro Sport Media.
Printed in India by Replika Press.

INTRODUCTION

Just when you thought it was safe again to go back inside a quality bookshop, along comes another offbeat soccer hardback (or football annual for grown-ups) from David Stuart and Robert Marshall, Scottish football writing's answer to Ernest Hemingway and Mary Shelley.

Hemingway drew much of his inspiration from living and drinking in the pulsating city of Havana in pre-Castro Cuba, and similarly David Stuart gets island inspiration writing and bevvying in the throbbing, edgy metropolis that is pre-independence Rothesay, Isle of Bute.

With the football fanzine entitled *Scotland Epistles, Bullshit and Thistles* Robert Marshall created a Frankenstein-like monster, whilst some of his Scotland away trips have also been gothic horror stories.

Anyway, hopefully you purchased and enjoyed our earlier tome from 2017 – *Scotland: Glory, Tears and Souvenirs*. *Scotland: Club, Country and Collectables* is part sequel to the aforementioned masterpiece (ahem) and part celebration of Scotland co-hosting (and participating in?) the 2020 European Football Championships.

We are two Tartan Army optimists (possibly in need of optometrists) who are continuing our sideways view of everything and anything relating to Scotland's national football teams but with an emphasis on how our clubs have contributed to the cause – not just the likes of Celtic, Rangers, Liverpool and Manchester United, but real *giants* such as Airdrie, Clyde, Motherwell, Partick Thistle and St Mirren.

However, whilst we express our appreciation of Don Revie's Scots colony at Leeds United and the dark blues who graced Stamford Bridge over the years, we also say thanks for the mementoes – the Corinthian minifigures of Gary McAllister

and Don Hutchison, the match badges (stinking or otherwise), the Caribbean postage stamps 'deifying' Scotland World Cup squads and the replica strips which just defy belief! There's no limit to the amount of factoids, trivia and junk, sorry, precious football souvenirs, that we hold on to and want to share with you.

Like before, we have done our utmost to make sure that the contents are factually correct – however, if you do spot any errors, we apologise and ask that you don't tell the publishers – a quiet word in our ear (or a bit of friendly stick on Facebook) will suffice.

So please enjoy, cherish and preserve this latest literary love affair with the 'Great Underachievers' and thank *you* for *your* support.

David and Robert

Danny McGrain challenges Brazilian full-back, Rivelino during a friendly defeat at Hampden Park, 30 June 1973

JOHN ROBERTSON
Scotland

By the end of the 1980/1 Season, this attacking midfielder had scored 53 goals in 316 League matches for his only club First Division Nottingham Forest. Now 29 years of age he has helped his team achieve victory in the League Championship, League Cup, European Cup and Super Cup. As Scotland's penalty expert, he made his international debut in 1978 against Northern Ireland and in 19 appearances for his country he has scored 6 goals, 4 of which were from the penalty spot.

KEY FEATURES

- An overview of football clubs [big and small, Scottish and English] which gives a flavour of the player contributions they have made to Scotland's international adventures

- An offbeat glance at Scotland's ongoing quest to win a major competition – or even qualify for one! Euro 2020 beckons

- A humorous look at a whole plethora of associated aspects of Scottish international football from statistical overviews, schadenfreude and weltschmerz to football collectables, personal experiences and nostalgic memories of a couple of supporters who actually enjoy suffering for the cause

- Extensive use of mostly colour images from the authors' own varied collections of football memorabilia

PART ONE: THE CLUBS

'No Again.....!'

51

- Stuart McKimmie
- ⭐ 27
- Aberdeen (S)

500,000

THE ALL-TIME GREATS

SCOTLAND

BILLY McNEILL
Defender   1961–72

PART TWO: AN ALTERNATIVE A TO Z

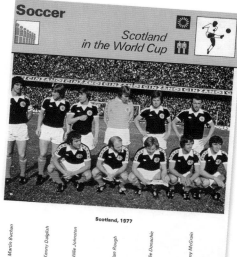

Scotland, 1977

ABERDEEN
The pride of Scotland

The emergence of Aberdeen as one of Scotland's leading club sides was confirmed last season when they took the Premier Division title. To emphasise their current stature, they now have 17 Scottish internationals on their books at Pittodrie.

BACK ROW (left to right): Neale Simpson (youth), Neale Cooper (youth), Alex McLeish (full), Jim Leighton (under 21), Bryan Gunn (youth), Bobby Clark (full), Dougie Bell (under 21), Mark McGhee (under 21), Drew Jarvie (full). FRONT ROW: Andy Watson (under 21), Stuart Kennedy (full), Alan Lyons (schoolboy), Willie Miller (full), Gordon Strachan (full), Eric Black (youth), Andy Dornan (under 21), John Hewitt (under 21).

SHOOT!

ABERDEEN

From the late 1970s through to the 90s it seemed as though every Scotland side had to have at least a couple of Aberdeen players involved. It hadn't always been thus although some of those early players did make their mark, not necessarily in caps and goals but in other unique ways.

Founded in 1903 it would only be five years before winger William Lennie was picked for Scotland for British Championship games versus Wales and Ireland in 1908, scoring the winner in the former. Donald Colman would be capped four times between 1911 and 1913 but he is better known for being the man responsible for the concept of the 'dugout'. As Aberdeen coach he was quite innovative in studying players' feet and their movement. To study this further during actual matches he devised the dugout – a sheltered area beneath pitch level in order to view this more clearly. The dugout has come a long

Alex Jackson of Aberdeen, Huddersfield, Chelsea and Scotland, one of the finest right-wingers in the history of the game. Jackson was a member of Scotland's never-to-be-forgotten 'Wembley Wizards' forward line of 1927–28 which crushed England 5–1.

Alex Jackson

way since. Incidentally, Donald's great-granddaughter Rachel Corsie has captained the Scotland women's football team in recent years.

Another winger, Alex Jackson, was capped three times as an Aberdeen player in the mid-1920s but would win a further 14 as a Chelsea player and indeed would be one of the 'Wembley Wizards' of 1928. Alex Cheyne, capped in 1929/30, is credited as the man who is responsible for the 'Hampden Roar', when with the annual fixture against England in 1929 tied at 0–0 and Scotland down to ten men, the crowd began to urge the home side on to victory with the noise gradually getting louder and louder. Cheyne would score direct from a corner kick (a speciality of his) in the 89th minute to give Scotland victory and indeed the British Championship, and so the 'Roar' was born; however, there are other claims as to the origin of this sporting phenomenon. Alex won five caps in total netting

Scotland v. England, 1929. Alec Cheyne's late winning goal direct from a corner-kick. Hughie Gallacher is ready to acclaim it.

Archie Glen (Aberdeen), leads out the Scotland 'B' Team at Dens Park

The 1960s and early 70s would see some more 'bit players', in the likes of Jim Forrest, Jimmy Smith and Davie Robb, being capped. However, Bobby Clark would gain his first cap in 1967 (against Wales in a British Championship/Euro qualifier double-header) and would stand between the sticks for 17 games in total. The 1974 World Cup finals would, however, only see ex-Aberdeen skipper Martin Buchan called up to the squad. Buchan gained the first two of his 34 caps at Pittodrie with the rest coming at Manchester United.

By 1978, things were beginning to change. Ally MacLeod had taken over the reins of the Scotland national side and Alex Ferguson took up his vacated seat at Aberdeen. MacLeod would take three Dons players on the Argentina adventure: veteran goalkeeper Bobby Clark, striker Joe Harper and full-back Stuart Kennedy. Kennedy would play in two of the matches in Argentina and somewhat controversially, Joe Harper would come on in the 73rd minute of the match versus Iran (as a replacement for Kenny Dalglish) whilst all of Scotland was screaming for in-form striker Derek Johnstone to be brought on.

BOBBY CLARK
Aberdeen

four goals. Also of note prior to World War II would be Benny Yorston – although capped only the once, against Ireland in 1931, he would be followed in that by his nephew Harry who would be capped once, versus Wales, in 1954.

The post-war years of the late 1940s and 50s would be a great, footballing boom time in Scotland, for not only would we see some of the biggest crowds ever to amass at football stadiums but also a variety of league champions, including Rangers, Celtic, Hibs, Hearts and Aberdeen.

Aberdeen would clinch the title in season 1954/55 and several players from the side would play for the national team, including Graham Leggat who would go on to forge a career in England with Fulham. Then there is the unfortunate Fred Martin. Goalkeeper Fred would travel to the World Cup finals in Switzerland in 1954, which started off with a narrow 1–0 defeat to Austria. However, Martin, like the rest of the Scotland side, was a bit shell-shocked to lose seven goals to defending champions Uruguay in their next and final game. Ten months later and he would be equally shocked to lose seven once more but to England this time at Wembley in a 7–2 British Championship mauling.

Also capped around this time were Paddy Buckley, Archie Glen and George Mulhall. Then there's my favourite, George Hamilton. George did travel to Switzerland for the World Cup but was never used; however, he is my favourite for having the audacity to score a hat-trick against Belgium (a team Scotland regularly fail against), as the Scots were 5–0 runaway winners in a friendly in the Heysel Stadium, Brussels, in 1951.

The Fergie era would see Aberdeen become the dominant side in Scotland and 1980 would have them not only win the league title for the first time in 25 years but also see the debuts of future Scotland mainstays in Alex McLeish and Gordon Strachan, as well as Steve Archibald. Willie Miller would also cement his place in the side too that year. In fact *Shoot!* magazine was able to publish a photo that year of the Aberdeen team in Scotland colours, such was their presence in the full and youth Scotland sides.

McLeish would represent Scotland more times in the 1980s than any other player, playing in 66 matches, with fellow central defender Miller following closely on 62 and

GOLDEN GOALS

WILLIE'S WINNER

G. HAMILTON SCOTLAND

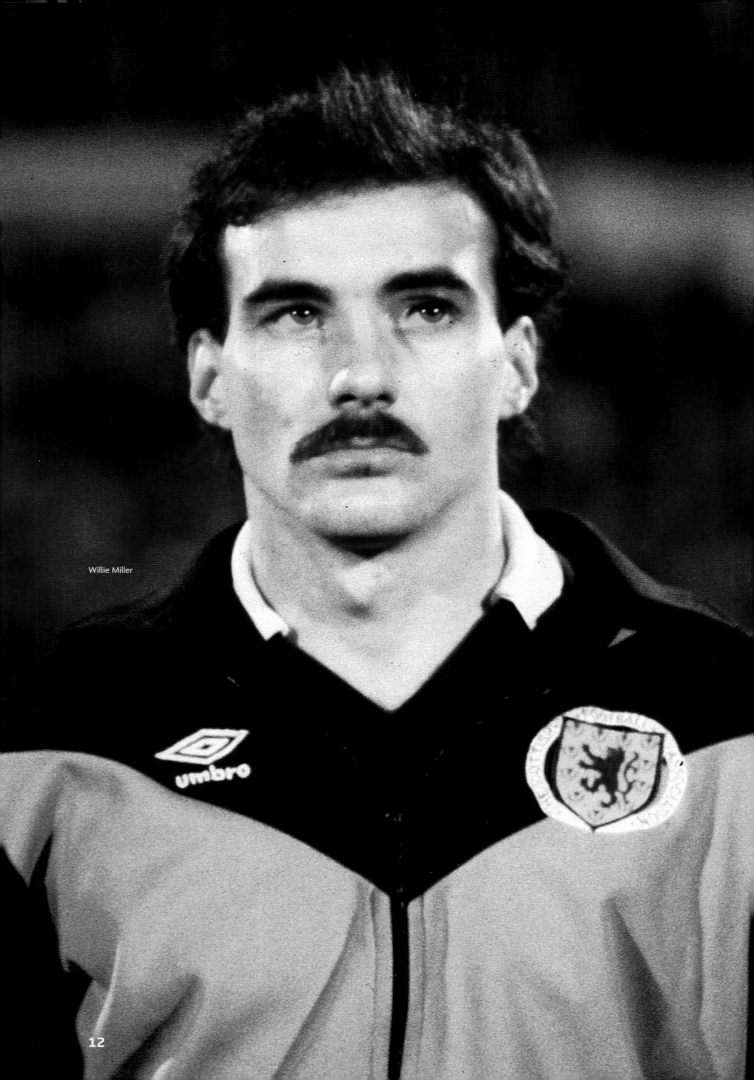

Willie Miller

then goalie Jim Leighton with 44. Aberdeen players past and present would be key to Scotland qualifying for, and appearing at, the Spain 82 and Mexico 86 World Cup finals with Aberdeen manager Alex Ferguson in charge at the latter in a caretaker capacity. Miller and McLeish would also captain their country on a number of occasions whilst Wee Gordon (Strachan) and Big Eck (twice) would go on to manage Scotland in the 21st century.

Aberdeen would win the European Cup Winners' Cup in 1983 versus Real Madrid in the Swedish city of Gothenburg. Of the starting 11 that night only John McMaster would not receive international recognition. It is perhaps surprising that the scorer of the winning goal, substitute John Hewitt, would never be capped at full level and would only win six caps for the Under-21 side. Dons fans will, of course, also point out the 'criminally ignored' winger Peter Weir who would only gain two of his six Scotland caps at Pittodrie.

As we head into the 90s, Ferguson, Strachan and Leighton had long moved on to English football. Willie Miller was injured against Norway on the night Scotland qualified for the 1990 World Cup finals and would retire within a year on a total of 65 caps. McLeish (who appeared at Italia 90) would also drop out (on 77 caps) but there would be one Dons player who succeeded in becoming a regular Scotland player in the early 90s. Right-back Stewart McKimmie would debut in 1989 but make his mark in March 1990 as he scored the only goal versus reigning world champions Argentina in a friendly at Hampden. McKimmie would make appearances at Italia 90 and Euros 92 and 96, amassing a total of 40 caps. Strachan's total, incidentally, was 50 caps and five goals.

Overall, Aberdeen players would come and go from the side in this period, with players such as Scott Booth and Duncan Shearer scoring some vital goals on our way to Euro 96, and indeed Booth would play at the finals but neither would really be seen as first-choice players. Eoin Jess was a forward that stood out in the early 90s but sadly injury and

inconsistent runs in the Scotland side meant his potential was never fully reached.

Billy Dodds would make his first forays into the Scotland side as an Aberdeen player for the 1998 World Cup qualifiers but would win more caps with both Dundee United and then Rangers. The 1998 World Cup squad would see Derek Whyte, then with Aberdeen, as a non-playing member, but one of the heroes of the 80s had returned to Pittodrie and indeed the Scotland side: Jim Leighton. Jim had won caps at Manchester United and Hibernian before returning to Aberdeen where he would win his last ten caps, reaching a total of 91, and he currently sits as Scotland's second-most capped player ever.

The early part of the 21st century were not great years for Aberdeen and subsequently very few Dons were picked for the national side. The recent resurgence under manager Derek McInnes, however, has seen some players emerge on to the international scene, in particular defender Scott McKenna (his debut versus Costa 'Bloody' Rica in March 2018) and maybe if their good form continues, we will see more.

SUPER STRACHAN!

'What an impact Gordon has made' He's helped Aberdeen to win the Scottish Premier League and is now a regular for Scotland.

THE ALL-TIME GREATS

SCOTLAND

ALEX McLEISH
Defender   1980–93

JIM BETT   37

DUNCAN SHEARER
Aberdeen

AIRDRIE

The first player ever to be capped for Airdrie also happened to be one of the founders of the club that formed in 1878 as the Excelsior Football Club. The change to Airdrieonians would come in 1881 but it would take goalkeeper James Connor another five years to win his one and only cap in 1886 in a 7–2 British Championship victory against Ireland in Belfast. However, James Connor does have a unique place in Scottish football history as the first Scottish goalkeeper to face a penalty kick. James McLuggage of Royal Albert would be the scorer of the first goal as Airdrie lost 2–0 that day on 6 June 1891.

The Scott brothers, inside-left Robert and left-back Matthew, were both given solitary caps four years apart, with Robert gaining his in 1894 versus Ireland and Matthew in 1898 against Wales. James Reid was Scotland's top league goalscorer in seasons 1912/13 and 1913/14 and as such was capped in 1914 against Wales. His next cap would come six years later after the end of World War I. James would win three caps altogether with his last coming in 1924, a 2–0 win against Ireland at Celtic Park.

However, in the early 1920s, Airdrie became a side to be reckoned with. They were runners-up for the Scottish title four seasons in a row with a very prolific forward duo of Willie Russell and the great Hughie Gallacher. Major trophy

Hughie Gallacher, the great Scottish centre-forward

success would come with the 1925 Scottish Cup win against Hibernian with Russell hitting both goals in the 2–0 victory. Of Airdrie's starting XI, six would win Scotland caps. James Reid we have, of course, mentioned and others such as Bob Bennie, Jock MacDougall and indeed Willie Russell would win a handful of caps between them.

Hughie Gallacher started at Queen of the South before moving to Airdrie in 1921. He would hit an amazing 90 goals in 111 league games with the Broomfield club. He would also be capped for Scotland on five occasions whilst with Airdie, netting five goals in total. Hughie (a 1928 'Wembley Wizard') would go on to play for Newcastle United and Chelsea among others and he currently sits third on Scotland's all-time goalscoring list with 24 goals (against England, Northern Ireland, Wales and France) in 20 games. Hughie would sadly take his own life in May 1957 at the age of 57.

Also playing in the 1925 cup final victory aged 18 was Bob McPhail. Bob would go on to be a legend with Glasgow Rangers but would win his first Scotland cap as an Airdrie player versus England in 1927. Bob would win 17 caps in total, scoring seven goals including two against England in the 3–1 win at Hampden in 1937 in front of 149,547.

Defender Jimmy Crapnell, 5ft 5in tall, would join the 'Diamonds', as they were known for their unique red and white strip, in 1926 and would play with some of the cup-winning side. However, with Gallacher and Russell both having moved south, Airdrie began

LAWRIE LESLIE, Airdrieonians and Scotland

to drop down the league table and indeed would never hit the heady heights of the early 20s again. Crapnell, though, would go on to win nine Scotland caps from 1929 to 1933, captaining the side on four occasions and is the club's most capped player.

The immediate post-war period would see a couple of players capped. Frank Brennan would gain the first of his eight caps in 1946 (in what was seen as a 'Victory International' versus Switzerland at Hampden) with Airdrie before moving on to Newcastle United where he would also collect FA Cup winners' medals in 1951 and 52.

Bobby Flavell would also win a couple of caps in 1947 and would hit a brace in a 6–0 victory away to Luxembourg. Bobby's career was halted on two occasions, first by the advent of the Second World War, but in June 1949 he left Hearts to join Millonarios of the Colombian League. The Colombian League was attracting a number of players from around the world at the time but was flouting international laws and was suspended by FIFA in 1951. Flavell returned to Scotland and was heavily fined by the SFA and banned from playing for over six months before signing for Dundee.

Presented by SCOTTISH DAILY EXPRESS

No. 25 IAN McMILLAN, Airdrieonians F.C.

1948 would see the arrival of club legend 'The Wee Prime Minister' Ian McMillan. Inside-forward McMillan would play 249 league games in his first spell with Airdrie, scoring a remarkable 109 goals. Ian's first cap came at age 21 and would be against England at Hampden in the 2–1 defeat of 1952. Fortune favoured him more in his second match as Scotland walloped the USA 6–0 at home, with McMillan netting a double.

Although included in the 22-man World Cup finals squad of 1954, the SFA would only travel to Switzerland with 13 players and so McMillan would be among those left at home on 'standby' as such. His fifth and final cap as an Airdrie player would be in the 1956 1–1 draw with England at Hampden. Teammate Hugh Baird would make his only Scotland appearance versus Austria at Hampden a few weeks later.

As for Ian, he would move to Rangers in 1958 but in his successful six years with the Ibrox club he would only add one more cap, in a World Cup qualifier versus Czechoslovakia in May 1961. The Scots would lose 4–0 in Bratislava and Ian along with a few others would not return to the side again.

Among the others was goalkeeper Lawrie Leslie who was making his fifth Scotland appearance. Lawrie had started out at Hibs but moved to Airdrie in 1959. He played in the first two matches of the 1960/61 Home Internationals but due to injury was unable to face England in April 1961. Sadly, one Frank Haffey took his place and the rest is history or indeed misery if you're Scottish. Lawrie would move to West Ham United in 1961 and would play for a number of English clubs before hanging up his boots in 1969.

The 1970s would see a revival of sorts for Airdrie as they produced a fine footballing side, with the likes of Drew Jarvie and Drew Busby among others, under the management of Ian McMillan. Jarvie gained international recognition winning three caps in 1971 under manager Bobby Brown, including a sub appearance at Wembley that year.

Jarvie would be the last player capped for the club known as Airdrieonians as they would cease to exist in 2002 and although there is a team which rose from the ashes of the defunct club, it is a pale shadow of what went before. Interestingly enough, Ian McMillan holds the position of Honorary President connecting the 'old' to the 'new'.

DREW JARVIE
(Airdrie)

ARSENAL

This club was founded by Scotsman David Danskin in 1886 and originally called Dial Square, before changing to Royal Arsenal, then Woolwich Arsenal and finally settling on the name we know today. It was as Woolwich Arsenal that their first players were to be capped for Scotland: Bobby Templeton and Thomas Fitchie in 1905 versus Wales at Wrexham. This was Templeton's only cap as a Gunner but he would win ten others with Aston Villa, Newcastle and Kilmarnock. Fitchie was to win two more caps with Arsenal and then a final one with Queen's Park.

Alex James had won four caps with Preston North End, including the Wembley Wizards triumph of 1928, before a move to Arsenal in 1929. Well known for his long baggy shorts, Alex enjoyed the London lifestyle that football afforded him. Midfielder James was the playmaker in the Arsenal side that would win four championships and two FA Cups in the early 1930s but would only make four more appearances for the national side.

Archie Macaulay had one cap to his name, won during a brief time with Brentford in 1947, but with Arsenal he would win the First Division championship in 1947/48 and would add to his cap tally, reaching seven in total. When he made his Scotland debut in April 1947 in a 1–1 draw with England at Wembley, starting alongside him and making his Scotland bow was Alex Forbes of Sheffield United.

Forbes would win five caps with the Blades before Arsenal came calling. Unfortunately for Macaulay, Forbes would take his place in the Arsenal side, winning the league twice and the FA Cup in 1950. Forbes is quite unique in that he also represented Scotland in ice hockey in his younger years. As for football, he gained nine caps during his time with Arsenal.

18 October 1958 was a special day in Scottish football history as it would see the debut of perhaps the finest player to ever grace the dark blue of Scotland, in Denis Law. However, there would also be three Arsenal players in the line-up that would win 3–0 at Ninian Park, Cardiff.

Tommy Docherty would be in the twilight of his career as such and had already gained 22 caps with Preston before joining Arsenal in August 1958, where he would add another two. Tommy would, of course, successfully manage Scotland for a brief period in the early 1970s.

Jackie Henderson had won five caps with Portsmouth and indeed was part of the standby squad for the World Cup finals in 1954. A move to Arsenal in October 58 saw him resurrect his international career and he

Alex Forbes (Arsenal and Scotland). One of many Scots who found fame with a Football League side. First recognised as a great wing half prospect while playing with Sheffield United. After playing a magnificent game against Arsenal was signed by the Highbury club and has become one of the finest wing halves in the game. Has played for Scotland several times. A brilliant ball player, is almost equally as good at inside forward.

Alex Forbes

The "Daddy" o' them a'

Alec James, a Wembley wizard. Helped put Arsenal on the map.

Alex James

Tommy Docherty

APRIL 1959

WORLD SPORTS

two shillings

Australia & S. Africa 2s. 6d.
U.S.A. & Canada 35 cents

Meet DAVID HERD
'Best centre-forward prospect in Europe' said Matt Busby

The Athletics Split	After Benaud . . . Gupte
Latest moves in Ireland's international crisis	Indian spinner spells danger to English batsmen

David Herd

IAN URE
(Arsenal & Scotland) (Copyright: Daily Mirror)

Ian Ure

GEORGE GRAHAM (Arsenal)

George Graham

Arsenal would finally win the 'double' in season 1970/71 and three players from that side would play for Scotland. Captain Frank McLintock already had three caps with Leicester City as well as a further three with Arsenal and would end that season with a total of nine. Frank said he should never have played against England at Wembley in 1971 as he was absolutely 'knackered'.

Goalkeeper Bob Wilson would be among the first to benefit from the rule change that allowed footballers to play for the country of their parents' birth and would make his Scotland debut versus Portugal in October 1971. Taking charge that night for the first time was Tommy Docherty, who also selected teammate George Graham, too. Wilson would only make one more appearance but George would gain 11 caps altogether, scoring three goals. Of course, George would go on to manage Arsenal rather successfully.

The last player to be capped at Arsenal, currently, is Charlie Nicholas. Charlie was one of Scotland's brightest hopes in the early 80s and in season 1982/83 he scored 48 goals in total for Celtic. Although Charlie was much loved at Highbury, he never quite hit the heights it was hoped he would. He would, however, gain 13 caps for Scotland during his time there but was never really a first pick in the side and often started out on the bench. Charlie is still the only Arsenal player to represent Scotland at the World Cup, playing against Denmark and Uruguay at Mexico 86.

returned to the side for a couple of matches.

The last of the Arsenal trio was David Herd. Herd had been with Arsenal since 1955 and would be from the 56/57 season the top scorer at the club, culminating in a tally of 29 in season 1960/61.

As for Scotland he would only ever be given five caps, scoring three goals. It is perhaps no coincidence that the man in charge of Scotland that day would be the major beneficiary of both Law's and Herd's greatest years: Sir Matt Busby. Busby would sign Herd in August 1961 and in 265 matches for the Old Trafford club he would hit an incredible 145 goals and yet would not be picked for Scotland during his time with Manchester United. At United Herd would win the league twice and was to hit a double in the 1963 FA Cup triumph.

Centre-half Ian Ure had been a major part of Dundee's championship-winning side of 1961/62 and moved to Arsenal in 1963, although he had won eight caps by this time, and at Highbury he was only to add another three.

STRIKER

EVERY MONDAY No. 102 DECEMBER 18 1971

WOLVES in colour

CLYDE BEST

BOB WILSON Arsenal and Scotland

Bob Wilson

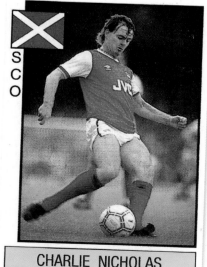

S C O

CHARLIE NICHOLAS

ASTON VILLA

Formed in 1874, Aston Villa were one of the founding teams of the Football League in 1888. James Cowan would win five league titles and two FA Cups in a 12-year period with the club from 1890 to 1902. James was also selected for Scotland on three occasions, in successive matches versus England from 1896 to 98, captaining the side in the last match. It was not unusual for the selection committee to choose their best players for the England match and use supplementary players for the Welsh and Irish matches in that era. Thomas Niblo was to win his only cap against England in 1904.

Jimmy Gibson would move south from Partick Thistle having already won four caps at the end of season 1926/27 and would captain the Wembley Wizards in their 1928 5–1 trouncing of England. He would gain four caps overall at Villa. Incidentally his father Neilly would play alongside the aforementioned James Cowan in all three of his Scotland games.

Another player bought from Thistle was George Cummings, a hard, fearless full-back whom Stanley Matthews apparently never really got the better of. George is a Villa legend, even though his career was halted in many ways by the advent of World War II. George gained six caps at Villa, adding to his three with the Jags. Playing alongside him in six of those matches was wing-half Alex Massie. Alex had joined Villa from Hearts in December 35 and was to win the last seven of his 18 caps at Villa Park.

After George's final cap in 1939 it would be 46 years before another Villan would play for Scotland. Striker Andy Gray had moved from Dundee United to Villa in October 1975 and a couple of months later he would make his Scotland debut versus Romania in a Euro qualifier at Hampden which ended 1–1. Despite his goalscoring exploits and indeed the PFA player awards, Andy was never really given many chances to shine for Scotland. Controversy does surround his absence from the 1978 World Cup squad, however. Ally MacLeod would only pick him once, which was in the first game after Argentina. Gray would score

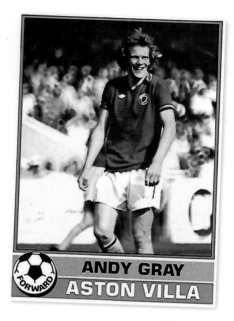

in the match versus Austria that was to be MacLeod's last game in charge. However, he would not be given a run of games under Jock Stein either and only won six of his 20 caps at Villa before he moved to Wolves for a then English record transfer fee of £1.49m.

George Cummings

Aston Villa would win the 1980/81 championship and would go on to win the European Cup the following year with three Scots among their side: Des Bremner, Ken McNaught and Allan Evans. It would only be Evans who would feature in a Scotland side, however. Prior to the 82 World Cup Jock Stein was unsure which was his best central defence pairing. Options included the likes of Alan Hansen, Willie Miller, Alex McLeish, David Narey and Paul Hegarty. Evans was thrown into the mix, too, and would play in three games before the World Cup. He and Hansen were partnered up for the opening game at the finals but slack play saw New Zealand snatch two goals when Scotland were coasting and Evans was never seen in the dark blue of Scotland again. Bremner had previously won his solitary cap with Hibernian in 1976. As for McNaught, his father Willie had won five caps with Raith Rovers in the early 50s.

In the modern game, players shift about so much sometimes that it's hard to recall who played where and when, but among the great and not so good (perhaps) in the last 20 years at Villa include Colin Calderwood

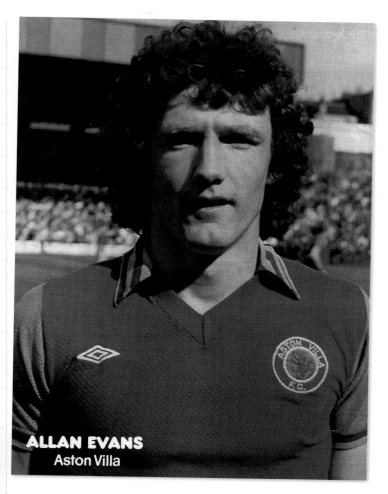

ALLAN EVANS
Aston Villa

for his final four caps, Shaun Maloney's first spell in English football, which saw him win six caps, and Barry Bannan who began his career with the Birmingham club and gained six caps.

Right-back Alan Hutton, however, hung in there. Signed by Villa in 2011, after his first season he was dropped from the first team, spending the following years out on loan and out of favour. Scotland manager Gordon Strachan would continue to pick Hutton even though he was not playing first-team football at the time. He won 29 of his 50 Scotland caps whilst at Villa Park before he retired from the international scene in November, 2016.

Having helped Villa win promotion via the play-offs at the end of season 2018/19 John McGinn has become a firm favourite with the side and by the end of that season had added six more caps to his then total of 15.

SCOTLAND v BELGIUM

Friday, 7 September 2018
Hampden Park
Glasgow
Kick-off 7.45pm

Official matchday programme £4

John McGinn in 1990 home kit

NOTHING MATTERS MORE

John McGinn

BLACKBURN ROVERS

Blackburn Rovers were founded in 1875 and like Aston Villa were one of the founding members of the Football League. Scottish selectors had been reluctant to use players from the English sides for the early internationals until 4 April 1896, when four were chosen to play against England at Celtic Park, Glasgow – Tom Brandon of Blackburn Rovers, James Cowan of Aston Villa, Thomas Hyslop of Stoke City and Jack Bell of Everton. Scotland would win 2–1 with Bell hitting the second goal. It is perhaps just as well they won or Anglos might have been barred for many a year after. As for Tom, this was his only cap.

Walter Aitkenhead won just the one cap for Scotland as they ran out 4–1 winners at Windsor Park, Belfast versus Ireland in 1912. Perhaps it might have been apt for Walter to have played at Hampden as Aitkenhead Road is one of the two main thoroughfares to the national stadium. I still await someone with the name Cathcart to represent Scotland.

Jock Hutton would add three caps to the seven he gained at Aberdeen in the mid-20s at Ewood Park. He would be part of the Blackburn side that won the 1928 FA Cup. It would be almost 70 more years until Rovers would lift a major honour. That title would be the English Premier League in 1994/95 and they would have one Scot leading them off the field and another leading the defence on it.

In October 1991, Kenny Dalglish had been lured back to football after an eight-month sabbatical by Blackburn owner Jack Walker. One of Dalglish's first signings was that of Colin Hendry. Hendry had been popular with Rovers fans in his first spell with the club in the late 80s and his return to Ewood from Manchester City was more than welcome.

He would go on to play his part in Blackburn's promotion from the then Second Division to the Premier League via the play-offs and then the title-winning season of 1994/95. He would win his first Scotland cap at the age of 27 in May 1993 in Estonia. Colin would lead Scotland to the 1996 Euros and 1998 World Cup finals during his time with Rovers, earning 35 caps, before moving on to Rangers, Coventry and Bolton and a total of 51 caps. Sadly, his Scotland career would end in ignominy due to a retrospective six-game ban for elbowing a San Marino player in a World Cup qualifier in which he also netted twice.

Kevin Gallacher was signed from Coventry City in 1993 and already had 14 caps to his name. Kevin missed most of the league-winning season due to a succession of injuries and only played in the one match. He would, however, represent Scotland at the Euro 96 finals and his goals helped the side on its way to France 98, particularly his double versus Austria at Celtic Park in April 1997. Kevin gained 30 caps at Ewood Park before moving to Newcastle United where he would win another ten.

Billy McKinlay had joined from Dundee United in 1995 and like Hendry and Gallacher would appear in both finals. However, rather oddly, he would come on as a sub in the first match versus the Netherlands at Euro 96 and then similarly come on in the first match at France 98 versus Brazil and fail to make another appearance at either tournament. Billy would win 15 of his 29 caps at Blackburn.

Scots would come and go in the Blackburn side around the turn of the century with the likes of Christian Dailly, Callum Davidson, Barry Ferguson and Paul Dickov all winning caps whilst plying their trade at Ewood. More recently the likes of Jordan Rhodes, Grant Hanley and Charlie Mulgrew have all had stints at Blackburn.

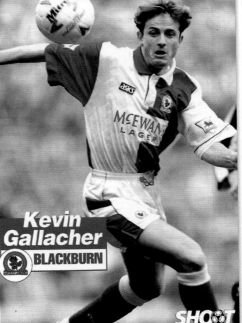

Kevin Gallacher

Paul Dickov

Colin Hendry

BLACKPOOL

Blackpool were formed in 1887 and it would take almost 50 years before they had a player representing Scotland. Defender Phil Watson was perhaps a strange choice for his only cap in November 1933 versus Austria at Hampden, as his club had been relegated to Division Two the previous season. Phil achieved 129 consecutive games for Blackpool from 1932/33 through to midway through 1934/35.

Alex Munro and Frank O'Donnell would play together for Scotland in a 3–1 victory over the Netherlands in Amsterdam in May 1938; both had won previous caps with Hearts and Preston respectively but these were to be their only ones with Blackpool. Munro would play in the first of three FA Cup finals that Blackpool and Stanley Matthews were involved in. The first in 1948 was lost 2–0 to Manchester United. Also in the side that day was Hugh Kelly who would win a cap in 1952 as Scotland whooped the USA 6–0 at Hampden Park.

Allan Brown had already won three caps with East Fife but would play alongside Kelly against the USA as a Blackpool player. Allan would win 14 caps in total scoring six times. He would also travel to the 1954 World Cup finals and play in both games against Austria and Uruguay. At Blackpool, Allan was unlucky to miss out on both the FA Cup defeat of 1951 and the victory in 1953 due to injury.

George Farm

HUGH KELLY

Goalkeeper George Farm would, however, play in both, although he did admit to being at fault for some of the goals conceded in the 1953 4–3 victory over Bolton. George was first capped versus Wales in 1953 and played seven games on the bounce; however, a 4–2 defeat to England at Hampden in April 1954 saw him lose his place to Fred Martin. George would not even make the squad of 22 for the World Cup finals in Sweden that year. It must have been a bit of a surprise five years later when he was called up for international duty once again and played in three games over the summer of 1959. After over 500 games for the Seasiders, George would move to Queen of the South whom he would go on to manage among others. In later life George would swap goalkeeping for lighthouse keeping at one point.

Although he had made his breakthrough in the Blackpool side in 1950 and played in both the 1951 and 1953 finals, Jackie Mudie did not make the Scotland team until 1956. He did make up for lost time, however, and would score nine goals in 17 matches in a two-year period. Jackie, standing at only 5ft 6in, was a bit small for a forward but like Mo Johnston for Italia 90 and Kevin Gallacher for France 98, his goals were absolutely vital in Scotland qualifying for the 1958 World Cup finals.

In a great game at Ninian Park, Cardiff, Wales and Scotland drew 2-2. In this picture, high-flying Jackie Mudie of Blackpool, Scotland's inside-right, gets his head to a ball while being tackled by Welshmen John Charles, who played inside-right, and Mel Hopkins, left-back. This was one of the season's finest internationals.

Jackie Mudie

Jackie scored in both victories over Switzerland and also hit a hat-trick against Spain, arguably the most important hat-trick ever by a Scotland player. Jackie played in all three games at the finals in Sweden and scored in the 3–2 defeat to Paraguay. After the World Cup the likes of Denis Law, David Herd and Ian St. John would take over the reins up front for Scotland. Jackie played with Blackpool all the way through to 1961, scoring 144 goals in 324 league games.

Blackpool would be relegated at the end of 1966/67 but on the final day of the season, a recent acquisition from Albion Rovers, Tony Green, would make his debut versus Liverpool. Tony was a left-sided attacking midfielder who was much loved at both Blackpool and Newcastle. Sadly he was out of the game by the time of his 26th birthday having suffered a knee cartilage injury in September 1972. He made six appearances for Scotland, his first four with Blackpool and the others at United. So loved was Tony by fans at Bloomfield Road and St James' Park he was inducted into the Hall of Fame at both clubs.

Charlie Adam had won a couple of caps by the time he signed on

permanently at Ian Holloway's Blackpool and he would play a major part in the Seasiders' brief revival and promotion to the top tier in 2009/10 via the play-offs, scoring with a free kick in the 3–2 Wembley win over Cardiff City. The following season he would hit many a spectacular goal but it would not be enough to halt Blackpool's slide back to the Championship. Charlie would be sold to Liverpool for £6.5m at the start of the next season.

Whilst at Bloomfield Road Charlie won a further ten caps but was unable to replicate his club form on the international stage and indeed never quite made his mark at Liverpool either. Capped around the same time at Blackpool were full-back Stephen Crainey, goalkeeper Matt Gilks and, winning his first two caps there, Matt Phillips, who in 2011 had appeared for England at the Under-20 World Cup finals in Colombia.

TONY COMES BACK TO A SCOTTISH CAP

LAST YEAR the future of Blackpool's Tony Green was very much in doubt. After an injury to an ankle, he was forced to spend over a year out of the game he loved so much. There were rumours that he would never come back. That he was finished.

But a few weeks after the start of this season, Tony ended any speculation when he played in a successful come back match against Everton. In five months, Tony has made a sensational impact on the First Division, even though his club have been struggling for League points.

By February, he was back to his best, and reward came in the shape of a full Scottish international cap against Belgium.

Now, though, Tony's future is again in doubt. But for different reasons. Blackpool look set for a speedy return to Division Two.

Last time they were there the club promised Tony a transfer if they didn't win promotion. This situation could arise again.

It's going to be a tough Spring for both club and player. Whatever Tony's future in the Football League, one thing is certain: he'll win many more international caps to go with his first one.

Tony Green

Danny McGrain

CELTIC

Celtic were founded in late 1887 and quickly established themselves as a force to be reckoned with via some decent acquisitions. Full-back Thomas McKeown and Willie Groves were both lured from Hibernian and were to be the first players to represent Scotland, playing in the 1889 7–0 thrashing of Ireland at Ibrox Park. Groves had already been capped and was to score a hat-trick in this match.

Both were to win more caps, each facing England in April 1890 as two of four Celts on display that day. Also in that side was another ex-Hibee James McLaren, who captained the team that day. The fourth player was James Kelly, whose family were to have a big say in Celtic's history over the next 100 years.

Kelly was the marquee signing for Celtic in 1888 when they convinced him to move from Renton. James was to captain Scotland on four occasions and won eight caps overall. After retiring James became a director of the club and chairman for a number of years. His son Robert Kelly was to be Celtic chairman during the Jock Stein era and indeed his grandsons were also to be directors of the club, although perhaps they are not as fondly remembered.

Dan 'Ned' Doyle had already played for the likes of Hibernian, Grimsby Town and Everton before joining Celtic in 1891. Dan would play a big part in Celtic's success in the following years, winning four championships and the Scottish Cup. He was capped eight times, playing against England on five occasions.

Although he was to be capped after Doyle, Willie Maley would be Doyle's manager in his last couple of seasons with Celtic. Maley won two Scotland caps, in 1893, despite being born in County Down, Ireland, playing in a 6–1 victory against Ireland at Celtic Park and a 5–2 defeat against England at the Richmond Athletic Ground, London. However, it is not as a Celtic player that his legacy is written but as Celtic manager for 43 years, winning 16 league championships, including six in a row, and 14 Scottish Cups.

Jimmy Quinn was a powerfully built striker for Celtic and would be the first Celt to score more than 200 goals for the club and is fifth on the all-time scoring list. He was part of the side that won six consecutive titles and five Scottish Cups. Jimmy was to play 11 times for Scotland, scoring seven goals. His first match was against Ireland at Celtic Park in March 1905 as Scotland won 4–0, with Quinn contributing one of the goals. He was to net four against Ireland three years later in Dublin and also score in the 2–0 victory over England at Hampden in 1910.

The scorer of the other goal against the English was a man who would serve Celtic for many a year as a player and later in life as assistant manager. Jimmy McMenemy joined Celtic in 1902 and played until 1920. He was to win 11 championships and six Scottish Cups with Celtic. Jimmy lies sixth in the all-time appearance list and seventh in the goalscoring. For Scotland, Jimmy's career stretched from 1905 to 1920 when he was 39 years old. He was only to gain 12 caps, though, scoring five goals, and was never on a losing Scottish side.

Alec McNair joined Celtic from Stenhousemuir in 1904 and played until 1925, capturing 12 titles and six Scottish Cups. As for Scotland, he was first capped in March 1906 as Scotland lost to Wales at Tynecastle and would go on to win 15 caps altogether, captaining the side on five occasions. His last three were won after a gap of six years due to the First World War.

Defender Willie McStay was to win four titles. When he left to join Hearts in 1929 he was succeeded in captaincy by his brother Jimmy. As for Scotland, Willie was to win his first ten of his 13 caps and was to captain the side on five occasions. He and Jimmy were both great-uncles to Celtic legend Paul McStay.

It is hard to fathom why Jimmy McGrory didn't win more caps – his goalscoring record at Celtic is phenomenal. Jimmy is the all-time top goalscorer, not just for Celtic but for any team in top-flight British football, with 485 league and cup goals. His great contemporary at the time was Hughie Gallacher, who in 20 games for Scotland scored 24 goals, only losing two games. As for Jimmy, his first cap in 1928 saw Scotland go down 1–0 at Firhill to Ireland. A year later and Gallacher was to put five by the Irish in a 7–3 victory in Belfast. Jimmy would have to wait until March 1931 for his next cap when he was to hit the second in a 2–0 win over England at Hampden. He was to score three goals in his next three games and was then to net a double against England in a 2–1 win in 1933. However, another loss to Ireland would be his seventh and final

Jimmy McGrory

cap, despite him hitting 50 goals in season 1935/36 in 32 games. Jimmy would go on to manage Celtic from 1945 until giving way to Jock Stein in 1965.

At the time of his death on 5 September 1931, following a collision with a Rangers player, goalkeeper John Thomson was only 22 years old and yet he had achieved so much by then. His Celtic debut came just after his 18th birthday and he quickly established himself as the Parkhead club's number one. By the end of the 1926/27 season he had collected a Scottish Cup winners' medal.

His first cap would come at the age of 21, coming against France in Paris in May 1930 with Scotland winning 2–0. He would then play in a 1–1 draw with Wales at Ibrox and a 0–0 draw with Ireland before what was to be his final match, the 2–0 win against England in March 1931 in which McGrory scored. A month later and John was to win his second Scottish Cup with Celtic, beating Motherwell. In total he was to play 164 games for Celtic in his short career and one is left thinking how much he could have achieved had fate chosen a different path for him.

Outside-right Jimmy Delaney signed for Celtic in 1933 and was gifted with speed and skill, and was well loved by fans of the club. His first cap was in a 1–1 draw with Wales in October 1935 in Cardiff. Jimmy would net a double versus Germany in a 2–0 win in October 1936, in a match that would see the Nazi flag fly over Ibrox. This was followed by a goal in a 2–0 victory over Ireland two years later. His last cap as a Celt was to come in a 3–2 victory over Wales in 1938. The war would, of course, interrupt his international career and shortly after the resumption of official play, Jimmy was at Manchester United.

Delaney and Celtic teammate George Paterson would be the only two players to gain official caps before and after the war. Jimmy was to win another six caps at Old Trafford, scoring three more goals. His grandson John Kennedy would also play for Celtic and Scotland but his international career was horribly ended after only 14 minutes due to a late tackle from Ganea of Romania in March 2004.

The immediate post-war years were not great for Celtic with only one league title won (1953/54) and two Scottish Cups (1951 and 1954), plus two successes in the

Bobby Evans

new League Cup competition (1956 and 1957), and so few caps came Parkhead's way. One player who would really buck the trend of Scotland sides being defensively dominated by Rangers players in this era was Bobby Evans. The red-headed defender signed for Celtic in 1944 and in October 1948 made his Scotland debut versus Wales in a 3–1 victory in Cardiff.

Bobby was to be a regular in the Scotland side for the next 12 years or so. He was to play in the qualifiers for the 1950, 1954 and 1958 World Cups. Bobby travelled to Switzerland for the 1954 finals but injury kept him out of both games. He played in all three games at the World Cup in Sweden 58, captaining the side in the final match against France. Overall Bobby was to win 45 caps with Celtic and was the Scotland captain for the last nine of those games. Evans was to leave Celtic for a brief spell with Chelsea in 1960 where he would add three caps to his total and continue to captain the side.

John McPhail was capped five times for Scotland with his first coming against Wales in 1949 in a match that doubled as a World Cup qualifier and British Championship game. John was to net the first in the 2–0 victory and then hit a brace versus Ireland at home a year later as Scotland won 6–1. However, Scotland suffered their first ever defeat at home to an overseas side versus Austria in December 1950, and McPhail and teammate Bobby Collins were among the scapegoats. McPhail was recalled to the side for a final time as they faced Ireland in Belfast in 1953 in another World Cup qualifier/British Championship game, with Scotland winning 3–1.

Bobby Collins only stood at 5ft 3in but the midfielder had the heart of a lion. Signed by Celtic at the age of 17 in 1949, Bobby was called up for Scotland duty the following year, playing in the opening two matches of the 1950/51 British Championship as Scotland swept Wales and Ireland aside 3–1 and 6–1. However, following the Austrian loss, his next cap would not come until away to Yugoslavia in May 1955. This 2–2 draw was followed a few days later with a 4–1 routing of Austria in Vienna.

Bobby would break his scoring duck, netting the winner in a World Cup qualifier against Switzerland in Basle in May 1957,

Jimmy Delaney

Bobby Collins

followed by two goals in a 3–1 win over West Germany shortly after. Collins would play in all three games at Sweden 1958, scoring in the 3–2 defeat to Paraguay. Bobby would move to Everton shortly after the World Cup. Overall Bobby would win 31 caps and score ten goals.

Neil Mochan and Willie Fernie were both to play in the 1954 World Cup finals, with both debuting just before the trip to Switzerland. Outside-left Mochan staked his claim in a 1–1 draw with Norway in Oslo in the May just before the finals, and forward Fernie a week later in a 2–1 win over Finland in Helsinki. They were both chosen to play as Scotland suffered a 1–0 defeat to Austria and a 7–0 humiliation to Uruguay. These were to be Neil's only caps. He would go on to coach at the club for many years. As for Fernie, he was to play 12 times for Scotland, including his final match, the 3–2 defeat to Paraguay in Sweden 1958.

Right-back Duncan MacKay was to play 14 games for Scotland with his first game, a 1–0 defeat against England at Wembley in 1959 and with his final game, a 3–2 reverse against Uruguay at Hampden in 1962.

May 1959 would see the first of the Lisbon Lions capped for Scotland and it was to be the headstrong Bertie Auld. Bertie was actually sent off on his debut against the Netherlands in Amsterdam for retaliation in the 93rd minute, as Scotland won 2–1. Another two caps were to be won just after this. Bertie moved to Birmingham City in 1961, returning to Celtic Park in 1964.

Celtic keeper Frank Haffey would earn his second cap and the nickname 'Hapless Haffey' following the 9–3 defeat to England in 1961 at Wembley. Making his debut at centre-half that day was Billy McNeill. Despite the result Billy was to retain his place in the Scotland team for the next few matches before losing out to Ian Ure from championship-winning side Dundee. Billy, though, would be back in the side for the 2–0 victory over England in 1962 and then the 1–0 victory in 1964 at Hampden, in which he would captain his country for the first time.

Having been with Celtic since 1957, Billy won his first trophy, the Scottish Cup, in April 1965 after netting the winner versus Dunfermline Athletic. At this point he was on 14 caps with only 15 more to go. Billy had a six-game run as captain including a World Cup qualifier against Poland at Hampden in which he opened the scoring, but ultimately Scotland lost 2–1. Injury would rule him out of the Italy game that was to follow a month later and Ronnie McKinnon of Rangers took over and was often chosen over Billy in the years that followed. Billy was only to play in three Scotland matches in the 1970s, all coming in the 1971/72 Home Internationals under Tommy Docherty, with the Scots beating the Irish and Welsh but losing 1–0 to England at Hampden – a bad tempered match in which Billy picked up his only booking for Scotland. Billy was to retire from playing a couple of years later but by this time he had won nine championships, seven Scottish Cups and six League Cups and, of course, the European Cup.

Pat Crerand was to win 16 caps with 11 coming in his early years at Parkhead. Tough-talking, tough-tackling Pat was also a gifted footballer with a great ability to find his man with an accurate pass. Crerand was drafted in to the Scotland side a month after the 9–3 game to face the Republic of Ireland in Scotland's opening 1962 World Cup qualifier. Pat would play 11 times for Scotland as a Celtic player winning eight games and losing three, including a 4–0 loss to Czechoslovakia in Bratislava where he was sent off. He moved to Manchester United in 1963, winning the European Cup in 1968, but only a handful of caps followed.

Stevie Chalmers and Jimmy Johnstone both made their debuts in a 3–2 defeat to Wales in Cardiff in October 1964. Chalmers's Scotland career was only to last five games, scoring three goals, including one against a

Brazil side that included Pele, with whom he famously swapped shirts in that 1966 World Cup warm-up match.

Jinky Johnstone's Scotland career is much more complicated and there's no doubt his paltry return of only 23 caps seems incredulous to those of us looking back. Too often Jimmy was given only a couple of caps in any given year, often losing out to the established Willie Henderson. Jimmy had hit a double in the 4–3 defeat to England at Hampden in May 1966 but even this didn't ensure him a run of games. He was also to score versus West Germany in a World Cup qualifier in Hamburg in 1969.

Of course, it all comes down to 1974 and the eternal question. Why didn't Ormond play Jinky at the World Cup? I don't suppose we'll ever know. Ormond had brought him in from the cold as such for the 1974 Home International series after he had been out of the team for almost two years. Jimmy had played against Wales as Scotland won 2–0 but then he found himself up the Clyde without a paddle. Despite the uproar, Ormond stuck by Jimmy and in return he got Johnstone's best performance in a Scotland shirt as they beat England 2–0 at Hampden a couple of days later. However,

there was to be no World Cup action for Johnstone. Surprisingly Jimmy did make two more Scotland appearances in the first two matches after the World Cup finals.

Bobby Murdoch's legacy seems to grow with each passing year as he is evaluated more and more as one of the best midfielders Scotland have ever produced. Bobby would gain 12 caps from 1965 to 1969, scoring five goals including that last-minute equaliser against West Germany in April 1969. Bobby would move on from Celtic to Middlesbrough where he helped mould future Scotland international Graeme Souness. Sweeper John Clark would be given four caps in 1966 and 1967 including the friendly versus Brazil.

BOBBY MURDOCH
CELTIC and SCOTLAND
SCOTCARD No. 18   SCOTTISH DAILY EXPRESS TOP FOR SPORT

Bobby Murdoch

The Wembley 1967 match featured a number of Celtic players. In goal was the 'Father' of the Lisbon Lions, Ronnie Simpson, making his debut at 36 years old. Ronnie was to win five caps overall. Full-back Tommy Gemmell had won his first cap in the 4–3 defeat to England of 1966 and was to be a regular in the side, playing in the right-back position rather than left-back, with Eddie McCreadie in the main taking over the left side. Tommy was to win 18 caps, scoring the one goal, versus Cyprus from the spot, and was famously sent off versus West Germany for putting his boot right up Helmut Haller's backside.

Willie Wallace and Bobby Lennox were also part of the 1967 side. Wallace had won three caps already with Hearts and added another three with Celtic. Bobby Lennox is another who was poorly dealt with for Scotland, only winning the ten caps, and was to score three goals including one in this match. Jim Craig was to win only one cap, in the USSR match, shortly after the Wembley game. Although he didn't take part in the Lisbon final, John Hughes was a regular for Celtic around this time and for Scotland he won eight caps from 1965 to 1969, scoring once against England at Hampden.

If the Lisbon Lions didn't win as many caps as they should have, the players that followed, commonly known as the 'Quality Street Gang', produced Scotland's most capped player ever as well as our greatest

FOOTBALL SCOT WEEKLY

JIMMY JOHNSTONE
(Celtic)

Jimmy Johnstone

Scottish Football ☐ ☐ ☐ ☐ COLOUR EXTRA
STARS IN ACTION — CELTIC

GEORGE CONNELLY · BILLY McNEILL · BOBBY LENNOX · KENNY DALGLISH

ever full-back. David Hay was to make his mark first, playing for Scotland at full-back in April 1970 against Northern Ireland in Belfast, two years after his Celtic debut. Eventually, though, it would be as a free-flowing midfielder that Hay would distinguish himself with Scotland, including some great displays at World Cup 1974. A move to Chelsea soon after would see Hay hit a run of ill fortune in terms of injuries, form, etc., and he was never to play again for Scotland. Davie's final cap total was 27.

10 November 1971 saw Kenny Dalglish come on as a sub up at Pittodrie against Belgium. A year later, making his fourth appearance, Kenny scored in the second minute to put Scotland ahead in a World Cup qualifier against Denmark at Hampden and from there he never really looked back. His Celtic/Scotland career was to span 47 of his 102 caps and 16 of his 30 goals. This would, of course, include the 1974 World Cup finals where he perhaps didn't do himself justice, but then there were wonderful moments against England, such as the Ray Clemence 'nutmeg' goal in 1976 and the second goal at Wembley in 1977, all celebrated with that wonderful, joyful smile that scoring brought to Kenny.

Lou Macari won six caps whilst with Celtic that all came in the reign of Tommy Docherty. Lou first appeared against Wales as Scotland won 1–0 at Hampden in May 1972. He would net two against Yugoslavia as part of the Brazilian Independence Cup and scored Scotland's first goal in the 4–1 win over Denmark in Copenhagen in 1972. This was to be his last match as a Celt as he would soon move to Old Trafford under Docherty. Overall he would win 24 Scotland caps, scoring five goals.

Willie Ormond would give Danny McGrain his first cap against Wales at the Racecourse, Wrexham, in 1973. Although a right-back with his club, he was soon to move over to the left and so began one of the most enduring Scottish full-back pairings of all time, consisting of Danny and Sandy Jardine of Rangers. This pairing would see us through to the 1974 World Cup where they formed a vital part of that fondly remembered side. On his return from West Germany, Danny was diagnosed as having diabetes but he was to take this in his stride. Danny as right-back was part of the Scotland side that defeated England in 1976 and 1977, but a foot injury in 1977

would see him out of the national side for almost two years, making his return against Belgium in December 1979 to win his 41st cap.

Having missed the 1978 finals, Danny was to make it to Spain 1982. He played in the majority of qualifiers and was to lead the side out at the 1982 World Cup finals in the match versus New Zealand. His final Scotland match was a sub appearance in the game against the USSR in Malaga. Danny won 62 caps in total and there are very few Scotland players that are admired and loved as much as him.

Much was hoped for George Connelly but sadly he was unable to fulfil his early promise due to mental health issues; however, the first of his two caps came on that magical night at Hampden in September 1973, as Scotland qualified for the World Cup in 1974. He was to suffer an ankle break in the 1973/74 season that was to see him miss the World Cup itself.

Along with McGrain, one other Celt was to make the squad for Spain 1982, winger Davie Provan. Provan had played in three of the 1982 qualifiers, scoring in the match

THE ALL-TIME GREATS
SCOTLAND
KENNY DALGLISH
Striker · 1971–86

Kenny Dalglish

against Israel at home, but overall he was to play second fiddle to John Robertson. He would not feature in the finals and indeed had actually won all of his ten caps by then.

One player whom it was felt should have been part of the squad at the time was midfielder and Celtic legend Tommy Burns. Tommy had been capped three times by the time of the finals but was left out by Jock Stein. He was only to gain eight caps, and perhaps had he been playing in England instead of remaining with Celtic he would have gained more recognition as well as caps.

Tommy Burns

Roy Aitken will never be among the list of great skilful Scottish players, but for sheer tenacity he will be up there. 'The Bear', as he was affectionately known, was used mainly as a defensive midfielder for Scotland. First capped in September 1979 versus Peru at home, it was not until 1983 that he came into Jock Stein's plans more. Although he didn't play in any of the early 1986 qualifiers, as the group was coming to its conclusion, he played in the two vital matches away to Iceland and then Wales, on that fateful night when we lost Jock Stein. He was also to feature in the play-offs against Australia and played in all three games at the 1986 World Cup finals.

After the World Cup Aitken was made captain by Andy Roxburgh and led the side to Italia 90. By the time of the tournament he was a Newcastle United player, having won 50 caps with Celtic. Roy captained the Scotland team in 27 of his 57 games and despite being a tenacious player he was only ever booked in the one match for the national side.

Charlie Nicholas made his memorable debut for Scotland against Switzerland in 1983 with a wonderfully taken volleyed goal, but for Scotland and Nicholas this was perhaps the zenith. Charlie was to win six caps at Celtic, with three coming in the Canadian tour of 1983, where he scored in the second match against the hosts. Charlie would go on to play for Arsenal and appear at the Mexico 1986 World Cup finals.

Charlie Nicholas

Paul McStay's Scotland youth career began quite spectacularly with the famous 5–4 schoolboys win at Wembley in 1980, where he netted two goals, and then he was part of the side that won the UEFA European Under-18 Championship, and so a lot was expected of him. Paul was first capped at the age of 18 in September 1983 in a friendly versus Uruguay – by the time Scotland next played Uruguay at the World Cup in Mexico, Paul would win his 15th cap. This was his only appearance at the finals. He was, however, a regular in the Scotland side, and after the 1986 finals and from the beginning of the Andy Roxburgh tenure he would become more so. Indeed, in the late 1980s he was to go on a run of 23 consecutive games that would take him through the 1990 World Cup. Paul was to score the opening goal of the 1990 qualifying campaign in the 2–1 win over Norway in Oslo.

Paul was also to play at the 1992 Euros in Sweden where he scored a memorable opening goal against CIS. Despite playing for Scotland up until 1997, he would not make the squads for the 1996 Euros or France 1998. Paul was capped 76 times for Scotland, scoring nine goals.

Maurice Johnston was only to win ten of his 38 caps during his time at Celtic Park, which included that double versus Spain at Hampden in the 1984 3–1 victory. He would, of course, not appear at the finals in 1986 after incurring Fergie's wrath in Australia. Murdo Macleod was to win only five of his 20 caps with Celtic, Brian McClair four of his 30 and Derek Whyte four of his 12, although Whyte would travel to the 1992 Euros as a Celtic player but would not feature.

Cultured midfielder John Collins had already won four caps with Hibernian and had also travelled to the World Cup finals in 1990 before signing with Celtic. John was

Paul McStay

to win 32 caps with the club, playing in all ten of Scotland's Euro qualifiers for 1996 and then in all three games at the finals in England. Overall, John was to win 58 caps with Scotland, scoring 12 goals, including that penalty versus Brazil at France 98 when he was with Monaco.

Paul McStay

Tom Boyd had won caps at both Motherwell and Chelsea before he joined Celtic in 1992. He was only to play in one game at the 1992 Euros, the 3–0 win over CIS, but was to be a mainstay of the side after this. Tom was to win 72 caps in total, including 38 consecutive caps from August 1995 to June 1999. This would, of course, take him through the 1996 Euros and France 98, where he would be unfortunate to concede an agonising own goal in the opening match of the finals.

Tosh McKinlay had to wait until he had moved to Celtic Park to gain a Scotland cap despite a number of good seasons with Hearts. Tosh was 30 when he made his debut against Greece in a vital Euro qualifier in August 1995. He would keep his place and featured in the matches against England and Switzerland at Euro 96. Tosh then played in all ten qualifiers for the 1998 World Cup and at the finals was to play in the Brazil and Morocco games, which were to be the last of his 22 caps.

John Collins

Overall the 1998 World Cup squad was to feature five other Celtic players. Craig Burley had won 20 caps at Chelsea by the time he joined Celtic in July 1997 for £2.5m. He was to win 16 more with the club with the peak being the moment he scored the equaliser versus Norway in Bordeaux, France. The trough came a game later, where the now bleached-haired Burley was sent off against Morocco as Scotland crashed out of the World Cup. Craig would win 46 caps altogether, scoring three goals.

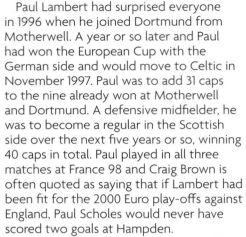

Paul Lambert had surprised everyone in 1996 when he joined Dortmund from Motherwell. A year or so later and Paul had won the European Cup with the German side and would move to Celtic in November 1997. Paul was to add 31 caps to the nine already won at Motherwell and Dortmund. A defensive midfielder, he was to become a regular in the Scottish side over the next five years or so, winning 40 caps in total. Paul played in all three matches at France 98 and Craig Brown is often quoted as saying that if Lambert had been fit for the 2000 Euro play-offs against England, Paul Scholes would never have scored two goals at Hampden.

Jackie McNamara and Simon Donnelly were among the younger players at France 98 but only defender McNamara was to make an appearance, playing in the Morocco game. Jackie would win 33 caps altogether from 1996 all the way to 2005. Simon would win only ten caps altogether. Goalkeeper Jonathan Gould was a squad member, too, winning two caps a couple of years later.

The final player from the squad was Darren Jackson. Darren had won 20 caps with Hibernian and played in most of the Euro 1996 qualifiers but did not feature at the finals. He was also a mainstay of the team that qualified for the 1998 finals, and although he didn't score many, he was involved in a number of goals on the way to France. His final eight caps came at Celtic, including two at France 98.

Celtic have, of course, provided many players for the Scotland side in the last 20 years but they are all marked with failing to get Scotland to a major tournament finals. Gary Caldwell was at Celtic when he netted the only goal against France in 2006. Scott Brown, of course, captained Scotland on many occasions, winning 50 caps. Then there were also the sublime moments that Leigh Griffiths gave us against England at Hampden a few years back. James Forrest, against Israel in November 2018, became the first Celtic player to hit a hat-trick for Scotland since Jimmy Quinn did so in 1908. Hopefully we won't have to wait so long for the next one.

James Forrest

RAEME SHARP

JANE ROSS
Manchester City WFC (ENG)
1,65 m 18-9-1989 DEBUT 2009

ndrew ROBERTSON

SCO

Darren FLETCHER

G. STRACHAN

ALAN McIL...

SCOTLAND

TOSH McKINLAY
SCOTLAND

DY JARDINE
EPS and SCOTLAND
SCOTTISH DAILY EXPRESS TOP FOR SPORT

Scottish Internationals

CAROLINE WEIR
Liverpool Ladies FC (ENG)
1,73 m 20-6-1995 DEBUT 2013

SCO

ALAN GILZEAN
(Dundee)

LEIGH GRIFFITHS

SCOTLAND

...ARSHALL

DAVE McPHERSON
ESCOCIA

Donachie

64 | 68
207

68
191 | 45

SHOOT! GOAL

SCOTTISH ALL STARS

DFIELDER

JAMES McARTHUR

JOE JORDAN
FORWARD ★

World Cup Appearances	
World Cup Goals	
International Appearances	27
International Goals	0
Height	5'9"

CHELSEA

Chelsea were formed in 1905 and within two years Scotsman David Calderhead became their manager. Calderhead had won a Scotland cap in 1889 with Queen of the South Wanderers and is Chelsea's longest serving manager, lasting until 1933, and would sign a number of notable Scots including the likes of Hughie Gallacher, Alex Jackson and Alec Cheyne.

Jock Cameron would be the first Scot to be capped with the Stamford Bridge club, achieving this in 1909 versus England at the Crystal Palace. Full-back Jock had been capped five years earlier as a St Mirren player. Angus Douglas would also win one solitary cap in 1911 versus Ireland at Celtic Park. Angus would go on to serve in the First World War but would sadly lose his life at the age of 30 to the flu pandemic of 1918.

The aforementioned Gallacher and Jackson, then of Newcastle United and Huddersfield Town respectively, were both part of the Wembley Wizards side of 1928, but at left-back that day representing Chelsea was Tommy Law. Tommy would return to Wembley two years later in his only other appearance for Scotland in a 5–2 defeat to England.

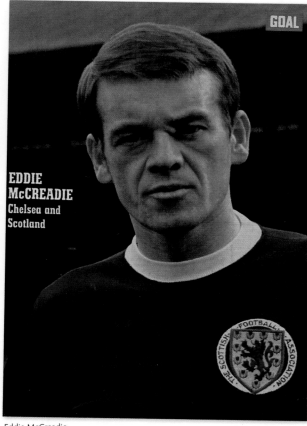

EDDIE McCREADIE
Chelsea and Scotland

Eddie McCreadie

John Jackson

Hughie Gallacher joined Chelsea from Newcastle in 1930 but despite being top scorer in the four seasons he was with them, he only gained one cap in 1934 in a 3–0 defeat to England at Wembley.

There were pre-war caps for goalkeeper John Jackson, winning four of his eight at Stamford Bridge having moved from Partick Thistle in 1933. Peter Buchanan was also to gain a solitary one in December 1937, scoring one as Scotland crushed Czechoslovakia at Hampden.

Post-war winger Bobby Campbell was to gain five caps, scoring once against Switzerland in 1950.

Among the great Chelsea side of the late 60s were a couple of Scots. Eddie McCreadie was one of the hard men in the flamboyant Chelsea side and would play 23 times for Scotland from 1965 to 1969, with his first match at Wembley in the 2–2 draw of 1965. He would, of course,

return there in 1967 as part of the famous 3–2 winning side. McCreadie played over 400 times for Chelsea and also managed them for a couple of years in the mid-70s.

Charlie Cooke was the other Scot in the side of the time. Charlie already had two caps when he joined from Dundee in 1966. He along with McCreadie would be part of the 1970 FA Cup-winning side and he would also win the European Cup Winners' Cup the following year. For Scotland, Charlie would win 16 caps in total from 1965 to 1975 but would never really get a regular run of games, with the majority of his caps coming in 1968 and 1969.

The late 70s and early 80s would see a decline in Chelsea's standing but a number of Scots had a role in the side's revival in the second half of the decade. Fiery striker David Speedie was signed from Darlington in 1982 and would play his part in Chelsea winning the Second Division title in the 83/84 season. Speedie would win his first Scotland cap in the Rous Cup victory over England at Hampden in 1985. His second

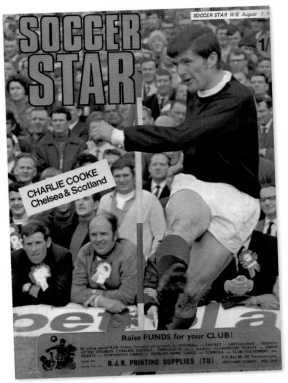

Charlie Cook

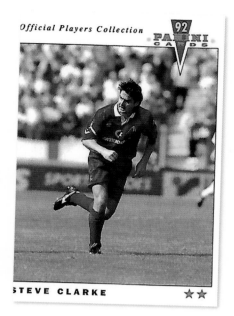

STEVE CLARKE ★★

match was the night of Jock Stein's death as Scotland drew 1–1 with Wales at Ninian Park, Cardiff. However, he was not really favoured by caretaker manager Alex Ferguson and would be left out of the squad for the Mexico 86 World Cup finals. He would win five caps at Stamford Bridge before joining Coventry City in July 1987 where he would double his cap tally.

Playing alongside Speedie for Chelsea and laying on a number of goals for him and his striking partner Kerry Dixon was Pat Nevin. Winger Nevin had a whole bundle of tricks and turns at his disposal and was very popular with Chelsea fans after his move to the London club from Clyde. Nevin did make a couple of sub appearances before Mexico but like Speedie was left out of the squad by Ferguson. He would gain another four caps at Chelsea before moving to Everton in 1988.

Right-back and current Scotland manager Stevie Clarke joined Chelsea from St Mirren in February 1987 and over the next ten years would play over 400 games for the club, winning the FA Cup, League Cup and European Cup Winners' Cup with them. Despite being Chelsea's first pick right-back, Clarke would only gain six caps with his first five coming in

1987 and a final one in 1994 in a friendly versus the Netherlands. The likes of Richard Gough, Stevie Nicol and Stewart McKimmie would keep Clarke out of the national side.

Joining Chelsea in 1986 from Hibernian, Gordon Durie is the only Chelsea player to appear at the World Cup finals for Scotland. Durie did so at Italia 90, playing in Scotland's victory over Sweden in Genoa. Durie would also at appear at Euros 92 and 96, as well as France 98, but with different clubs.

Striker John Spencer would join from Rangers in 1992, winning 13 caps, and would play at Euro 96. Interestingly Spencer would gain 14 caps in total and play against 14 different sides. Craig Burley would also feature at the 1996 finals and although predominantly a midfielder for Chelsea, often turned out for Scotland at full-back in the early part of his career. By the time of his move to Celtic in 1997 he had amassed 20 caps and would win more at France 98.

Sadly, in these modern times, only one player has been capped for Scotland whilst on the books at Chelsea this millennium and that would be Warren Cummings, who made a second half appearance versus a Hong Kong League Select XI in 2002, which is 45 minutes more than he ever did for Chelsea.

Gordon Durie • Chelsea

Linwood (Clyde)

Tommy Ring

CLYDE

Clyde were formed in Glasgow in 1877 and although until recently they occupied the bottom tier of Scottish football, they have won the Scottish Cup on three occasions. William Walker would be the first Clyde player to represent Scotland in 1909; however, lining up against him that day would be Jack Kirwan of Ireland, who was his teammate at Clyde. Scotland won 5–0.

Daniel Blair would win seven of his eight caps whilst at Shawfield, including a 2–0 victory over England at Hampden in 1931. Daniel had taken the long way round to play for Clyde – having been born in the nearby Parkhead area of Glasgow, he began playing football in Canada and the United States, turning out for such clubs as Willy's Overland Motor Works and the Providence Clamdiggers. Billy Boyd would play alongside Daniel in two matches and would score against Switzerland in a 3–2 victory in Geneva, also in 1931.

Clyde's first Scottish Cup victory would come in 1939, defeating Motherwell 4–0 in the final at Hampden in front of a crowd of 94,000. Keeping goal that day was Jock Brown who had only conceded one goal in the whole competition, a penalty kick in a 4–1 mauling

of Rangers in the third round at Ibrox. Jock would win one cap versus Wales in November 1938, with Scotland winning 3–2. Jock's sons Peter and Gordon both played for Scotland at rugby union – Gordon, of course, being better known as 'Broon frae Troon'. Jock's brother Jim would also represent the USA at the World Cup in 1930, scoring a goal against Argentina.

The immediate post-war years would see solitary caps for Jimmy Campbell in a Victory International versus Belgium, Hugh Long versus Northern Ireland in 1946 and Alex Linwood, who would score in a 2–0 World Cup qualifier victory versus Wales in 1949. Leslie Johnston would earn two caps and scored in a friendly versus Switzerland in Berne, in 1948.

1955 would bring cup success to the Shawfield side as they beat Celtic 1–0 in a replayed game at Hampden. The first match ended in a 1–1 draw and was the first ever Scottish Cup Final broadcast live on BBC TV. The scorer of the winning goal was one Tommy Ring. Outside-left Tommy had already won five Scotland caps by the time of the Scottish Cup victory. In an era with the likes of Willie Ormond and Billy Liddell, Tommy's 12-cap haul is quite remarkable considering he was a Second Division player for five of the caps. He would play in all of Scotland's qualifiers for the 1958 World Cup but would be replaced by Stewart Imlach for the finals in Sweden. Tommy would score two goals for Scotland – one in the famous 4–2 defeat to Puskas's Hungary in 1954 and one against England at Wembley in 1957 in the first minute in a 2–1 loss.

Two other players from the 1955 cup-winning side also played for Scotland. Left-back Harry Haddock was given his debut in the aforementioned Hungary game at Hampden. He then played in Scotland's next four games, including further defeats to England and Hungary in Budapest. Harry then lost his place as John Hewie of Charlton Athletic made the left-back berth his own for a number of years. Harry would be included in the 1958 World Cup finals squad but would not play in any of the matches.

However, inside-forward Archie Robertson would. Archie won his first cap alongside Haddock in the 1955 3–0 victory over Portugal at Hampden. He would also score first as Scotland thumped the mighty Austrians 4–1 in Vienna in May 1955. Competition was stiff for the Scotland team at this time, though, and Robertson would go a couple of years without being picked, but on his return, Scotland would beat Switzerland 3–2 at Hampden to qualify for the 1958 World Cup finals, with Archie netting the opener.

Robertson would initially lose his place to Jimmy Murray of Hearts in Sweden. Murray would be the scorer of Scotland's first ever finals goal but injury would see him miss the next match in Sweden and Archie was chosen to replace him. Scotland would lose narrowly 3–2 to Paraguay, but Murray would return for the final match and so for Robertson his World Cup was over as was his Scotland career.

Ring, Haddock and Robertson would all be part of the Clyde team that would lift the Scottish Cup once more in 1958. A John Coyle goal would win the cup final versus Hibernian. Coyle would also travel to the World Cup finals that year but would not play, nor would he at any point play for Scotland.

Also in the cup-winning side was inside-forward George Herd. George had made his debut for Scotland at Hampden just the week before but unfortunately had a miserable debut with England winning 4–0. George would

Harry Haddock, smiling skipper of Clyde

Harry Haddock

be forgotten about when it came to the World Cup finals that year, but in 1960 he would return to the national side and would be given a run of four games in which he would score one goal against Hungary in a 3–3 draw in Budapest. George would go on to play for Sunderland for many years but would not gain any more caps. He would also be the last Clyde player to be capped for Scotland. John McHugh would make the squad for a friendly in the mid-60s and Harry Hood would travel around the world with a Scotland XI in 1967.

GEORGE HERD

George Herd

However, youngster Pat Nevin would, in 1982, win the Under-18 UEFA European Youth Tournament with Scotland and be named player of the tournament. Pat would, of course, go on to play for the likes of Chelsea, Everton and Tranmere Rovers and gain 28 Scotland caps in total. His manager at Clyde at the time, Craig Brown, would also go on to serve Scotland with distinction, leading them to the Euros in 96 and to France 98.

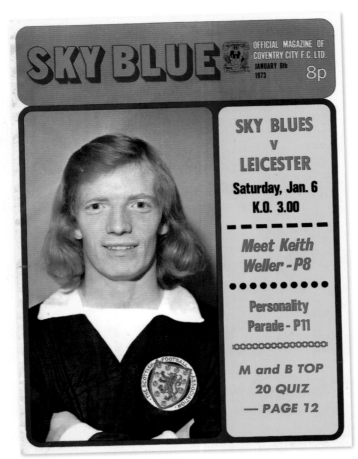

Willie Carr

COVENTRY CITY

Coventry City were founded in 1883 as Singers FC, becoming Coventry City in 1898. Jimmy Hill would lead them to the English top flight for the first time in 1967. Midfielder Willie Carr, the inventor of the 'Donkey Kick' free kick, would sign that year and in 1970 would play in all of Scotland's four games. Scotland would remain unbeaten but two 0–0 games and two 1–0 victories were not much to shout about. Carr didn't play in 1971 but was recalled by Tommy Docherty for a couple of matches in 1972, including the Doc's final one, a World Cup qualifier against Denmark at Hampden. At the end of Willie's time with the national side he remained unbeaten in his six games.

If Doc's successor didn't fancy Carr in his squad he did cap a couple of his Sky Blues teammates. Striker Colin Stein already had 17 caps to his name, scoring nine goals, all coming with Rangers. Colin played

Tommy Hutchison

in Willie Ormond's first four games in charge, mostly as a sub, but was then discarded. However, he was named in Ormond's preliminary squad of 40 for the World Cup in 1974 but would not travel to West Germany.

Someone who did travel was teammate Tommy Hutchison. Tommy was rather oddly built for a Scottish winger in that he was 6ft tall. He had joined Coventry from Blackpool where he had enjoyed five seasons. Tommy would make his Scotland debut on 20 September 1973 and that night would be part of the side that would make history by qualifying for the 1974 World Cup finals with the 2–1 victory over Czechoslovakia.

Tommy would only make two appearances at the finals, coming on as a sub in both the Zaire and Yugoslavia games. He would play in the first few games after the World Cup and would score from the penalty spot as Scotland beat East Germany 3–0 in a friendly at Hampden in October 1974, but would turn villain a month later, as he missed a penalty against Spain that would cost dearly in terms of qualifying for the 1976 Euros. By late 1975 his Scotland career was over and yet there are many who would say he played some of his best football beyond this point.

February 1978 and Ally's army were on their way to Argentina and in a friendly versus Bulgaria at Hampden, not one but two Coventry players were on show. Jim Blyth would be between the sticks and striker Ian Wallace would come on for Kenny Dalglish in the 65th minute and hit the winner as Scotland ground out a 2–1 win. Blyth would play one more game (versus Wales in May 1978) and would concede a late own goal from a terrible Willie Donachie back pass that he would have no chance from but which would taint his Scotland reputation. Jim did travel to Argentina as second choice to Alan Rough but would never feature in the side again.

Ian Wallace had moved to Coventry in 1976 after a couple of seasons at Dumbarton. He would become their top goalscorer in the following seasons and indeed would move to reigning European champions Nottingham Forest in 1980 for £1.25m. However, despite his goal

JIM BLYTH
COVENTRY & SCOTLAND

Shoot!

Kevin Gallacher
COVENTRY

TOPPS SALUTES
S
IAN WALLACE

for Scotland he would not feature again under Ally MacLeod and would only gain two more caps, all before his move to Forest.

Forward David Speedie would win a handful of caps towards the end of the 80s. Following this Kevin Gallacher would win ten of his 53 caps at Coventry. These appearances would include his three at the 1992 Euros, coming off the bench in the first two matches versus the Netherlands and Germany. He would start the third and final game as Scotland beat the CIS – as the remaining countries of the Soviet Union were temporarily known at the time. Kevin would, of course, go on to make a greater impact for Scotland after his move to Blackburn in 1993.

Like Gallacher, Eoin Jess would make a finals appearance whilst berthed at Coventry but it would only be the last six minutes of the defeat to England at Euro 96. Jess's stay at Coventry would last just over a

year and three caps before he returned to his beloved Aberdeen.

Gary McAllister moved to Coventry from Leeds United for £3m in July 1996 and would lead Scotland to the 1998 World Cup finals. Sadly, though, injury would rule him out of the finals themselves but his penalty against Belarus in the 1–0 victory in Minsk would prove invaluable to the successful campaign. Gary would only play in one game after the World Cup and sadly was booed by some sections of the Scotland crowd as they fell behind 2–0 to the Czech Republic in a Euro qualifier at Celtic Park in 1999. Gary would quit international football after this. Colin Hendry would win a few caps in a very brief spell with Coventry in the early part of the millennium and he currently stands as the last City player capped for Scotland.

DERBY COUNTY

Derby County were formed in 1884 and were one of the 12 founder members of the Football League. However, it would not be until 1932 that left-winger Douglas 'Dally' Duncan would be capped for Scotland in October that year. Dally would score on his debut as the Scots were humbled 5–3 by Wales at Tynecastle Park, Edinburgh. Dally, though, would retain his place and was a regular in the Scotland side over the next few years.

Dally would score seven goals for Scotland, including both in the 2–0 victory over England at Wembley in 1935. Both these goals came from corners by future Derby player Charlie Napier who was then with Celtic. Also on that day Hughie Gallacher was playing in his only Scotland match as a Derby player. Napier

Charlie Napier

would win two of his five caps at the Baseball Ground and indeed he would score in the first of these, a 3–1 win over Ireland in Belfast playing alongside Duncan. Also scoring that day was David McCulloch of Brentford, who would win two caps at Derby in 1938.

The post-war era would see the fiery Billy Steel move from Morton to Derby in 1947 for £15,500, a then British record. Billy was a quick, sharp and instinctive type of player, although not often liked by his teammates for his sharp tongue. Billy would gain 14 of his 30 caps at Derby, having already won three at Morton. 1949 would see Scotland win all four of their games and Billy scored in three of these, including the 3–1 victory at Wembley. In 1950 Billy would, surprisingly, move back to Scotland and Dundee for a then Scottish record of £22,250.

It would be another 20 years before a Derby County player was capped for Scotland. Brian Clough and Peter Taylor had taken over at the Baseball Ground in 1967 and would win the Second Division in 1968/69 and then the First Division in 1971/72. A smattering of Scots were among this side, including former international Dave Mackay plus John McGovern, Archie Gemmill and John O'Hare.

Forward O'Hare was first capped in 1970 and scored on his debut versus Northern Ireland in Belfast. John would score five goals for Scotland in his 13 games, three of which were match-winners. However, Clough's refusal to allow O'Hare and Archie Gemmill to travel to Brazil in 1972 for the Independence Cup matches would see O'Hare lose his Scotland place completely.

It's quite ironic that Scotland legend Archie made his Scotland debut in the mud of the Stade Sclessin in Liege against Belgium in February 1971, given the state of the pitch at the Baseball Ground in the early 70s most Saturdays, it seemed. Archie and O'Hare would score the goals on the night of the 2–1 victory over Portugal in Docherty's first match in charge in October 1971 but like O'Hare, Docherty would not choose Gemmill again after the summer of 1972. Archie wouldn't come back into the reckoning until over three years later in October 1975, becoming

"Dally" Duncan eludes Crayston (England). Wembley, 1936.

Dally Duncan

GOAL GETTER

Billy Steel

Billy Steel

JOHN O'HARE
Derby County and Scotland

JOHN now has 13 full Scottish caps . . . but there's nothing unlucky about that! It's unlikely that the stocky Derby forward will stay on this figure for very long, even though he was left out of the team that beat Denmark in October.
John's international debut was in the 1970 Home Championships. He played in all three of the games, scoring on his first outing against Northern Ireland.

Scotland were unbeaten tournament, and John was After that, Scotland hit losing seven out of their ne . . . this resulted in Manage being dismissed.
John is one of the few p era still in favour.
Tommy Docherty appre hard-running of the Derby

THE ALL-TIME GREATS

SCOTLAND

ARCHIE GEMMILL
Midfield   1971–81

a ready-made replacement for the banned Billy Bremner in midfield. He would play a major part in the side over the next few years, however, with 22 of his 43-cap total coming whilst at Derby, but his finest Scotland moment would come as a Nottingham Forest player.

Already in that side was Bruce Rioch. Rioch along with Archie had won the 1974/75 First Division under Dave Mackay who had taken over from Clough. Rioch had burst into the Scotland side and along with Don Masson of QPR formed a great partnership in the midfield. Rioch was well known for his powerful shot and racked up six goals in his first 14 caps before moving to Everton for one season in 1977/78. He would head back to Derby in September 1977 and within a month he would be joined by Don Masson.

Managing Derby at the time was Tommy Docherty and Rioch and Masson were to fall foul of his wrath and spent a lot of their time on the sidelines. By the time of Argentina, both players had lost a lot of self-belief and confidence and Masson in particular was a shadow of his former self at the World Cup finals. The Peru defeat, during which he missed a penalty, would be his last cap. Only three of his 16 caps came whilst at Derby and arguably they were his worst performances.

As for Rioch, despite playing in the win versus the Netherlands in Mendoza, he too would not play again after Argentina, and both would soon leave Derby too.

Christian Dailly would move to County in 1996 and would win his first Scotland cap in May 1997. Christian would win 13 caps with Derby and would play in all three games at France 98 before moving to Blackburn in August that year. Since then, as Derby have moved back and forth from the Premier League to the Championship many Scots have plied their trade at Pride Park, including the likes of the three Craigs – Bryson, Forsyth and Burley (10 caps), plus Chris Martin (15), Ikechi Anya (8), Kris Commons (7) and Gary Teale (7), though not forgetting Stephen Pearson, Johnny Russell and Kenny Miller.

BRUCE RIOCH

DERBY

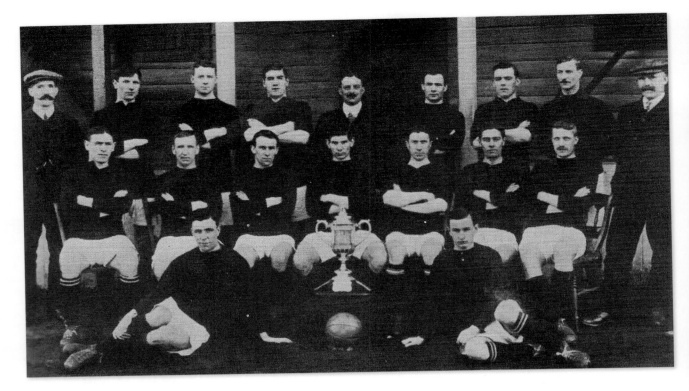

DUNDEE

Dundee FC were formed in 1893 and within six months of their first league match, not one but three of their players were chosen to represent Scotland in March 1894 in Belfast. Forward Alex Keillor had already been capped for Scotland whilst playing at Montrose and would win a further four with Dundee. Playing alongside him in the 2–1 victory were goalkeeper Frank Barrett and defender Bill Longair, who were to win two caps and one cap respectively.

1910 would bring Scottish Cup success for the only time in the club's history and three players from the cup-winning side would gain Scotland caps; however, only one was to come after the event. Winger Jack Fraser won his only cap in 1907 in a 3–0 victory over Ireland. John 'Sailor' Hunter would score the winning goal in the cup replay against Clyde as Dundee ran out 3–2 winners, but had won his only cap a year before in a 3–2 defeat to Wales in Wrexham.

Inside-forward Sandy MacFarlane was capped five times between 1904 and 1911. Although not part of the cup-winning side Robert Hamilton was at Dundee that season and added one more cap and two goals to his ten caps won at Rangers. With 15 goals in total Robert currently sits equal seventh with James McFadden on the all-time Scotland scoring list.

Although Dundee players would be capped in the 1920s and 30s it was not until the 1950s and 60s that Dens Parkers were to win the bulk of their caps. Billy Steel was bought from Derby County for a Scottish club record fee of £22,500 in 1950 and he was part of the Dundee side that would lift the Scottish League Cup in 1951 and 1952. Within a couple

Billy Steel (Scotland, Morton, Derby County, Dundee) one of the post-war greats.

of months of signing for Dundee, Billy hit four goals in a 6–1 rout of Northern Ireland at Hampden and in the following April was in the side that won 3–2 at Wembley. He would add 13 caps to his tally of 17 already won at Morton and Derby; however, he also holds the ignominious record of being the first Scotland player to be sent off – versus Austria in Vienna, 1951.

Defender Doug Cowie would also be part of the League Cup successes and captained the team for much of the 50s. Doug would win 20 caps and appeared at both the 1954 and 1958 World Cup finals. Doug played in both the matches in 1954 and the opening two games in Sweden, which would mark his final appearance for Scotland.

Also in the squad for 1958 was goalkeeper Bill Brown. Bill had played in the 1951 League Cup Final, too. Incredibly Bill's first cap would come in Scotland's final World Cup game versus France. Scotland lost 2–1 but Bill went on to win another three caps with Dundee before moving to Tottenham Hotspur and double glory.

November 1961 and with Dundee remarkably heading towards a sensational league championship title, defenders Ian Ure and Alex Hamilton were drafted into the Scotland side. Their first game was a 2–0 victory at home over Wales and then both players would play in the 1962 World Cup play-off match versus Czechoslovakia in Belgium. A third Dundee player, winger Hugh Robertson, would win his only cap in that 4–2 extra-time defeat at the Heysel Stadium in Brussels.

Hamilton would take part in a hat-trick of consecutive wins over the Auld Enemy from 1962 to 1964 and won 24 caps altogether. Ure would gain eight caps at Dens including the Wembley 1963 victory. Alan Gilzean would hit 169 league goals in 190 games for Dundee but he did not feature in the Scotland side until November 1963, as Scotland walloped Norway 6–1 at Hampden. However, Alan did not make a goalscoring debut as Denis Law nabbed four and Dave Mackay the other two.

Doug Cowie (Dundee)

ALAN GILZEAN, Dundee

It was in his third game that Gilzean would hit the back of the net for Scotland as his header clinched victory over England at Hampden in April 1964. He followed this up with a double against West Germany in a 2–2 friendly draw in Hanover. He made it four goals in five games in November 1964 as Scotland beat Northern Ireland 3–2 at home. This was to be his last appearance as a Dens Park player as he moved to White Hart Lane and a successful time with Spurs a month later. His final tally would be 22 caps and 12 goals. In season 1965/66 Charlie Cooke would win the first couple of his 16 caps (versus Wales and Italy) before moving to Chelsea and league winner Andy Penman won his only cap, also – versus the Netherlands at Hampden.

League Cup success was to come again to Dundee in 1973 with a 1–0 victory over Celtic, and three of that side would gain Scotland caps. Forward Jocky Scott had by this time won his two Scotland caps playing for Bobby Brown's side in defeats against Denmark and the USSR in 1971. Goalkeeper Thomson Allan was also to win two Scotland caps, both in the run-up to the 1974 World Cup finals, where he would be understudy to David Harvey. Skilful midfielder Bobby Robinson would win four caps either side of the finals but was not to be included in the squad that travelled to West Germany.

With the exception of Robert Connor's one cap in 1986 (versus the Netherlands) no Dundee player would represent Scotland again until this century, when first Gavin Rae and then Lee Wilkie were to gain caps. Midfielder Rae had been capped late into Craig Brown's tenure as manager of the national team and would be joined in the side early into Berti Vogts's reign by defender Wilkie. Lee played in most of the 2004 Euro qualifiers but his last match was to be the humiliating 6–0 defeat to the Netherlands in the play-offs in 2003. The likeable Wilkie, who won 11 caps in total, would suffer serious injury in the following months and never returned to the side. That was also to be Rae's eighth and final cap as a Dundee player, although he did gain another three each with Rangers and Cardiff City.

DUNDEE UNITED

Dundee United were formed as Dundee Hibernian in 1909, switching their name to United in 1923. It would only be with promotion in 1959 that they were to become an established First Division side. The arrival of Jim McLean at Tannadice Park as manager in 1971 would herald the most successful period in United's history, peaking with winning the Premier Division in 1982/83 and reaching the semi-finals of the European Cup the following year.

Seven players from that side would grace the Scotland team. In April 1977 David Narey replaced John Blackley in the 76th minute of a 3–1 home friendly win over Sweden and in doing so became the first United player to be capped. However, this was to be Willie Ormond's last game in charge and the subsequent Ally MacLeod whirlwind era would see no second cap for Narey, nor for any of his teammates.

In November 1978, Jock Stein would bring back Narey into his Scotland side in his second game in charge and, of course, in 1982, David would create Scottish football history by hitting that marvellous shot past a bewildered Brazilian goalie at the World Cup finals in Spain. He was to win 35 caps,

David Narey

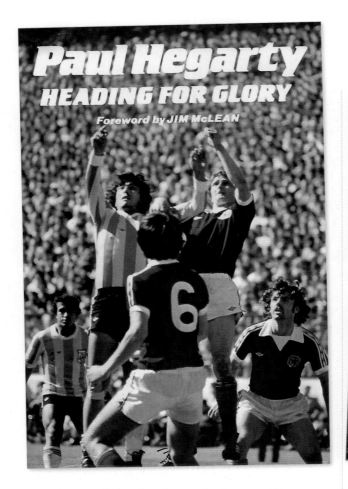

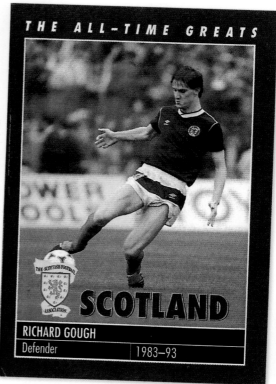

THE ALL-TIME GREATS

SCOTLAND

RICHARD GOUGH
Defender   1983–93

including matches at the 1986 World Cup, finishing his Scotland career in 1989. Jock Stein was quick to promote Narey's defensive partner Paul Hegarty to the national side, too. Hegarty would win his first cap in the 3–0 British Championship defeat to Wales at Ninian Park in May 1979 and within a month, another four caps would follow, but there was to be only three more for him thereafter.

Eamonn Bannon had been at Hearts and then Chelsea before heading to Tannadice, and his first cap came in a 3–1 defeat at Hampden to Belgium in a Euro qualifier in December 1979. It was to be another four years before the skilful midfielder returned to the side, playing in all three Home Internationals in May and June 1983. Once more, though, he was absent from the side until Alex Ferguson took over and Eamonn would play the final two of his 11 Scotland games at the Mexico 86 World Cup finals.

PAUL STURROCK Dundee United

Paul Sturrock was another United player who would begin his Scotland career in a defeat to Wales, this time at

the Vetch Field, Swansea, in 1981. Paul won 20 caps in total, scoring three goals for Scotland, and was part of the squads for Spain 82 and Mexico 86 where he appeared in the Denmark and Uruguay games.

Richard Gough would make his Scotland debut in a 2–2 draw in March 1983 versus Switzerland in a Euro qualifier at Hampden. Given his later commanding performances for Spurs, Rangers and indeed Scotland as a central defender, it is surprising that Richard's early matches for Scotland were at right-back. He was to win 26 caps with the Tannidice club, playing in all three games at Mexico 86. Of course, before Mexico he would score the goal that would give Scotland victory (and the trophy) in the inaugural Rous Cup game versus England at Hampden in 1985.

On the other wing, at left-back in Mexico was Maurice Malpas. Malpas would really be the last great Dundee United player to remain at Tannadice throughout his career and be recognised for Scotland whilst playing over 600 games for his club. For Scotland he would win 55 caps and play in the World Cup finals in Mexico and Italy (where he would be the sole Dundee United player), and at the Euros in Sweden, 1992.

Davie Dodds was also capped, making two appearances in 1983 and scoring in a 2–0 victory over Uruguay in a friendly at Hampden. These players would represent United at their peak, winning over 150 caps between them whilst at Tannadice.

When Scotland qualified for the Euro finals for the first time in 1992, four United players were included in the squad, as well as a former 'Arab' in Kevin Gallacher. Forward Gallacher's first four caps came at United and all in 1988. Kevin would go on to win 49 more with Coventry, Blackburn and Newcastle.

Of the four United players who travelled to Sweden 92, midfielder Jim McInally, following on from Maurice Malpas in 1984, was the next to be capped – in April 1987 as Scotland were walloped 4–1 by Belgium in a Euro qualifier in Brussels. Jim would win ten caps but was only on the winning side twice, including the 3–0 victory over CIS at the 1992 finals. David Bowman won the first of six caps in one of the warm-up games for the Euros versus Finland at Hampden, when only 9,275 were in attendance.

115 INTERNATIONAL

Billy Dodds

Team	Scotland
Position	Forward
Born	5 February 1969
Place	New Cumnock
Height	1.73 m
Weight	68 kg
Club	Dundee United
Previous clubs	Chelsea, Partick Thistle (loan), Dundee, St Johnstone, Aberdeen

- Billy started off his club career with Chelsea. However, it wasn't until a return north of the border that he blossomed into a prolific goalscorer.
- Billy won his first cap against Latvia in October 1996. But it was in a game with another East European team that he really made his mark, coming off the bench to net two goals against Estonia in October 1998.

BILLY McKINLAY
Dundee United

Big things were expected of Duncan Ferguson and he was indeed seen as potentially leading the line for Scotland all through the 90s. Unfortunately, it was not to be and he would end up with a cap tally of seven, four of which came at United. He would play just over ten minutes of the match versus the Netherlands in Sweden and his final cap at Tannadice would be versus Germany at Ibrox Stadium, where he would famously hit the bar with an overhead kick. Sadly that was as good as it got for Ferguson.

There would only be two more United players capped in the 1990s as the club's stock began to slide. Midfielder Billy McKinlay first featured for Scotland in 1993 in what was Craig Brown's first official game in charge. McKinlay repaid this by scoring within 15 minutes as Scotland beat Malta 2–0 in an 'academic' World Cup qualifier in Valetta and as a United player would score four in total in 14 games before moving on to Blackburn. McKinlay would gain some of these caps whilst playing in the second tier of Scottish football.

Towards the end of the 20th century Billy Dodds slotted into the Scotland side and although he hadn't scored in his first four caps won at Aberdeen, he would net a double in his first outing as a United player versus Estonia to help Scotland to a 3–2 win in a Euro qualifier at Tynecastle Stadium, Edinburgh. Another couple of goals saw Scotland gain vital wins as they headed towards the Euro 2000 play-offs. Billy appeared in the two play-off matches against England in November 1999 without scoring and these were to be his last as a Dundee United player.

The new century would see success for Dundee United in the Scottish Cup in 2009/10 but they rarely pushed for honours the way they had before. A total of 12 players would be capped thus far, amassing a total of 29 caps between them. Among them were goalkeeper Paul Gallacher, forward Steven Thompson, Charlie and Lee Miller, David Goodwillie and others. However, on the plus side, the current Scotland captain Andy Robertson would win his first two caps whilst at Tannadice.

EVERTON

Founded in 1878 as St. Domingo FC but a year later renamed as Everton, they were one of the founding members of the Football League in 1888. Jack Bell would become the first Scot to be capped whilst at the Goodison Park club in 1896, scoring a vital goal in a 2–1 victory over England at Celtic Park, Glasgow. Jack had already won a couple of caps with Dumbarton before the three he would win at Everton. He would go on to win five more with Celtic. Playing alongside him in 1898 versus England was clubmate John Robertson; sadly it was to end in a 3–1 defeat and this was to be Robertson's only cap.

Alex 'Sandy' Young would win two caps in 1907 which followed his FA Cup-winning goal in 1906, as Everton lifted the trophy for the first time. Sandy is one of Everton's all-time top goalscorers but, sadly, after finishing with football, he would be convicted of manslaughter in Australia for the killing of his brother in 1916. He would pass away in 1959 in an Edinburgh asylum.

Neil McBain would win two caps in the early 1920s but he is mainly notable for being the oldest player, at 51, to appear in a Football League match, when as manager of New Brighton he turned out during an injury crisis in March 1947. Winger Torry Gillick, in-between stints at Rangers, would win five caps, scoring three goals, and perhaps without the intervention of World War II would have won more.

Right-back Alex Parker had already won 14 caps as a Falkirk player before moving to Everton in June 1958. His one and only appearance as an Evertonian was versus Paraguay at the 1958 World Cup finals. Alex would go on to win the league with Everton in season 1962/63. Also playing at the World Cup in 1958 was Bobby Collins, who moved to Everton after the finals. Whilst at Everton, Bobby would win six of his 31 caps in the couple of years that followed, scoring three of his ten goals.

Along with Parker three other international Scots were involved in Everton's championship-winning side of 1962/63. Alex Young's cap tally of eight is another one of those that it is hard to rationalise; after all, he won the Scottish First Division twice with

Tiny Scottish international Bobby Collins moved from Celtic to Everton last season for a fee of £25,000, and made a great difference to the forward line. Only 5 ft. 3 in., Collins takes size 4 in boots.

Bobby Collins

Alex Young

Hearts and the English title with Everton, scoring 24, 23 and 22 goals respectively in these triumphs. He would only play once whilst at Goodison, at Hampden Park in June 1966, in a World Cup warm-up for England-bound Portugal.

Defensive midfielder Jimmy Gabriel moved from Dundee to Everton in 1960 and won his first cap just over six months later in a 2–0 defeat to Wales in Cardiff. His second and last would come three years later as Scotland cruised to a 6–1 victory over Norway with Jimmy coming on for Jim Baxter at half-time. Also playing that night was winger Alex Scott who had signed from Rangers in February 1963. Scott had won several titles and honours with Rangers including 11 Scotland caps and was part of the 1958 World Cup squad. With Everton he would win the league title within a few months and along with Gabriel and Young the FA Cup in 1966. His cap tally at Goodison would see him win 16 in total.

Bruce Rioch would have a brief spell at Everton from December 1976 to September 1977, before returning once more to Derby. He was to play and captain Scotland six times in this period, including the memorable victory at Wembley in 1977 and two of the matches in that year's South American tour. Another Scotland midfielder in Asa Hartford would pitch up at Everton in winter 1979 after a three-game spell with Brian Clough's Nottingham Forest. Asa was to add eight caps to his final total of 50 during his two-year spell at Goodison, including a number of 1982 World Cup qualifiers plus the victory at Wembley in 1981.

Goalkeeper George Wood was one of many that were expected to take over from Alan Rough in goal for Scotland but in many ways a 3–1 defeat to England at Wembley in May 1979 put the kibosh on that one. However, George does have one claim to fame as the first goalkeeper to concede a full international goal to football superstar Diego Maradona at Hampden in June 1979! George would win three caps at Goodison and added another whilst at Arsenal in 1982, where he was also chosen to be part of the 1982 World Cup finals squad.

Graeme Sharp

Andy Gray moved to Everton in November 1983 and in a two-year spell would win the FA Cup, the league and the European Cup Winners' Cup. As for Scotland, in May 1985 he was to win his only cap at the club, in a World Cup qualifier versus Iceland in Reykjavik – his 20th and final cap.

Graeme Sharp is one of the most loved players at Goodison Park from the 1980s, winning a host of honours with the club including two titles, scoring 159 goals in 426 appearances, making him second only to the great Dixie Dean in the goalscoring stakes. As for his 12 caps for Scotland – ho-hum. Scotland had a host of strikers around this time but scoring goals was not at a premium for any of them it seemed. Sharp's goal return was one solitary hit versus Malta in his final match. He would make an appearance at Mexico 86 in the 0–0 draw with Uruguay.

Winger Pat Nevin had a four-year spell at Everton (1988–1992) but would not be selected for Italia 90. However, he was a regular in the Scotland side that qualified for the Euros in 1992 under manager Andy Roxburgh. Nevin would get some game time in Sweden, making two substitute

Pat Nevin

Stuart McCall

appearances versus Germany and the CIS. Eight caps were won at Goodison before he would move on to Tranmere Rovers, where he was to win another 14 caps and would finish with a total of 28 overall.

Stuart McCall was picked for both Scotland and England Under-21s on the same day in 1984 whilst at Bradford City and chose the latter. However, fortune favoured Scotland as Stuart did not get any game time and subsequently opted for Scotland. He moved to Everton in 1988 and made his Scotland debut versus Argentina in March 1990. Quite quickly, Stuart established himself in the side and

would play in all three games at Italia 90 and hit that wonderful scrambled goal versus Sweden in Genoa. In all he was to win 11 caps at Everton before moving on to Rangers.

Although no Evertonian would represent Scotland at France 98, by the time of the 2000 Euro play-off match versus England at Wembley in November 1999, three Goodison players were on show. John Collins had first been capped in 1988 as a Hibernian player and had memorably scored that equalising penalty versus Brazil in the Stade de France at World Cup 98. He was to win his final six caps at Everton, with the Wembley 1999 match being his final one.

In defence was David Weir who had joined Everton from Hearts in 1999 having already won nine caps. David would go on to win 43 caps whilst at Everton which included a two-and-a-half-year break after quitting during the Berti Vogts era. David would eventually win 69 caps in total. Don Hutchison would win ten caps whilst at Everton and they were to be his most prolific in terms of goals, netting five, including winners versus Germany in Bremen in April 1999 and versus England at Wembley in November 1999.

In this century a number of caps have been won by Scots at Everton, including Scot Gemmill winning 13 of his 26, defender Gary Naysmith 32 of his 46 and forward Steven Naismith winning 26, too. Of course, there is one extra-special player who has also sent us into rapturous moments like Hutchison did in 1999: the one and only James McFadden, a man who grew in stature every time he stepped on to the pitch on Scotland duty.

McFadden would play at Everton from 2003 to 2008 and like Hutchison had his most fertile period in the Scotland team whilst at Goodison. James hit 13 goals in 33 games, including unforgettable strikes versus the Netherlands in the 2004 Euro play-offs, that goal versus France in Paris in September 2007 and a scintillating third versus the Ukraine at Hampden the following month. He would return to Everton in 2011 but was ravaged by injury and would only play a few more games, and alas his Scotland career was over by this time, too. His final tally was 48 caps and 15 goals.

INTERNATIONAL 115

Don Hutchison

Team	Scotland
Position	Midfielder
Born	9 May 1971
Place	Gateshead
Height	1.85 m
Weight	75 kg
Club	Everton
Previous clubs	Hartlepool United, Liverpool, West Ham United, Sheffield United

❀ Don is one of three English-born players, the others being keepers Jonathan Gould and Neil Sullivan, in the Scottish squad. He made his international debut as a sub against the Czech Republic in March 1999.
❀ Don's favoured position is in central midfield. But he can also do a job up front, as he proved with his stunning goal in a surprise 1-0 friendly win over Germany in April 1999!

James McFadden

FALKIRK

Falkirk were formed in 1876 but were not elected to the Scottish League until season 1902/03. However, by then two players had already been capped. Defender Jock Drummond was chosen to play against Ireland in Belfast in March 1892 (the Scots won 3–2) and would go on to play for Scotland a further 13 times; however, by the time of his second cap he was a Rangers player. Jock's main claim to fame is he is known as the last outfield football player to wear a cap whilst playing in first-class football! Six years later and goalkeeper William Watson was given a run-out against Wales in a 5–2 win at Fir Park, the home of Motherwell FC, for his only cap.

Falkirk were to finish league runners-up in both 1907/08 and 1909/10. Archie Devine had hit 13 goals in 25 games in the latter season and was to hit a late winner versus Wales in March 1910 at Rugby Park, Kilmarnock, in his only international. Teammate John McTavish was to play his solitary Scotland game a fortnight later in a 1–0 defeat to Ireland in Belfast.

Scottish Cup success was to come to Falkirk in April 1913 and three of that side were to be capped for Scotland. A month before the

Robert Orrock

John McTavish

final, full-back Robert Orrock made his only Scotland appearance on 3 March down at the Racecourse Ground, Wrexham, which would end in a 0–0 draw. Almost a fortnight later Jimmy Croal and Tommy Logan were part of the Scotland side that won 2–1 in Dublin versus Ireland. Logan would go on to score one of the two goals that would bring victory to Falkirk in the cup final versus Raith Rovers played at Celtic Park in front of a 45,000 crowd. Like Orrock, centre-half Logan would only play the one Scotland game but Croal would go on to feature in another two. Within weeks of the cup final, Logan was on his way to Chelsea, where he would be joined by Croal a year later. Both were in the Chelsea side that reached the 1915 FA Cup Final, losing to Sheffield United.

1925 would bring a cap for Tom Townsley, with the centre-half captaining Scotland on the occasion, a 3–0 victory over Wales at Ninian Park, Cardiff. Two years later and Robert Thompson won his only cap versus England in a 2–1 defeat at Hampden. Robert would go on to serve in the RAF in the Second World War and in the early 50s would manage Dutch side Ajax. Likewise, centre-half Alex Low would win but one cap in 1933 as Scotland lost 2–1 to Ireland at Celtic Park.

May 1955 and Scotland had been hammered 7–2 by England the month before, so a wholesale clear-out was demanded and right-back Alex Parker of Falkirk was slotted into the defence. Out of the next 11 games Parker was to play in ten, and only one of which would see Scotland defeated, a 3–1 loss to Hungary in Budapest. The arrival of Eric Caldow on the scene, however, would see Parker lose his place in the side, as 1957 began.

April 1957 would see Alex win the Scottish Cup with Falkirk after a replay against Kilmarnock and by October, Parker was back in the Scotland side. Caldow moved to left-back with John Hewie of Charlton dropping out of the side. Later that month Parker would line up alongside teammates Jimmy McIntosh and winger Eddie O'Hara to play the Netherlands in an Under-23 match. However, once more Parker was out of the Scotland side after they went down 4–0 to England at Hampden in 1958 and indeed this was to be his last cap as a Falkirk player. He and O'Hara would head south to Everton where Parker would win the First Division title in 1962/63.

There was just one more cap for Alex, as injury to the re-established Hewie saw him play against Paraguay at the World Cup finals in Sweden. The fee for Parker and O'Hara would free up money for Falkirk to buy the promising John White from Alloa. John would not remain at Brockville for long, only playing 30 league games and scoring 11 goals. He would also make an immediate impact on his Scotland debut, scoring within the first minute against West Germany in a 3–2 home victory at Hampden in May 1959 – a crowd of 103,415 turned up for that friendly match. John was to add three more caps during his time with Falkirk and was to score a second goal versus Northern Ireland in October 1959. Later that month he signed for Tottenham Hotspur, where he would win the 'double' in 1960/61 and another 18 caps, before his untimely death in 1964.

It was to be almost 50 years later that a Falkirk player would win a Scotland cap again. Defensive midfielder Darren Barr would come on as a second half sub versus Northern Ireland in 2008 in a friendly that would end goalless at Hampden during George Burley's reign as manager. Darren was retained in the squads for the next few matches but no further caps came his way and he continues to be the last Bairn capped for Scotland.

Alec Parker (Falkirk)

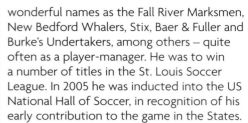

GREENOCK MORTON

Greenock Morton were formed in 1874 as Morton Football Club and added the name of their home town in 1994. Morton were one of the founding members of the Scottish Second Division in 1893 and first gained promotion to the First Division in season 1899/1900. However, by that time three players had already earned a cap each.

First up was Greenock-born Robert Fleming, who turned out versus Ireland in 1886. Scotland would win 7–2 with Charles Heggie of Rangers netting four. Fellow Greenockian Rab MacFarlane was the next to play for Scotland, this time versus Wales in 1896 up at Carolina Port, which was home to Dundee FC at the time. Scotland would win 4–0. So perhaps there wasn't too much for goalkeeper MacFarlane to do. He would go on to play for, among others, Third Lanark, Everton, Celtic, Aberdeen and Motherwell.

Peter Campbell was another to face Wales in his only match, also. It was not unusual for the best players to be picked for the England game and more of a second string chosen for the Welsh and Irish games. Peter played in the 1898 match at Fir Park, Motherwell, which ended in a 5–2 victory over the Welsh. Peter would be part of the Morton side that won promotion in 1900.

Alex McNab

Morton would win the Scottish Cup in season 1921/22, but the season before, Alec McNab would win his only two Scotland caps, playing in a 2–0 victory over Ireland in Belfast and a 3–0 win over England at Hampden, in which Alan Morton of Rangers scored. Wing-forward McNab was part of the cup-winning side but by 1924 things had gone sour at Morton and he moved across the Atlantic to play football. Alec played for teams with such wonderful names as the Fall River Marksmen, New Bedford Whalers, Stix, Baer & Fuller and Burke's Undertakers, among others – quite often as a player-manager. He was to win a number of titles in the St. Louis Soccer League. In 2005 he was inducted into the US National Hall of Soccer, in recognition of his early contribution to the game in the States.

Only one more player was to be capped before the advent of World War II and that was to be forward Danny McRorie in October 1930, as Scotland drew 1–1 with Wales at Ibrox. Within a month, Danny was a Liverpool player; however, this did not work out and he was soon on his way to Rochdale, then Runcorn, as well as returning to Morton briefly.

Greenock-born Billy Campbell had played for Morton in the war years and was capped for the first time in May 1946 against Switzerland. Some records count this as a Victory International; however, the SFA classify it as a full international. Either way Scotland were to win 3–2 and Campbell would go on to play versus Northern Ireland that year and then three games in 1948. Billy Steel would earn his first three caps at Cappielow, but as they came in 1947, Campbell would not play alongside him. Steel would net three goals in these matches, before winning further caps with first Derby County and then Dundee.

Autograph...
BILLY CAMPBELL   (Morton F.C.)
31

BILLY CAMPBELL   JIMMY COWAN

ANDY RITCHIE STEPPED BACK TO GO FORWARD

A £15,000 transfer to Morton seemed to single a downward trend in Andy Ritchie's career. But the former Celtic player responded in sensational fashion.

Instead of accepting a life in football away from the spotlight, Ritchie grabbed star billing — and set the First Division alight.

The big, powerful winger earned the applause by scoring 22 goals in his first season at Cappielow, and played a key part in Morton's storming finish to the season which earned them fourth spot.

It was a dramatic turn about for Ritchie, who never really established himself at Parkhead despite being tipped for the top.

Now Morton face the problem of keeping the big clubs at bay as Ritchie continues to hit the goals trail.

If they are forced to sell the former Celt eventually they will have the consolation of receiving a fee probably five times greater than the one they paid Celtic.

Morton legend goalkeeper Jimmy Cowan was first capped in April 1948 versus Belgium, a week before he and Campbell had lost 1–0 in a Scottish Cup Final replay to Rangers in extra time. Jimmy was to make the yellow goalkeeping jersey of Scotland his own over the next four years, playing in 25 out of 27 matches. Jimmy played in both the Scottish victories at Wembley in 1949 and 1951. Scotland would win 3–1 in the 1949 match but such were the heroics performed by Jimmy that day, defying England attack after attack, he is seen in pictures being carried off the field on the shoulders of supporters. What makes Jimmy's cap count even more remarkable is that in season 1949/50 he was playing in the Second Division.

Another Greenock-born player in Tommy Orr was to represent Scotland twice in the 50s, too. Tommy had lost in the 1940 Scottish Junior Cup Final to Maryhill as part of the Morton Juniors side, and like Cowan and

Campbell, he too played in the Scottish Cup losing side of 1948. His two caps came in the Irish and Welsh Home Internationals of 1951. Tommy scored in the first as they won 3–0 in Belfast and although they were to lose in the second match, a 1–0 defeat by Wales at Hampden, he played alongside Cowan and former teammate Billy Steel that day. Tommy would make 340 appearances for Morton before retiring in 1958. His son Neil would also play for Morton, making almost 220 appearances for the club, and would win seven Scotland Under-21 caps.

No other Morton player has been capped since the 50s, but Joe Jordan, Joe Harper, Mark McGhee and David Hopkin would all win caps after starting out at Cappielow, although fans of the club will tell you that Andy Ritchie (1979 Scottish Football Writers' Player of the Year) was the greatest of them all, but he was never to pull on the dark blue of Scotland other than one Under-21 cap and one appearance in a 'League International'.

Jimmy Cowan (Morton and Scotland). Earned almost immortal fame at Wembley in 1949 when, almost single-handed, kept brilliant England attack at bay and thus laid foundations of a shock Scottish victory. First senior club was St. Mirren but 'guested' for Morton during war and later signed for them. Is now regarded as finest goalkeeper Scotland has produced in last decade and is automatic choice for his country.

Jimmy Cowan

HEARTS

Heart of Midlothian FC were formed in 1874 and 13 years later in 1887 Tom Jenkinson was to be the first Hearts player to be capped for Scotland. Tom would score the second goal in a 4–1 victory over Ireland at the first Hampden Park.

Hearts were to be quite successful in the years that followed and would win the league in 1894/95 and 1896/97 as well as lift the Scottish Cup in 1891, 1896, 1901 and 1906. Davie Baird was the only player to play in the first three finals and had begun his Scotland career in March 1890, playing against Ireland in Belfast. In the same side and also making his debut was formidable club captain Isaac Begbie. Scotland would win 4–1. Baird would win three caps, scoring a goal in a 6–1 rout of Wales in 1892 at Tynecastle Park, Edinburgh. Begbie would go one better than Baird and win four caps.

Bobby Walker was one of the early Hearts greats, the first player to hit over 100 goals for the club. He first played for Scotland in March 1900 and would play his final match in April 1913, having amassed 29 caps in total. Bobby would score eight goals for Scotland, including

Wardhaugh (Hearts)

the winner versus England at Bramall Lane, Sheffield, in 1903.

In 1907 he and clubmate Charlie Thomson were the only two 'home Scots' to play against England at Newcastle in a 1–1 draw. Thomson had made his Scotland debut in 1904 in a 1–1 draw with Ireland in Dublin. Thomson would gain 12 caps whilst with Hearts and captain the side on eight of these occasions. He was to go on and play for Sunderland and gain 21 caps in total. Like Walker, Thomson was to play in the 1901 and 1906 cup triumphs.

Then there's Jock White who would only gain two caps, in 1922/23, and to this day is the only Albion Rovers player to be capped. His other cap came, of course, at Hearts. Goalkeeper Jack Harkness was to gain nine of his 12 caps whilst at Hearts in the late 20s but by then had already taken part in the Wembley Wizards match of 1928 during his time with Queen's Park.

Another worth mentioning is Barney Battles Junior, whose father, Barney Battles Senior, had gained three caps with Celtic in the early part of the century. As for Junior, he gained

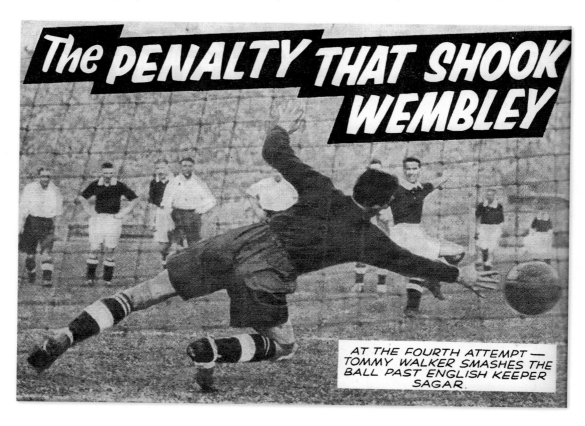

AT THE FOURTH ATTEMPT — TOMMY WALKER SMASHES THE BALL PAST ENGLISH KEEPER SAGAR.

two international caps — one for the USA in 1925 and on his return to Scotland, a Scottish cap in 1930. Right-back Andy Anderson would gain 23 caps from 1933 to 1938, playing in 23 of the 25 internationals in this period.

One of Hearts's all-time legends was the elegant Tommy Walker. Tommy gained his first Scotland cap aged 19, playing in a 3–2 victory over Wales at Pittodrie in late 1934. Tommy would only gain 21 caps, scoring eight goals, including two against England. The first was a late penalty in a match at Wembley in 1936 where the ball kept getting blown from the spot. Tommy took it at the fourth go to help earn a 1–1 draw. His second goal against the English came two years later, back at Wembley, as Scotland defeated the Auld Enemy 1–0.

Tommy was to win one last cap in 1946 versus Switzerland, but there is no doubt, had it not been for the war, Tommy would have won many, many more. At Hearts he would never win any major honours as a player but as manager, he would win all three Scottish trophies. Under Tommy's guidance Hearts would win the league in seasons 1957/58 and 1959/60, the Scottish Cup in 1956 and the League Cup four times.

Throughout the 50s Hearts were sometimes suspect in defence but up front was a different matter, with the legendary 'Terrible Trio' of Jimmy Wardhaugh, Willie Bauld and Alfie Conn, who between them would score over 900 goals for the club, but for Scotland would only win an aggregate total of six caps. Bauld would be first capped, appearing three times in 1950 and scoring two goals, in friendlies against Switzerland and Portugal. Wardhaugh made his debut in the famous match versus Hungary at Hampden in 1954, with a second cap to follow in 1956 against Northern Ireland. Conn would play against Austria in May 1956, scoring Scotland's goal in a 1–1 draw at Hampden but would never be selected again. Of course, at the time they would be competing against the Hibernian 'Famous Five' forward line for caps. However, you do get a sense of a west of Scotland bias at the time, too.

Wing-half John Cumming would win nine caps from 1954 to 1960 and the great Dave

Hearts' blond bombshell—Alec Young, a delightful forward

Mackay would win four of his paltry 22 with Hearts as well, including playing against France at the 1958 World Cup finals. Forward Alex Young would win only seven caps whilst at Hearts and only one more at Everton, but perhaps like many a forward of this era they were up against the greatest player of his or any other generation, in Denis Law, for a place in the side.

And then there was inside-forward Jimmy Murray, who was thrust into the side as Scotland faced England at Hampden in April 1958 and who would be one of the few to be retained after the 4–0 mauling by the Auld Enemy. Murray would start in Scotland's first match at those 1958 World Cup finals and indeed netted the equaliser versus Yugoslavia in Vasteras, and in doing so became the scorer of Scotland's first ever goal at a World Cup. Jimmy would miss the next game but played in the 2–1 defeat to France and that would be it for his Scotland career.

The 1960s would see full-back David Holt gain six caps, future Lisbon Lion Willie Wallace would earn his first three caps as a Hearts player and goalkeeper Jim Cruickshank would

DONALD FORD

gain one cap in the 60s and another five in the 70s. Hearts striker Donald Ford would travel to the 1974 World Cup finals but all of his three caps were won prior to the team's departure to West Germany. Incidentally, Donald would go on to represent Scotland at cricket, too.

The second half of the 1980s would see some great club players emerge at Tynecastle and they came agonisingly close to lifting the league title in 1986. The likes of Henry Smith, John Colquhoun, Gary Mackay, Craig Levein and John Robertson were all part of that side and were all capped.

Colquhoun would play two friendlies in the late 80s, and Smith would play in three and was the third-choice goalkeeper at the 1992 Euro finals. Gary Mackay would famously score on his Scotland debut versus Bulgaria to send a

GARY MACKAY
Heart of Midlothian

euphoric Republic of Ireland to the 1988 Euro finals; however, he would only win four caps in total.

Defender Craig Levein would play for Scotland from 1990 to 1994, gaining 16 caps in total; however, there's no doubt that had he not suffered from persistent knee injuries during his career, his Scotland total would have been more. Craig played against Sweden at the World Cup finals in 1990, and lining up alongside him that night at right-back was his defensive partner Dave McPherson. McPherson had joined Hearts in 1987 from Rangers and would appear in all three games at Italia 90, playing in the middle of defence in the final match versus Brazil. By the time of the 1992 Euro finals, McPherson had travelled back along the M8 motorway to Rangers once more, where he would win the last seven of his 27 caps.

Hearts's prolific goalscorer of the era, John Robertson, was unlucky in that Mo Johnston, Ally McCoist, Gordon Durie and others were ahead of him in the queue for the coveted striker roles. However, with Johnston more or less slipping out of the side after Italia 90, Robertson was given his chance as Scotland geared towards the 1992 Euros. Robbo would hit two goals in his first two matches, ensuring Scotland would beat Romania and Switzerland in their opening matches of the qualifying campaign, but despite this he would become a bit-part player in the side, often being used as a sub rather than starting games. John would be left out of the squad for the finals, with the likes of Brian McClair, Kevin Gallacher and Duncan Ferguson being included.

In 1994 Dave McPherson travelled back along that M8 to Hearts, with young central defender Alan McLaren moving in the opposite direction. McLaren had by this time made over 180 appearances for the Tynecastle side following his debut in 1987. He had also been capped for Scotland, coming into the side before the 1992 Euros, but was to be a non-playing member of the squad that travelled to the finals in Sweden. He was to

Craig Levein

win 14 caps with Hearts and a further ten with Rangers.

Due to Rangers's financial dominance of Scottish football in the 1990s and beyond, a lot of young Scottish talent was bought up by the Ibrox side and Hearts in particular would see some of their most talented players end up directly or indirectly at Rangers, including the likes of Neil McCann, Paul Ritchie, Allan Johnston, Andy Webster and, in later years, Lee Wallace, with all gaining Scotland caps.

No Hearts players would feature in the Euro 96 squad, although their former goalkeeper Nicky Walker would travel to the finals as a reserve. Defender Davie Weir, though, would play at France 98 and memorably hit a long pass to Craig Burley for the equaliser versus Norway in Bordeaux. Weir would win ten caps at Tynecastle, a further 42 at Everton and then a final 17 with Rangers for a total of 69 caps.

Steven Pressley would buck the usual trend, however, starting out at Rangers and winding his way to Tynecastle via Coventry City and Dundee United in 1998. His first cap would be awarded in 2000 in a friendly versus France. Initially capped by Craig Brown,

Pressley would gain the bulk of his 32 caps in the Berti Vogts era, but a number came during Walter Smith's subsequent tenancy, too. He is currently Hearts's most capped player. Also gaining a number of caps around the same period were the likes of Scott Severin (8 of 15), Colin Cameron (11 of 28) and Gary Naysmith, who would begin his cap tally at Hearts (4 of 46) before moving on to Everton.

Goalkeeper Craig Gordon made his debut in May 2004 in a friendly win versus Trinidad and Tobago – at Hibs's Easter Road stadium – towards the end of the Berti Vogts era. Over the next few years, however, under Walter Smith and then Alex McLeish, Craig would become Scotland's number one. Gordon would play 23 times for Scotland as a Hearts player, before he moved to Sunderland in August 2007, including that memorable win over France at Hampden in a Euro qualifier in October 2006. Playing alongside him that day was the aforementioned Steven Pressley, and another clubmate in Paul Hartley. The Berti Vogts era had come and gone without the skilful midfielder being considered for national service; however, Walter Smith picked him for his first game and Hartley would become a major part of Smith's Scotland side, gaining 11 caps, before he moved on to Celtic, where he gained a further 11, finishing with 25, with the last three coming at Bristol City.

In recent years, a number of Hearts players have played for Scotland, including the likes of Christophe Berra, who has gained a few more caps to add to the three he initially won in 2008 at the start of his career with Hearts. Utility player Callum Paterson began his international career with Hearts in 2016 (in a friendly versus Italy), whereas 'veteran' striker Steven Naismith looks like finishing his Scotland odyssey whilst at Tynecastle.

HIBERNIAN

Hibernian were formed in Edinburgh in 1875. Their first Scottish Cup success would come in 1887, but prior to that two players who would subsequently lift the trophy with Hibs, in James Lundie and James McGhee,  had become the first club players to be capped for Scotland. They both appeared against Wales, for their only caps, in April 1886 as Scotland beat the Welsh 4–1 at the First Hampden Park.

Jimmy Dunn

Two more players were to be capped from the successful cup-winning side: James McLaren and Willie Groves were chosen to play against Wales in March 1888 on Easter Road, but not quite where the ground is now – the first international in the capital. Groves would hit the fourth goal in the 5–1 victory but along with McLaren and other Hibs players of the time moved to the newly formed Celtic in Glasgow. Both would win two caps each whilst with Celtic, with Groves hitting a hat-trick versus Ireland in 1889 in a 7–0 victory.

Scottish Cup success would once more come to Hibernian in 1902 and was followed by a championship in 1902/03 and several players from this era were duly capped. Right-half Bernard 'Pat' Breslin was the first to be capped in March 1897 in a 2–2 draw versus Wales in Wrexham. Clubmates John Kennedy and Pat Murray were also in the Scotland side that day but both would leave Hibernian before the cup success.

Inside-left Pat Callaghan would win his only cap versus Ireland in Belfast in March 1900 as Scotland ran out 3–0 winners. Playing in goal that day as a Hearts player was Harry Rennie, winning the first of his 13 caps; however, 11 of those would come whilst at the Easter Road side. A broken leg was to rob William McCartney of his place in the Scottish Cup line-up but he would play his part in the league-winning side the following season, and his one and only cap came in a 1902 5–1 victory over Ireland in Belfast. The final player to be capped was full-back Archie Gray, who won his only cap versus Ireland at Celtic Park in 1903 as Scotland lost 2–0.

George Stewart was also part of the league-winning side, scoring nine goals. He was to play for Scotland in March 1906 as they lost to Wales at Tynecastle, home of Edinburgh rivals Hearts. However, a month later he was part of the Scotland side that defeated England 2–1

at Hampden Park in front of Scotland's (and possibly the world's) first 100,000-plus crowd. His last two caps were to be as a Manchester City player.

Goalkeeper Bill Harper was to win the first nine of his 11 Scottish caps whilst at Hibs, the other two coming at Arsenal. His first came in March 1923 (a 1–0 win over Ireland in Belfast) and he would play in the following eight games, only suffering one defeat, against Wales in 1924. He lost his place in October 1925 to Rangers goalie Willie Robb, who in 1927 won his only other cap as a Hibee.

Jimmy Dunn was to win five of his six Scotland caps whilst at Easter Road. The last of the caps was as part of the famous 'Wembley Wizards' side of 1928 where he was one of only three home-based players. Jimmy was part of the famous forward line that all measured under 5ft 7in, and his display was to earn him a move to Everton, where he was to gain only one more cap. His son Jimmy Jr would win the FA Cup with Wolves in 1949.

The post-Second World War period would prove to be the most successful in the history of Hibernian FC, with three championships coming their way in 1947/48, 1950/51 and 1951/52, and although this was the time of the 'Famous Five' forward line, a number of more defensive players were also capped.

Left-back Davie Shaw would be the first Easter Road player to be 'officially' capped after the war, lining up alongside his brother Jock of Rangers in a friendly match versus Switzerland in May 1946. (The next set of brothers to play in the same match would be Gary and Steven Caldwell versus Slovenia in Celje in 2005, with Gary plying his trade at Hibernian at that time.) Davie would gain nine caps altogether and played with his Hibernian right-back counterpart John Govan in five of his six caps. A run of five games together was broken up with another Hibee in Hugh Howie filling in for Govan in a match down in Cardiff versus Wales in October 1948. Scotland were to win 3–1 with Howie scoring.

Wing-half James 'Bobby' Combe was to win three caps, all in 1948, and would score in a 2–0 friendly victory over Belgium at Hampden, which makes him a genuine hero in my book or indeed in this book. Five Hibernian players were in that particular side. Shaw was part of the 1947/48 championship winners, and Govan, Howie and Combe would take part in all three.

Shaw (Hibs)

All of the Famous Five would win the three titles, with the exception of Bobby Johnstone who would 'only' gain the second two. Winger Gordon Smith first signed for Hibernian in 1941 and would play with the club until 1959. Even after this he had time to win championships with both Hearts and Dundee and is surely one of the finest players ever to grace a football field in Scotland. However, for Scotland he didn't quite shine the same and often was left out in favour of Willie Waddell of Rangers, and so he would only win 19 caps. His first official cap came in 1946, his last in 1957, but there would be a number of years – 1949, 1950, 1951 and 1953 and 1954 – where he would not be chosen, so he was not a consistent part of the side either. In 1955, however, Gordon would play six games, scoring three of his four goals and indeed captaining the side in two matches. The first captaincy was in a stunning 4–1 victory over

Gordon Smith

Austria in the Prater Stadium, Vienna, where a bewildered/belligerent Austrian spectator threw a punch at him.

Eddie Turnbull would be the next to be selected for national duty, his first match coming in the aforementioned Belgium game of 1948. Remarkably the majority of his caps would come in 1958, when he was aged 35. A World Cup-destined Scotland had been pummelled 4–0 by England at Hampden in April that year and so Eddie was drafted in to play in the heart of the defence, and would indeed play in all three games at Sweden 1958. He would eventually receive his actual caps almost 50 years later, as at the time, the SFA only handed out physical caps for British Home International matches, until a campaign led by Gary Imlach on behalf of his father Stewart Imlach, who also played at the 1958 World Cup finals, saw this wrong rectified. Eddie would go on to manage Hibs and would create the great side of the 1970s known as 'Turnbull's Tornadoes'.

Centre-forward Lawrie Reilly would make the greatest impact of the Famous Five, playing 38 times for Scotland and scoring a remarkable 22 goals. His first match was in October 1948 versus Wales in Cardiff. The first goal that day (Scotland won 3–1) is officially credited to teammate Hugh Howie; however, video evidence would suggest that there

Reilly (Hibs)

was contact from Reilly for the strike and even some contemporary newspapers gave it to him. Interestingly, on this same day, two of the other Famous Five were scoring in a 6–2 mauling of Partick Thistle, as there was a full card of league football in Scotland that Saturday as well.

Reilly would score in his second international as Scotland defeated England 3–1 at Wembley in April 1949. He would score six times in total versus England, and late goals against Northern Ireland and England in 1953 would earn him the nickname 'Last Minute Reilly'. However, Lawrie was unlucky to miss out on the World Cup finals in 1954 due to a bout of pleurisy and sadly a knee injury saw him lost to Hibs, Scotland and football as a whole aged 29. He is still Scotland's fourth all-time top goalscorer and Hibernian's most-capped player.

Bobby Johnstone would make his international bow in April 1951 versus England and would also score in that 3–2 victory at Wembley, as did Reilly. Like Reilly, Johnstone was injured at the time of the 1954 World Cup finals and was originally part of the travelling party of 13 before withdrawing from the squad. He would move to Manchester City in 1955 but by then had won 13 caps, scoring seven goals, and was to go on and win four more caps, netting a double versus Wales in November 1955.

Only one Hibernian player would make the 1954 World Cup finals and that was to be winger Willie Ormond, the last of the Famous Five to be capped. Like Johnstone, Ormond would score on his debut – versus England in April 1954. Sadly, though, this was to be in a 4–2 defeat at Hampden. Ormond was to win his fourth and fifth caps versus Austria and Uruguay at the Switzerland finals. Remarkably his sixth and final cap would come in 1959 in a 1–0 defeat away to England. Willie would, of course, go on to manage Scotland rather successfully, leading them to the World Cup finals in 1974 where they were to remain unbeaten.

Goalkeeper Tommy Younger had been with Hibs since 1948 and indeed had won the 1951 and 1952 titles with the club; however, it was to be May 1955 before he was capped, in a 3–0 friendly match victory over Portugal at Hampden. Tommy was to then

Willie Ormond

Tommy Younger, Scotland and Hibernian goalkeeper

go on a run of 24 consecutive internationals, including eight while with Hibernian, before moving to Liverpool in June 1956.

In the 1960s the likes of Neil Martin and Peter Cormack had been capped whilst with Hibs before moving to England for successful club careers, but Pat Stanton would win his first cap versus the Netherlands in 1966 and remain with the club until 1976, captaining the side for many years. He would win the majority of his 16 caps in the period from 1969 to 1971.

Eddie Turnbull returned to the club as manager in 1971 and although some of the team he would mould were already there, under him Hibs became an exciting team to watch and challenged the Old Firm, particularly Celtic, for the major honours at the time. A League Cup win in 1972/73 and two successive Drybrough Cup trophies would be their only tangible successes, although many a Hibee will count the 7–0 crushing of Hearts at Tynecastle on Ne'erday 1973 as more than tangible.

Alex Cropley would gain two caps in 1971 (Euro qualifiers versus Portugal and Belgium) in Tommy Docherty's first games in charge, but two leg breaks at Arsenal and one at Aston Villa would hamper his career. Nevertheless, he is fondly remembered at Villa Park, as is Des Bremner, who would win his only cap in April 1976 (versus Switzerland) before going

HIBERNIAN

PAT STANTON
WING HALF

on to win the English title and the European Cup with the midlands club.

A double leg break would also hamper John Brownlie's Scotland career, having won six caps prior to this injury in January 1973. There are many who would argue that as an overlapping full-back, JB was as good as Danny McGrain and Sandy Jardine in their prime. Sadly, he would only win one more cap in December 1975 in an 'academic' Euro qualifier versus Romania.

On the opposite flank at left-back in the Hibs side was Erich Schaedler, well known for his turn of speed and ruthless tackling. Erich was the son of a German prisoner of war and would play his only Scotland game in his father's homeland in a pre-World Cup finals friendly in Frankfurt. Erich, though, would make the 1974 World Cup squad that travelled to West Germany.

Hibs central defender John Blackley would play at World Cup 1974 in the opening match versus Zaire in place of the injured Martin Buchan, who would return for Scotland's other two matches in the tournament. Blackley had also played in the win versus England at Hampden in May 1974. He was to win four caps around this time and a final three in the last months of Willie Ormond's tenure as Scotland manager. Ally MacLeod would regularly have Blackley as a squad player but he would not make it to Argentina in 1978. Winger Arthur Duncan was the last Tornado to be selected for Scotland, winning six caps in a four-month spell in 1975.

World Cups 1978 and 1982 would come and go with no Hibs players in the squads. However, goalkeeper Alan Rough would travel to Mexico 1986 whilst with the club and had indeed won the last two of his 53 Scotland caps whilst with the Easter Road side. The other two goalies in Mexico were Jim Leighton and Andy Goram, both of whom would wind up at Hibernian, adding to their caps count with the Edinburgh side. Leighton was to win 23 of his 91 caps at Easter Road in the period from 1993 to 1997. As for Goram, his first few

John Brownlie
HIBERNIAN and SCOTLAND

caps came at Oldham Athletic before moving to Hibs in 1987, where he would win a further 11 caps before his transfer to Rangers in 1991.

Goram along with John Collins would be non-playing members of the 1990 World Cup finals squad. Collins had by this time won four caps, starting out in a friendly versus Saudi Arabia in February 1988, where he scored in the 2–2 draw. Collins would move to Celtic later in the year and was to go on to win 58 caps in total.

Darren Jackson and Jim Leighton would travel to the Euros in 1996 as Hibs players but neither would be picked by Craig Brown at the finals, although both had played their parts in qualifying. Jackson would win his first 20 caps whilst at Easter Road from 1995 to 1997 but was to take part in the 1998 World Cup finals as a Celtic player.

In the next 20 years or so Hibernian would produce some decent players but few would fulfil their real potential at the club, often moving on to win the majority of their Scotland caps. Hibernian have produced some gifted players in this time, such as Garry O'Connor, Steven Fletcher and Scott Brown, who would all win their early caps at Easter Road.

It is perhaps a reflection of the times that the player to win the most caps at Easter Road in this century is Gary Caldwell, who would win 20 of his 55 caps from 2002 to 2006 whilst in the Scottish capital. Despite all his achievements, central defender Caldwell was seen by many as being not much more than a half-decent player.

Hibernian would finally win the Scottish Cup again in 2016 and in true tradition three of the side would go on to win Scotland caps – Lewis Stevenson, Dylan McGeough and John McGinn, who is carving out a good career in England.

Official Players Collection

MURDO MacLEOD ★★★★

Jeff Blackley

KILMARNOCK

Kilmarnock were founded in 1869 and are the oldest professional football club in Scotland. Sandy Higgins was to be the first Kilmarnock player to represent Scotland in 1885. Sandy would hit a hat-trick in an 8–2 drubbing of Ireland at the First Hampden Park and like many a player of the time was never selected again. He would go on to play for Derby County and Nottingham Forest before returning to Kilmarnock. He would pass away on 17 April 1920 on the same day Killie were to lift the Scottish Cup for the first time. His son, also Sandy, was with Kilmarnock at the time but did not play in the final. Sandy Jr would win four caps whilst with Newcastle United.

John 'Kitey' McPherson was next for international honours, playing in a 5–1 victory over Wales in March 1888. John would win more caps with Cowlairs and Rangers, finishing with a total of nine.

In 1898 Kilmarnock would win the Scottish Second Division (as they were to do the following season – promotion was not always mandatory at that time) and reach the final of the

GEORGE ROBERTSON, Kilmarnock F.C.   Topical Times

Scottish Cup for the first time, only to lose 2–0 to Rangers. A number of players from that side were capped for Scotland.

James 'Bummer' Campbell would be the first, his debut coming against Ireland at Celtic Park in a 2–1 victory in March 1891. The following year would see David McPherson, brother of the aforementioned John, win his only cap in a 3–2 win over Ireland in Belfast.

Although he didn't play with John in this match, his brother was in the cup-winning Rangers side of 1898.

John Johnstone was another player who would net on his debut and never play again, as he scored the fifth goal in a 5–2 victory over Wales in March 1894 on the occasion of the first international held at Kilmarnock's Rugby Park. On 19 March 1898 (a week before the Scottish Cup Final) Robert Findlay would also play in his only international, a 5–2 win over Wales at Fir Park, Motherwell. George Anderson, who would be the only player capped 'post-final', appeared in an 11–0 trouncing of Ireland at Celtic Park in 1901. Incidentally, Mr Anderson was not the only player not to score that day, whilst Sandy

McMahon of Celtic and Robert Hamilton of Rangers both hit four each.

Outside-right Bobby Templeton would be capped with Aston Villa, Newcastle United and Woolwich Arsenal all before his six caps with Kilmarnock from 1908 to 1913. His only goal would come in his debut in 1902 in a 2–2 draw with England at Villa Park, Birmingham. Around the same time William Agnew and James Mitchell were also capped three times each, with all three Killie players appearing in a 5–0 victory over Ireland at Dalymount Park, Dublin, in March 1908.

Kilmarnock's first Scottish Cup success in 1920 would bring no more Scotland appearances down Ayrshire way. However, the 1929 Scottish Cup winners would have two in their number who were to win caps, namely Hugh Morton and Joe Nibloe.

Full-back Nibloe would be the first to be capped, in the April 1929 match versus England at Hampden, in which Alex Cheyne would net the winner direct from a corner in the 90th minute. Joe was also to take part in the 1932 victory over the Auld Enemy, as the Scots won 2–0 at home. He took in a couple of overseas tours – in 1929 to Norway, Germany and the Netherlands as the Scots ventured abroad for the first time, and in 1931, playing in Austria, Italy and Switzerland. Joe still stands as Kilmarnock's most-capped player with 11 in total. He was also to win the FA Cup with Sheffield Wednesday in 1935. Teammate Morton played his only two Scotland games in the aforementioned matches versus Germany and the Netherlands in 1929.

Kilmarnock would be runners-up in the Scottish First Division in seasons 1959/60, 1960/61, 1962/63 and 1963/64, and would become champions on the last day of the 1964/65 season. Goalkeeper Robert 'Campbell' Forsyth would start that season between the sticks both at Rugby Park and Scotland, having made his debut versus England in April 1964, when an Alan Gilzean goal gave the Scots a victory at home. Forsyth was to win three more caps in the winter of 1964, playing Wales and Northern Ireland, with a World Cup qualifier versus Finland in-between. These were to be his last caps as he suffered an ankle injury in the last few weeks of the season, and so Bill Brown took over in goal for Scotland whilst Bobby Ferguson took his slot at Kilmarnock.

TOMMY McLEAN

Ferguson would also be capped for Scotland on seven occasions from November 1965 to November 1966. Scotland manager Bobby Brown would opt for Celtic keeper Ronnie Simpson for his first game in charge and although Ferguson would move to West Ham United for £65,000, which was a world record fee for a goalie at the time, no more Scotland caps would come his way.

Jackie McGrory would also play in the 1964 World Cup qualifier against Finland at Hampden alongside Forsyth for his debut and would make two more appearances for the national side, but competition for the centre-half spot would see him lose out to the likes of Billy McNeill and Ronnie McKinnon. Jackie would, however, play over 300 times for Kilmarnock.

Winger Tommy McLean was playing in his first season when Killie won the league and would play well over 200 games for the club. Tommy would, of course, go on to an even more successful time with Rangers but remarkably all his caps would come with the Ayrshire club. His first cap came in October 1968 in a friendly versus Denmark. However, with competition from the likes of Jimmy Johnstone and Willie Henderson, among others, Tommy did well to win five more caps, scoring in the 5–3 win over Wales in Wrexham in 1969. That goal was the only one by a Killie

JIM STEWART (Killie)

player in the 20th century for Scotland. Wee Tom played in the opening two matches of the 1970 British Home Internationals before losing out in the England game to Celtic's Jinky Johnstone.

Full-back Billy Dickson would only play in a couple of games in the championship- winning season but would go on to play over 200 matches for Killie in total. He was also to play alongside McLean in the Home Internationals series of 1970 but unlike Tommy, Billy would play in the 0–0 match versus England at Hampden in front of a crowd of 137,438. Another couple of caps would come his way at the end of Bobby Brown's time as manager, as Scotland lost in both Denmark and Russia in the summer of 1971.

Goalkeeper Ally Hunter gained the first two of his four caps as a Kilmarnock player

– in the friendly versus Peru at Hampden in April 1972 and the Yugoslavia match in the Brazilian Independence Cup in Belo Horizonte in June of that year. Hunter joined Celtic in 1973 and put in a great performance versus England that year, but the 'letting in' of a poor goal versus Czechoslovakia on the night Scotland qualified for the 1974 World Cup finals saw Hunter dumped by manager Willie Ormond. His replacement at Kilmarnock, Jim Stewart, would be a non-playing member of the 1974 World Cup squad and was to gain his first cap three years later in Chile, as Scotland played (and won 4–2) in the controversial friendly in the Estadio Nacional, Santiago. His only other cap came as a Middlesbrough player in October 1978 versus Norway in a Euro qualifier at Hampden.

As the 20th century ended it was two ex-Rangers players who were to win caps, with Ian Durrant gaining nine and Ally McCoist his last two (i.e. numbers 60 and 61). It is a bit surprising given the number of goals that he scored for the Ayrshire club that Kris Boyd was never capped at Killie, either in the early part or latter period of his career. Steven

Naismith would gain the first of his many caps at Rugby Park, replacing Boyd late on as Scotland were winning 2–0 in the Faroes in June 2007. Right-back Stephen O'Donnell has taken his chances in the last year or so, starting against Peru in Lima in the summer of 2018, and may well be the player to overtake Joe Nibloe in the Killie cap count if he remains at the club.

IAN DURRANT

LEEDS UNITED

Leeds United were formed in 1919 shortly after the forced disbanding of the Leeds City club by the Football League due to allegations of payment irregularities during the First World War. One of the surprising things about Scots being capped whilst playing for Leeds is that the first player to do so was Bobby Collins in 1965. Don Revie, ironically a future England manager, would bring about an era of unprecedented success for Leeds and ultimately Scotland, which would see the Elland Road club provide five players for the 1974 World Cup finals squad.

One of Revie's first signings was Bobby Collins in 1962. Bobby had been previously capped for Scotland 28 times, first at Celtic and then with Everton, and had last been capped in 1959. His return to the international scene to face England at Wembley in 1965 came in the same year he won the Football Writers' Player of the Year award, although he would only win three more caps. Collins also played alongside fellow Leeds and Scotland legend Billy Bremner when he made his debut in the dark blue of Scotland on 8 May 1965, as Scotland drew 0–0 with European champions Spain in a friendly match at Hampden.

Billy's early Scotland career was a bit stop-start as he regularly missed games, possibly due to FA suspensions or just not being released by his club, as they wielded that kind of power back then. Generally he would play in most of the important games, i.e. World Cup qualifiers, England games, etc. Bremner was made captain on the occasion of his 13th cap, taking over the mantle from John Greig, who was still in the side as the Scots faced Denmark in a friendly in Copenhagen in October 1968. Billy would go on to captain Scotland 39 times, making him second on the all-time list behind George Young of Rangers on 48.

At the time of Leeds's epic European Cup semi-final with Celtic in 1970 none of the Yorkshire club's players were released for the British Home Internationals, and indeed from April 1970 to April 1971 no Leeds player turned out for the national side. However, there was never any doubt of the tenacious Billy's loyalty to the Scotland cause and he would lead the side to the 1974 World Cup finals, the pinnacle of his Scotland career. Of course, with Billy there came his drinking and his boisterous nature that put him at odds with the beaks at the SFA and which saw his downfall in September 1975 in ironically the same city he was first bestowed the captaincy of the side: Copenhagen. Billy was banned from playing for Scotland for life, as were others, but whilst there was to be a reprieve/return for some, there wasn't for Billy. A sad end to one of the most committed of Scots over the years.

The next Elland Road player after Billy to become involved was not a Revie signing and is perhaps the least known of Leeds's Scotland players at this time. Full-back Willie Bell had been at Leeds United since 1960, joining from Queen's Park. He would play over 200 times for his club but only twice for his country — against Portugal in a 1–0 defeat and a 1–1 draw with Brazil, both at Hampden in June 1966. Eddie Gray, perhaps the most skilful player of Revie's era, first played for Scotland on 10 May 1969, but sadly Scotland were soundly beaten 4–1 by old rivals England at Hampden that day. Eddie would only win 12 caps for Scotland, which is rather surprising

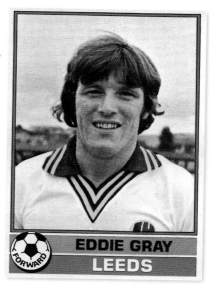

PETER LORIMER (Leeds)

given his talent; however, competition for a place on the wing was always healthy with Jimmy Johnstone, Charlie Cooke and Tommy Hutchison latterly among the contenders, but injury would also rule him out sometimes, too. Eddie would be left out of the Scotland squad for the 1974 World Cup finals.

In Scotland's last game of the 1960s Peter Lorimer made his international bow, coming on as a sub in the second half in a 2–0 defeat to Austria in Vienna. Peter was well renowned for his thunderbolt of a shot, as can be seen in the World Cup game against Zaire in Dortmund in 1974 when he scored Scotland's opener. Peter would play over 700 times for Leeds and 21 times for Scotland, scoring four goals.

Keeping goal at the World Cup in 1974 was David Harvey. Harvey had been with Leeds since 1965 but found himself second choice behind the erratic Welsh goalkeeper Gary Sprake. However, by 1972 he found himself first choice and was called up for Scotland by Tommy Docherty in November 1972 to face Denmark. Scotland won 2–0 with Peter Lorimer netting a goal before being sent off, but the 'Doc' would leave and replacement manager Willie Ormond would choose Bobby Clark, Peter McCloy and Ally Hunter before Harvey would return almost a year later. Harvey became first choice, had some good performances at the World Cup and looked set to be the number one for years to come; however, he was injured in a car accident in the 1974/75 season and this saw him lose his place at Leeds and Scotland. He did get his chance again in late 1975, playing two Euro

qualifiers against Denmark, but the following year saw Alan Rough between the sticks and Harvey was forgotten about. Incidentally at Leeds United, David Stewart took his place for a while and he too was capped for Scotland versus East Germany in September 1977.

The final two players to make up the five for World Cup 74 were Revie signings from Scottish clubs. Joe Jordan was bought from Morton for £15,000 in 1970 and would make his Scotland debut as a sub against England on 19 May 1973, which we lost 1–0. However, his fourth appearance in the blue of Scotland would be his most memorable, coming on for Kenny Dalglish at Hampden in September 1973 to score the winning goal against Czechoslovakia and so send us to the World Cup finals in 1974. Joe would also have a successful World Cup, scoring against Zaire and Yugoslavia. Jordan would play his part in Scotland winning the 1976 and 1977 British Home Internationals championship and would play his final and 27th cap, as a Leeds player, at Anfield, Liverpool, as the Scots beat Wales 2–0 to qualify for Argentina 78 – a game in which he had a big hand in Scotland winning. Joe would, of course, go on to play 52 times for Scotland in total.

Gordon McQueen, a bargain buy from St Mirren in 1972 for £30,000, made his Scotland debut against Belgium, on 1 June 1974 – a fortnight before our opening game at the

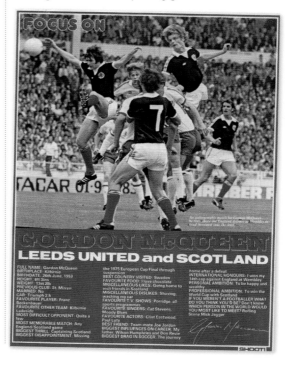

World Cup finals. Scotland lost this World Cup warm-up 2–1. He would not take part in the 74 World Cup but was part of the squad. McQueen's biggest moment in a Scotland jersey was that thunderous header versus England in May 1977. His lowest would be crashing into the post versus Wales in May 1978 that kept him out of the Argentina World Cup finals. However, by the time of that 1978 World Cup, Revie had left Leeds (for England then the United Arab Emirates), as had Jordan and McQueen (for Manchester United), which meant there was no Leeds player in Ally MacLeod's squad for South America.

Frank Gray (Eddie's younger brother) had been first capped in April 1976 (in a friendly versus Switzerland) but would not return to the side until Jock Stein's second reign as manager began in October 1978. Gray would be consistently picked by Stein over the next few years, often playing at left-back opposite Danny McGrain on the right. He also won seven caps whilst at Nottingham Forest from late 1979 to the end of the 1980/81 season when he returned to Elland Road. Gray travelled to the 1982 World Cup finals and played in all three of Scotland's games, whilst a Leeds player, but was to miss a late penalty against Belgium in Brussels in a Euro qualifier that would have given Scotland a 3–3 draw in December 1982. By the summer of 1983 he had played his final Scotland match, having won 32 caps in total.

Left-winger Arthur Graham was one of the players 'banned' along with Bremner in Copenhagen, during his time with Aberdeen FC. He joined Leeds United in 1977 and was a firm favourite with fans. It was Ally MacLeod who brought him into the Scotland side for his debut in the same DDR match that David Stewart made his debut. However, Argentina would come and go before he was back in the side and when Jock Stein took over, Graham was given an extended run in the team. Unfortunately, competition from the likes of John Robertson and Davie Cooper would see him squeezed out and he won his 11th and final cap in Swansea in May 1981, as Scotland lost 2–0 to Wales.

The 1980s would see a further decline in Leeds's fortunes and it would be 1989 before another player was to be capped for Scotland. Gordon Strachan joined Leeds United in March 1989 and was made captain shortly after. Leeds would win the title the following season with Strachan being an ever-present in the side. Gordon was not picked for the 1990 World Cup finals but did play his part in the qualifying for the 1992 Euros and won eight caps whilst with Leeds. Having won his 50th cap (in a Euros warm-up match versus Finland) and suffering from back problems Strachan called it a day on his international career just before the finals. Incidentally, only 9,275 were at Hampden that March evening to witness what would be Strachan's international swansong.

Leeds had won the old First Division title that season with Strachan earning the Football Writers' Association Footballer of the Year award, but another integral part of the Leeds midfield as well as the Scotland side at the time was Gary McAllister. McAllister had already won three caps and had been a non-playing squad member at Italia 90 by the time he arrived in Yorkshire in July 1990. He would win 41 of his 57 caps whilst at Elland Road, playing at the 1992 and 1996 Euro finals, before moving to Coventry City in July 1996.

There have been some other players capped at Leeds since then but few would make the impact that those before them had. David Hopkin, Dominic Matteo, Barry Bannan, Robert Snodgrass, Liam Bridcutt and Ross McCormack have all played for Leeds United and Scotland, but perhaps only Snodgrass is fondly thought of by the Tartan Army.

LIVERPOOL

Liverpool were formed in 1892 following a dispute between the Everton FC committee and John Houlding. Everton shipped to Goodison Park and Houlding, the owner of Anfield, founded Liverpool FC.

George Allan signed for the club in 1895 from Leith Athletic and quickly got among the goals, scoring 25 in 20 league games, helping Liverpool gain promotion with a further three in the Test matches (play-offs). His only cap came in 1897, lining up against England at Crystal Palace. Scotland would win 2–1. Allan was to return north for a spell with Celtic before heading back to Liverpool in 1899, but sadly he was forced to quit the game due to failing health and would succumb to tuberculosis in October of that year at the age of 29.

During his two years at Anfield, forward Hugh Morgan was to add to his one cap won at St Mirren in March 1898, by gaining his second versus England at Villa Park in 1899, as Scotland went down 2–1. Left-back Billy Dunlop signed for Liverpool in 1895 from Paisley side Abercorn for a princely sum of £35 and was to play for Liverpool until 1909. He was to win two First Division championships with the club in 1900/01 and 1905/06. His only Scotland cap would come in the 1906 2–0 victory over England at Hampden.

BILLY LIDDELL
Liverpool and Scotland

Captaining the side that day was Alex Raisbeck. Alex had joined Liverpool from Stoke City in 1898 and was such a commanding figure at centre-half, even though he only stood at 5ft 10in, that he was made captain of the side aged 21. He would lead Liverpool to the two First Division titles already mentioned and a Second Division one when they fell out of the top tier in the 1903/04 season, returning immediately the season after as champions.

Raisbeck was not only held in high respect down in Merseyside but with the SFA selectors, also. He was picked for national duty on only eight occasions from 1900 to 1907; however, seven of those matches were against England, for whom they would generally pick their best players. Only the 1905 game was missing from his CV in that period. He would captain the side four times and was beaten but once, in 1904. Raisbeck would leave Liverpool in 1909 for Partick Thistle as he longed to head back home to Scotland. At Firhill, he is remembered as one the early greats for the Jags, but would return to Liverpool in his later years as a scout before passing away in 1949.

The First World War would disrupt many players' careers and among those were three Scots at Anfield who would win national honours. Left-back Donald McKinlay would sign for Liverpool in 1910 and would remain with the side for almost two decades. Donald was to captain the side through their league successes of 1921/22 and 1922/23 but was to grace the Scotland side on two occasions, both coming in 1922 versus Wales and then Ireland.

Playing alongside Donald in both games was goalkeeper Kenny Campbell, although by then a Partick Thistle player – Kenny had signed for Liverpool a year after McKinlay. Kenny was first capped in 1920, playing in all three matches of the British Championship that year, but would move on from the club as he finally lost his place in the side to the Liverpool great Elisha Scott after many years of competing with one another. He was to win another five caps with Partick Thistle.

Forward Tom Miller had signed for the club in 1912 and would win his first cap whilst at Liverpool and net a double to give Scotland a 4–2 half-time lead at Hillsborough in 1920. However, the match ended 5–4 to England. Miller was to win two more caps at Manchester United. Wing-half Jock McNab would take part in the two championship seasons alongside McKinlay and was picked for Scotland on one occasion in 1923 versus Wales at Love Street, Paisley. Prior to World War II, Jimmy MacDougall was the only other Liverpool player to be capped, making two appearances in 1931 – in Austria and Italy no less.

The war would prevent outside-left Billy Liddell from achieving many caps and triumphs with Liverpool, with the league championship of 1946/47 being his only success, but he is still remembered as one of the Liverpool greats. Billy signed in 1938 and would remain with the club until 1961. Although he wouldn't play his first official game for the side until 1946 Billy had already won eight wartime caps for Scotland and was to go on to win 29 official caps, too, scoring eight goals in the process. Billy would be denied a place at the World Cup finals twice as Scotland withdrew from the 1950 World Cup, having announced they would only go if they became British champions, whilst he was not chosen by the selectors for the 1954 finals.

Goalkeeper Tommy Younger signed for the club in 1956 from Hibernian in the midst of his 24-game unbroken sequence for his country that would end after Scotland's second of three matches at the 1958 World Cup finals – versus Paraguay in Norrkoping. His last 16 caps were won during his time at Anfield.

Bill Shankly's era would see in the beginning of a great period for Liverpool that would stretch 30 years or so, with numerous title and cup triumphs, both domestic and European. In the 1960s a number of Scots featured in his sides but their cap count was quite limited.

Ian St John signed for Liverpool in 1961 having already won seven Scotland caps whilst with Motherwell. Ian was to win two championships with Liverpool and would score the winner as the Anfield side won their first FA Cup in 1965. He would win a further 14 caps whilst at Anfield, scoring eight goals in the process. However, he was to be dropped from the side after the 2–2 draw with England at Wembley in 1965. Despite scoring, Ian was made to be the scapegoat as Scotland failed to make it four successive wins against the English – with the old enemy finishing that game with nine fit men and one walking wounded, in those long-gone days of no substitutes. On hearing he was dropped from the squad for forthcoming World Cup matches Ian 'misspoke' and instead of slighting the Scottish selection committee, it came across that he never wanted to play for Scotland again. Sadly, he was granted his 'wish'.

WITH THE COMPLIMENTS OF **Ty·Phoo TEA** LTD., BIRMINGHAM 5

IAN ST. JOHN
(Liverpool and Scotland)
Moving from Motherwell to Liverpool in May 1961, Ian St. John was already an international player. His total so far is four League caps, six 'Under 23' caps and 21 full International caps.
His achievements include scoring the fastest hat-trick in Scotland in the time of 2½ minutes. Ian St. John has also collected two League Championship medals in 1964 and 1966 and a 2nd Division Championship medal in 1962.

Ron Yeats also signed in 1961 and was immediately made captain of the side. The powerfully built defender would lead Liverpool to a Second Division championship, two First Division titles and the FA Cup, too. As for Scotland, in an era of Billy McNeill, Ian Ure and others he was cruelly ignored, only being picked twice, versus Wales in 1964 and Italy – in a vital but unsuccessful World Cup qualifier – in 1965.

Goalkeeper Tommy Lawrence was also part of the successful 60s side but like Yeats found himself way down the pecking order, with only three caps coming his way. Perhaps this was more to do with his bulky size rather than his goalkeeping ability as he was affectionately known as the 'Flying Pig' down Liverpool way.

Tommy Lawrence

Shankly described Peter Cormack as the 'final piece of the jigsaw' when he signed him in 1972 as the club chased their first trophies of the 70s. Peter would win two league titles, the UEFA Cup twice and the FA Cup and would travel to the World Cup finals in 1974. Despite all this success Peter would not add to his nine-cap tally won with Hibernian and Nottingham Forest.

Kenny Dalglish

With the Shankly era ending, Bob Paisley took over and he would surpass his predecessor's achievements. Having won the European Cup in 1977, Bob Paisley signed three Scots who would go on to make a great impact at the club in its quest for further European success.

Bob signed Kenny Dalglish from Celtic for £440,000 in August 1977 to replace Kevin Keegan. It was a veritable steal as Kenny's time would see Liverpool win six league titles, three European Cups, one Super Cup and a host of other domestic trophies. Kenny had come to Anfield having already played at the World Cup in West Germany, with a cap total of 47 and goals totalling 16. He would go on to play a further 55 times for Scotland, scoring another 14 goals, and with 102 caps is Scotland's most capped player. He also stands as the country's top goalscorer alongside Denis Law on 30. Kenny played at both the 1978 and 1982 World Cups, scoring a goal in each, but injury would keep him out of World Cup 86.

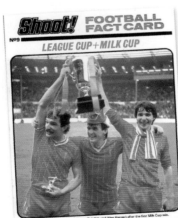

Little was known about Alan Hansen by Liverpool fans when Paisley signed him from

Partick Thistle a month after the signing of Dalglish. Centre-half Hansen strode gracefully through his 14 or so years with the Reds and would collect two more titles than Dalglish. Had he been a 'Sassenach', Hansen may well have won close to 100 caps for England, such was his standing among the English media and football fraternity, but he never seemed to fit into the Scotland set-up. At the time Scotland was blessed with a host of great centre-halves in Miller, McLeish and Narey, who were all based in Scotland – and Jock Stein often seemed to be unsure of his best central pairing. Inconsistent game time, sometimes caused by his perceived frequent call-offs, and indifferent performances saw Hansen never being 'taken to' by his home support, and his one World Cup finals ended in disaster when he and Willie Miller contrived to collide and concede a goal to the USSR in the vital group match at Spain 82. He won a total of 26 caps from 1979 to 1987.

The fiercely competitive Graeme Souness was signed from Middlesbrough in January 1978 and was to captain the Liverpool side to great success in the early 80s. Souness had already won three caps during his time at Ayresome Park in season 1974/75 but had fallen out of the picture for a few years. Ally MacLeod had brought him back into the fold in early 1978 but he wasn't a fully established player by the time of the finals. However, after a disastrous first two matches in Argentina, there was a clamour for his inclusion in the last match versus Holland. Scotland would win and Souness cemented his place in the side. The arrival of Jock Stein would solidify this as he and Stein built up a good rapport. Souness would win 37 caps in his time at Anfield and captain the side in the final two matches at World Cup 82. Overall, Souness would captain Scotland 27 times in his 54 matches, including his final two at Mexico 1986.

Playing alongside Souness, Dalglish and Hansen at the World Cup in 1982 was free-scoring midfielder John Wark. Wark at that time was part of Bobby Robson's great Ipswich side that won the FA Cup in 1977/78, the UEFA Cup in 1980/81, as well as pushing Liverpool for a number of league titles. Wark netted a double versus New Zealand at the Spain finals and had, overall, won 26 caps, scoring seven goals, before signing for Liverpool in March 1984. His time at Anfield **would see him as the**

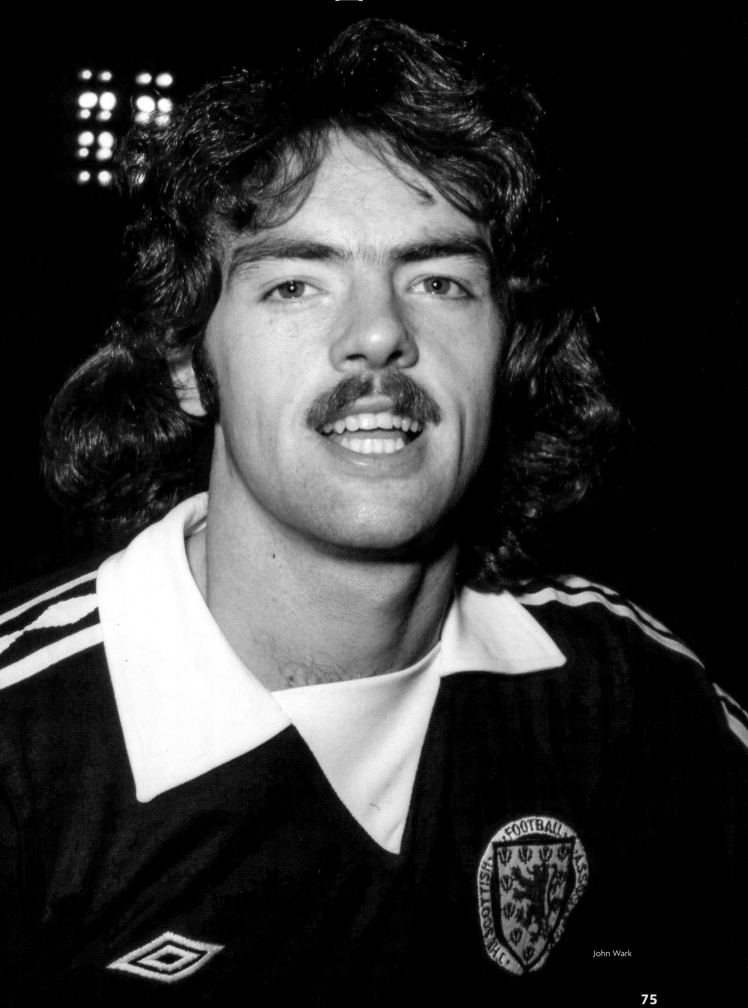

John Wark

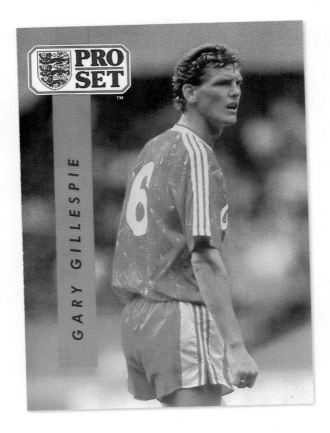

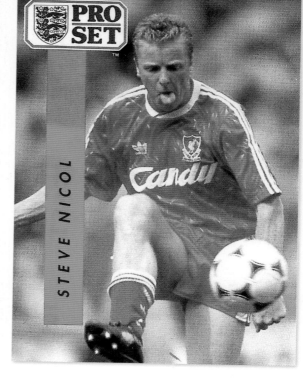

club's top goalscorer in his first full season with 27 goals, but injury would see diminishing returns over the next few seasons and he was only to add three more caps to his total.

Steve Nicol was another player about whom many English observers were surprised at his lack of Scotland caps – he would only win 27. Competition was quite strong at the time with the likes of Richard Gough playing at right-back and later on Stewart McKimmie. Nicol, however, would play in all three games at the 1986 World Cup finals and perhaps had the only real chance created by Scotland in that most frustrating of matches as we failed to net against ten-man Uruguay.

Gary Gillespie was another who could not transfer his splendid league form to international level for Scotland, playing in 13 games from 1987 to 1990, including an appearance versus Brazil at the Italy World Cup finals. However, two own goals might not have helped his cause too much.

The Premier League years have seen a decline in Scots at Anfield, with Danny Wilson winning more caps than games played with Liverpool: five as opposed to two. Charlie Adam had a disappointing spell at Liverpool after his successful time with Blackpool, adding only six caps to his total. Mercifully, though, in the last couple of years we have seen left-back Andy Robertson put in some magnificent displays for the club after signing from Hull City. He has since been given the captaincy of the national side and has added a number of caps following his move to Anfield and long may that continue.

Andy Robertson

MANCHESTER UNITED

Manchester United were originally a railway club formed as the Newton Heath LYR FC in 1878 and were renamed in 1902 as Manchester United. Sandy Bell would be the first United player to represent Scotland, winning his only cap as Scotland ran out 4–1 winners versus Ireland in Belfast in March 1912. South African-born Sandy was to win two league titles with the club in 1907/08 and 1910/11, as well as their first FA Cup triumph in 1909. Sandy would also win the league with Blackburn Rovers in 1913/14.

Only two more players would be capped by Scotland before the advent of the Second World War. Tom Miller would add two caps to one he had already won at Liverpool, including a 3–0 victory versus England at Hampden in 1921. The following year, Neil McBain was to play in the reverse fixture at Villa Park as Scotland won 1–0 and would go on to win two more caps with Everton.

Winger Jimmy Delaney had already won ten caps with Celtic, with nine of them coming prior to the commencement of World War II, when Matt Busby brought him to United in 1946. Delaney would add another five caps to his total and an FA Cup winners' medal in 1948. Jimmy scored for Scotland in the first of those matches as Scotland beat Belgium 3–1 in 1946, giving him a goal tally of six.

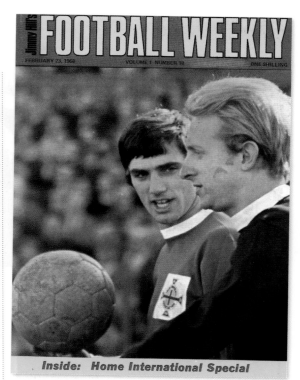

Inside: Home International Special

Denis Law

Following the Munich Air Disaster one of the players thrust into the Manchester side was a young Scots forward called Alex Dawson. Dawson would be replaced in 1960/61 by David Herd from Arsenal, who despite his quite phenomenal scoring record with the Reds never added to his cap tally of five. However, an Aberdeen Schoolboys teammate of Dawson's would make a great impact on the Old Trafford side and Scotland: Denis Law.

Busby had been desperate to sign Law before he had gone to rivals Man City in 1960 and was glad to help him escape from his torrid time in Italy with Torino. Denis would win the FA Cup with United in 1963, supplying one of the goals with Herd scoring the other two as they beat Leicester City 3–1. He was to play for Scotland, whilst at Old Trafford, 35 times, scoring 25 of his Scotland total of 30. He would hit 11 goals in total in season 1962/63 alone and was to captain the side versus Spain as the Scots routed the Spaniards in the Bernabeu 6–2 in the June of 1963. He would play in the 1963, 1964 and 1967 victories over England – as well as the 1962 win when he was at Torino. He was to win two titles at United in 1964/65 and 1966/67 but would be injured for the epic 4–1 Wembley victory in the 1968 European Cup Final.

One player who would take part in that European match as well as the FA Cup and league title wins was Pat Crerand. Pat had already won 11 caps with Celtic when he

Jimmy Delaney

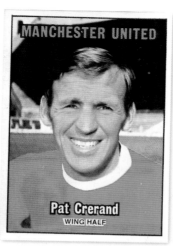

Pat Crerand
WING HALF

joined United in 1963. He was known as a fiercely competitive player but he was also appreciated for his great passing, creating many a chance for the likes of Law, Charlton and Best. Pat would only win five caps whilst at Old Trafford and would more or less quit the national side due to a lack of game time. In this era, only the first 11 were guaranteed a game and often the 12th man would sit in the stands frustrated at being unable to take part in the match, even when injury meant teams often played with less than ten men or indeed carried on with the walking wounded shoved out to play left-wing or similar.

Tommy Docherty would make a great impact at Old Trafford in the 1970s but before that, as Scotland manager, he gave a number of caps to United players and some he would recruit during his time at the club. In his first match in charge versus Portugal in October 1971 he was to give George Graham, then of Arsenal, his first cap. George would win his first eight caps at Highbury. Docherty would sign him when he took over as United manager; however, George was to win only four more caps under Willie Ormond, notching a double versus Wales at Wrexham in May 1973.

Given a sub appearance against Portugal was Martin Buchan, then of Aberdeen. By February 1972 Buchan had moved to Manchester United and would go on to give long service to the club, captaining the side to FA Cup victory in 1977 and playing over 450 games for the Red Devils. As for Scotland, Buchan would appear at both the World Cup finals in 1974 and 1978, playing in five of the six matches and captaining the side on two occasions. He would win 32 of his 34 caps at Old Trafford.

It was Docherty who recalled Denis Law back to the Scotland cause after

an absence of almost three years to face Peru in 1972, as well as winger Willie Morgan, who had won his first cap at Burnley in October 1967 and was hitherto forgotten about. He had signed for Man United in 1968 just after the European Cup triumph and although United's standing was to fall in the following years, 'Willie on the Wing' was well beloved by the fans. He was to win 20 caps with United, including playing all three matches at World Cup 1974. His most sublime moment in a Scotland shirt would be his perfectly flighted cross with the outside of his foot for Joe Jordan to score versus Czechoslovakia in September 1973.

Lou Macari made his Scotland debut as a Celtic player in the 1972 Home International versus Wales, and by early 1973 Docherty had signed him on at Old Trafford. Although he would be capped under Willie Ormond nine times, he was never favoured by him, missing out in the World Cup in 1974 and excluded for a number of years, too. Ally MacLeod would immediately reinstate Macari to the squad, something he may have regretted a year or so later as Lou would apparently lead disgruntled voices about bonuses in Argentina and then with Scotland in free-fall, Macari was selling stories to the British tabloids. Macari would remain at United for over ten years.

When Scotland stepped out on to the pitch at Estadio Mineiro, Belo Horizonte, to play Yugoslavia in the Brazilian Independence Cup in June 1972, Buchan, Law, Morgan and Macari were all in the side, and making his debut was Partick Thistle's Alex Forsyth. Full-back Forsyth had been part of Thistle's League Cup-winning side in October 1971 and he was to find himself at Old Trafford in December 1972 as one of Docherty's first signings. By this time Alex had won four caps and was to add another six to his total in the next few years, but with

ARGENTINA 78

LOU MACARI
SCO

SCOTTISH DAILY EXPRESS
TOP FOR SPORT

MARTIN BUCHAN
MANCHESTER UNITED and SCOTLAND
SCOTCARD No. 3

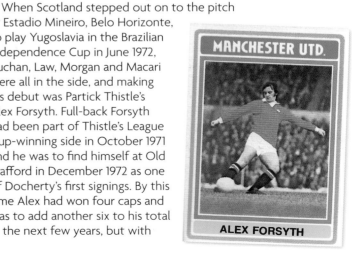

MANCHESTER UTD.

ALEX FORSYTH

Danny McGrain and Sandy Jardine dominating the full-back positions chances were limited for Alex and he would not be part of the 1974 World Cup squad.

There can be few players who would only win 15 caps for Scotland yet be loved as much as Jim Holton was. Holton had signed for Docherty from Shrewsbury in January 1973. By May of that year Willie Ormond had installed him in the Scotland side and he was to play in all three of the Home Internationals series; however, by the September he was the stuff of legends. His commanding presence in the air and tough tackling had endeared Scotland fans to him, too, and rising above the defence to score the equaliser against Czechoslovakia is an enduring moment for many a Scotland supporter of that era. Jim would play in all three games at the 1974 World Cup finals, lining up alongside his defensive partner Buchan in the Scotland side for two of those. Jim looked set to play for Scotland and United for years but he was to break his leg twice in a matter of months and sadly he was to play only one match after World Cup 1974. His time at United would peter out and Jim would go on to play for Sunderland, Coventry City and even the Miami Toros.

In early 1978 United manager Dave Sexton signed both Joe Jordan and Gordon McQueen from rivals Leeds United. Both, of course, had established Scotland careers and with the World Cup coming up later that year both had their eyes on taking part in the tournament. For Joe everything seemed to go to plan as he hit the opener against Peru in Cordoba in June but then, of course, 'the wheels fell 'aff the barra'. For McQueen they had already done so, as he clattered the post against Wales in May that year, thus missing the World Cup.

McQueen would win 13 of his 26 caps at Old Trafford, with ten of them coming after the

JIM HOLTON

1978 World Cup. His final cap would come a year before the World Cup in Spain 82 and so he was never to appear at any finals, despite being in the 1974 and 1978 squads. As for United, he would play over 200 games and win the 1983 FA Cup with them.

Jordan would win 20 of his 52 caps at Old Trafford but would move to AC Milan in 1981, and so no Manchester United player would be part of the 1982 Scotland World Cup squad. Joe would, of course, play his part, netting against the USSR, thus scoring at his third World Cup finals in a row.

United had two Scottish players on show at the 1986 World Cup finals in Mexico. Arthur Albiston had joined United from school in 1972 and was to win three FA Cups with the side in 1977, 1983 and 1985. As for Scotland he had won his first cap versus Northern Ireland in Belfast in April 1982 but may well have felt disappointed when George Burley of Ipswich Town was chosen ahead of him in subsequent games. However, Arthur was to continue to win caps over the next few years but would have been a bit surprised to find himself lining up against Uruguay in Mexico. It would be his last match for the national side but Arthur would play for another couple of years for United and is still attached to the club as part of the MUTV team.

The torrid Uruguay game is perhaps best known for Gordon Strachan being crudely tackled by Jorge Barrios in the first minute. Strachan had signed for United from Aberdeen in August 1984 and was to win 14 of his 50 caps there, including most of the qualifiers for Mexico 86 and all three games in the actual finals. Strachan scored in the match versus Germany and in an iconic moment pretended to jump the hoarding behind the goal in his celebration. Sadly, Scotland were to lose the match 2–1. Gordon's

Gordon Strachan

Joe Jordan

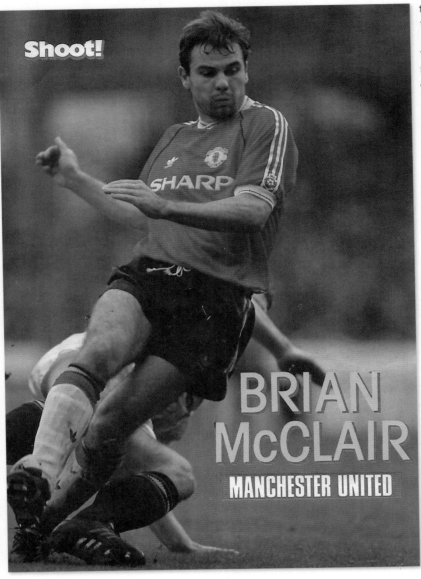

Shoot!

BRIAN McCLAIR

MANCHESTER UNITED

to return to Scotland duty after a gap of three years.

Brian McClair had won four caps by the time he had signed for United for £850,000 in 1987. He was to go on to have a great career at United, playing over 470 games for the club, winning four Premier League titles and a host of other trophies in his 11-year spell at Old Trafford. As for Scotland he never seemed to fit in or produce the consistent displays that he did for his club side. Having won 15 caps by the time of Italia 90 and having played in several of the qualifiers, he fell out of favour with manager Andy Roxburgh and never made it to the World Cup finals. McClair was, however, part of the 1992 Euro finals squad, playing in all three games and he scored his first Scotland goal versus the CIS, which was his 26th match for his country. Only another four caps were won by Brian as Scotland failed to qualify for World Cup 1994.

Midfielder Darren Fletcher would become a regular in the Scotland side before he was fully established at Old Trafford. Berti Vogts had already promoted many a young player to the Scotland side long before they were ready and some thought Darren seemed another example; however, in his second appearance he was to score the winner against Lithuania that would see Scotland through to the 2004 Euro play-offs. Darren quickly became an integral part of the Scotland side for the years that followed and was to captain the side 34 times, winning 80 caps in total. He would, of course, also establish himself in the Manchester United side, playing in well over 300 games. His cap count at United was 66, which would have surely been more had he not been stricken with ulcerative colitis, eventually having surgery in early 2013, keeping him out of football for almost a year. Darren left United in 2015, having joined as an 11-year-old two decades before, to join West Brom where he would win 12 caps and then Stoke City, gaining a further two.

Currently young Scott McTominay is beginning to establish himself in the United set-up with some good performances in central midfield and will surely be an integral part of the Scotland side for years to come.

final match as a United player was to be the 2–0 World Cup qualifier win over France at Hampden in 1989.

Jim Leighton would follow Strachan and, of course, manager Alex Ferguson from Pittodrie to Old Trafford in 1988 and although initially he seemed to be doing well, a serious of high profile mistakes saw Fergie drop Leighton for the 1990 FA Cup Final replay. United would win the replay but from then on he was on his way out of the club. Jim was to win 13 of his 91 Scotland caps whilst with the Red Devils, including the 1990 World Cup qualifiers and finals, where he would play in all three games. Jim moved to Hibernian in 1993 where he was

Darren Fletcher

Scotland

Back row: Tommy Burns, Graeme Sinclair (Dumbarton), David McNiven (Leeds United), Trevor Ross (Arsenal), Drew Brand (Everton), Paul Sturrock (Dundee United), Arthur Albiston (Manchester United), George Burley (Ipswich), Tony Fitzpatrick (St. Mirren). Front row: Eric Ferguson (Dundee; Physio- therapist), An... Roy Aitken (C... (Aberdeen), J... Dave Provan... Donnie MacK...

Scotland v England, Stark's Park, Kirkcaldy, 30th April, 1989

Football HAMPDEN HEROE
SOUVENIR

Here's a sight to set all Scottish hearts beating with pride ... the men in Dark Blue just before that magnificent victory against England at Hampden.
They are (Back row, left to right): McClaren (Leeds), Stewart (Kilmarnock), Harvey (Leeds), Allan (Dundee), Hutchinson (Coventry).
Middle row: Manager Ormond, Shaedler (Hibs), McGrain, (Celtic), Smith (Newcastle), Hay (Celtic), Jardine (Rangers), Jordan (Leeds), Blackley (Hibs), Holton, Buchan (both Manchester United), Lorimer (Leeds).
Front row: Trainer Allan, Ford (Hearts), Dalglish (Celtic), Bremner (Leeds), Law (M... (Manchester United), Johnstone (Celtic) and t...

...ccer
Scotland in the World Cup

...cotland ..... as the World Cup team line up at Ram... match with Israel, in Februar...
...t): Alex McLeish, John Wark, Graeme Souness, ...ohn Robertson, Kenny Burns, Frank Gray, Danny... ...and Archie Gemmill (Captain...

ENTRY OF

CINZANO CINZANO CINZANO CINZANO CINZANO C

SCOTTISH TEAM POOL 1973

ls International match: England v. Scotland. Played at White Hart Lane, London, March 16th, 1968.
o right): R. Sherry (assistant team manager), A. Bruce, G. Souness, J. Harrower, T. Livingstone, A. R
Helam, R. Cairns, D. Macfarlane (team manager). Front row (left to right): M. Pollock, R. Miller,
T. Sinclair, B. Laing, J. McGorley and J. Robertson

Motherwell FC were founded in 1886 when two local works sides, Glencairn FC and Alpha FC, decided to merge to establish a side to represent their hometown. George Robertson would be the first of the Steelmen to play for Scotland. Left- winger George was picked to play against Wales at Rugby Park in 1910, with Scotland winning 1–0. George would go on to play for Sheffield Wednesday and gain a further three caps, playing in victories over Wales and Ireland and a defeat to England in 1913.

In the late 20s and early 30s Motherwell were regularly challenging for the league title and were to lift it in 1931/32. They were runners-up on four occasions around this time and came third four times, too. This would, of course, lead to international recognition for some of their players.

Goalkeeper Allan McClory was the first to be capped in October 1926 as Scotland defeated Wales 3–0 at Ibrox. However, Jack Harkness of Queen's Park and then Hearts would dominate the goalkeeping position up until the 30s, so McClory would only get two more caps – versus Ireland in 1928 as Scotland lost 1–0 at Firhill, Glasgow, and then a final appearance in 1934 as Scotland defeated Wales 3–2 at Pittodrie, Aberdeen. McClory had six ever-present seasons for 'the Well', including four consecutively.

MITCHELL'S CIGARETTES

G. STEVENSON
(MOTHERWELL)

Inside-forward George Stevenson was another who would play for Motherwell for many years, amassing well over 500 games for the club. George gained the first of his 12 caps in October 1927 as Scotland drew 2–2 with Wales at the Racecourse Ground, Wrexham. George would score as Scotland beat England 2–0 at Hampden in March 1931 in front of a crowd of 129,810, with Celtic great Jimmy McGrory netting the other. George played his final game versus Ireland in Belfast in 1934, having scored four goals in total. After the war, George would take up the mantle as Motherwell's manager, leading them to League Cup (1950/51) and Scottish Cup (1951/52) success.

Allan Craig also served Motherwell greatly. From the beginning of the 1925/26 season to the end of 1931/32, out of a possible 266 games, he missed only six. In 1929, centre-half Craig took part in Scotland's first ever overseas tour, playing in two of three games against Norway and the Netherlands, with Scotland winning the former 7–3 and the latter 2–0. His final cap would come in a 3–0 defeat to England at Wembley in 1932.

Solitary caps would be handed to John Murdoch versus Ireland at Windsor Park in February 1931 and Hugh Wales against Wales (ironically) in a 5–2 defeat at Tynecastle in October 1932, plus two to Willie Telfer in successive matches versus Ireland – away in 1932 and at Celtic Park in 1933.

In their 1931/32 league title success Motherwell's striker Willie MacFadyen would hit 52 league goals, which is still a Scottish League record today, and with 251 league goals for the club, he is also in the top ten for top-flight league goals in Scotland. However, Willie was up against the likes of Hughie Gallacher and Jimmy McGrory for caps, so sadly only won two and, of course, he scored in both.

On his debut in October 1933 at Ninian Park, Cardiff, two other Steelmen lined up beside him – John Blair and John McMenemy, who was the son of Celtic great Jimmy McMeneny. Jimmy had won 12 caps from 1905 to 1920 but for John this would be his only cap. Scotland were defeated 3–2 by Wales and a month later, Willie lined up with teammate Duncan Ogilvie for his only cap versus Austria in a friendly match at Hampden that ended 2–2.

As mentioned earlier Motherwell would enjoy success in both the League Cup and Scottish Cup in the early 1950s and a number of players from these sides were to be capped, also. Playing in both cup successes was centre-half Andy Paton, whose first cap came in January 1946, which is in some places considered a Victory International and therefore sometimes discounted; however, the Scottish and Belgian FAs both count these as official. The match ended 2–2. It would be a further six years until Andy would be capped again, this time as Scotland toured Scandinavia in May 1952, beating Denmark 2–1 but losing 3–1 against Sweden. Wilson Humphries, who would score in the 1952 Scottish Cup Final

JOHN BLAIR,
Motherwell F.C.   TOPICAL
                                   TIMES

John Blair

as Motherwell walloped Dundee 4–0, made his only Scotland appearance in the latter match. He did not play in the 1950 League Cup Final.

Similarly, Jimmy Watson had a long wait between caps – his first would come in October 1947 as Scotland lost 2–0 in Belfast. His second and last, as a Huddersfield Town player in 1953, saw him return to Windsor Park but come away with a 3–1 victory in a Home International/World Cup qualifier double-header. Watson appeared in both finals, scoring in the Scottish Cup Final.

Also on the Scottish Cup scoring list that day was Willie Redpath. Left-half Willie also played in the 1950 League Cup win and was capped nine times for Scotland from 1948 to 1952. Scotland would win seven of those nine games, including a 3–2 win at Wembley in April 1951. The following month Redpath travelled with Scotland from Mount Florida to Europe as they beat France 1–0 at Hampden and Belgium 5–0 in Brussels, before coming back down to earth with a thump as they lost 4–0 to Austria in Vienna.

Jim Forrest would only play in the 1950 League Cup Final, scoring once, as Motherwell beat Hibernian 3–0 at Hampden. Jim, who married George Stevenson's daughter, would have to wait a while for his one cap, which came at Hampden in April 1958 against England. Had events turned out differently perhaps, Jim could have found himself on his way to Sweden and the World Cup finals, but a 4–0 defeat by the old enemy saw an overhaul of the side and Jim was left out in the cull.

Bobby Ancell had taken over the reins of Motherwell from Stevenson in 1955 and brought through a number of young exciting players, collectively known as the 'Ancell Babes', and although they would not win any honours, they did finish third in the league in 1958/59. Not quite a Babe but Ian Gardiner, at age 29, won his only Scotland cap versus Wales in 1957. However, May 1959 would see three young guns as such all make their Scotland debuts in a friendly international versus West Germany at Hampden.

Andy Weir would net only six minutes into his debut, although John White of Falkirk had done likewise in the first minute. Scotland would win 3–2 but this would be Weir's only goal in six games and it was also to be his only taste of victory. His other five games were all

Autograph...
WILLIE REDPATH   (Motherwell F.C.)

in 1960, with draws against England and Hungary and defeats to Poland, Austria and Turkey.

At centre half versus West Germany was Bert McCann, who was to win five caps, with the final one coming in the 9–3 defeat to England at Wembley in 1961. Ian St John would be the most famous of the 'Ancell Babes' and he was to win his first seven caps whilst at Fir Park, before winning a further 14 at Liverpool. Ian would score nine goals for Scotland but only one during his spell with Motherwell, coming in the 3–2 friendly match defeat at home to Poland in 1960.

1960 would also bring three caps for inside-forward Willie Hunter, who also scored on his debut versus Hungary in Budapest as Scotland drew 3–3. Like Weir, he is one of only 11 Scottish players to ever play Turkey at the time of writing.. Defender John Martis would play his only game in Hunter's last, versus Wales at Ninian Park in October 1960. 55,000 saw Wales win 2–0. Pat Quinn made his debut versus England at Wembley in 1961 but did go on to play in three more games, including two World Cup qualifiers versus the Republic of Ireland.

The late 60s and early 70s would see few caps come Motherwell's way, although Tom **Forsyth would win the first of his 22 caps**

I. ST. JOHN

Ian St. John

WILLIE PETTIGREW
★ FORWARD ★

whilst at Fir Park, against Denmark in a Euro qualifier in 1971. Predatory Fir Park striker Willie Pettigrew would also win five caps, scoring in his first two games, both at Hampden, versus Switzerland (after only two minutes) in April 1976 and Wales a month later.

Scottish Cup success would return to Motherwell in that most memorable of finals, as they beat Dundee United 4–3 in 1991. The scorer of one of the goals would be Phil O'Donnell, who was to win his only Scotland cap versus Switzerland in a World Cup qualifier at Pittodrie in September 1993. Davie Cooper had enjoyed a new lease of life at Fir Park following his years with Rangers and indeed won his last two of his 22 caps with Motherwell in season 1989/90. Sadly, both he and Phil would tragically die prematurely, with Cooper passing away in 1995 after suffering a brain haemorrhage aged 39 during the filming of a training video. O'Donnell would collapse late in a game against Dundee United in December 2007 and would be pronounced dead shortly after due to a cardiac arrest aged only 35.

Defender Tom Boyd also played in the 1991 cup final and had already won the first four of his 72 caps prior to that game. He had made an immediate impact on his debut after coming on as a sub in a Euro qualifier versus Romania in September 1990 by playing a part in the winning goal.

Japan in May 1995 would see three players from the Well take part in the opening match of the Kirin Cup against the hosts, which ended 0–0. Full-back Rob McKinnon had made his debut a full two years before against Malta but would make one more appearance after this match.

Defender Brian Martin was well loved at Motherwell, as he was at other clubs he played for, in the way he was able to read the game and seemed almost effortless

with his composed style of play. He would also play against Ecuador in Japan as Scotland won 2–1, but with the likes of Colin Hendry, Colin Calderwood and Alan McLaren available, Martin never made it back into the side.

Midfielder Paul Lambert would, however, make the grade as such, but these two Kirin Cup caps would represent his Motherwell haul. A move from Fir Park to Borussia Dortmund would see him win the Champions League in 1997 as well as reach a total of 40 caps overall, with the majority coming in his time with Celtic.

Scotland's talisman for the early part of the century would be James McFadden, who began his career at Fir Park in 2000 and was to win the SPL Young Player of the Year award in season 2002/03. Berti Vogts gave James his first Scotland action in the 2–0 defeat to South Africa as part of the Hong Kong Reunification Cup in 2002. James was to miss the team flight home due to a late-night drinking session, but thankfully Berti would forgive him and persevere with McFadden. Only four of his Scotland caps came at Motherwell, however, before he moved to Everton in 2003.

One of the great moments early in Faddy's Scotland career was the well-worked goal with Darren Fletcher versus the Netherlands in the Euro play-offs in November 2003 that would give Scotland victory that day. Former teammate Stephen Pearson was to make his international bow that same day, coming on as a late substitute. This would be Stephen's only cap with the Steelmen but another nine were to follow with Celtic and Derby County.

DAVID COOPER
Motherwell

Quite a few Motherwell players have made their debuts for Scotland overseas and Chris Cadden also did so in the summer of 2018 as he played in matches against Peru and Mexico. With a number of young Motherwell players breaking through to the Scotland Under-21s will we have to wait for another foreign junket for them to make their mark at full level?

NEWCASTLE UNITED

Newcastle United were formed following a merger of Newcastle East and West End in 1892. The early part of the 20th century was very successful for the club, winning three championship titles in 1904/05, 1906/07 and 1908/09. They would also win the FA Cup in 1910 after a replay, and after being runners-up the year before. A number of Scots would be among their ranks, with six playing in the FA Cup Final win of 1910.

Defender Andy Aitken would take part in the first of the league triumphs and was the first Newcastle player to be capped for Scotland, playing in the 1901 match versus England at Crystal Palace, which ended 2–2. A year later and in only his second international, at Villa Park, he was to take to the field as captain, in another 2–2 draw with England. Six of Andy's Scotland caps at Newcastle were against England. He would go on to win another three each at Leicester Fosse and then Middlesbrough, with four of those against the Auld Enemy.

Also taking the field in that 1902 game, for his only Scotland appearance as a Newcastle player, was one Robert Smyth McColl, better known as R S McColl, founder of the newsagent chain. McColl had also bagged 13 goals in 11 internationals in his Queen's Park days. He would be reinstated as an amateur and win another cap with Queen's Park in 1908. McColl had left Newcastle by the time of their first league success.

Teammate Ronald Orr was on the scoresheet in 1902 and was to play in the 1–0 defeat to England in 1904 at Celtic Park. Ronald was part of the first two league-winning sides. Representing Aston Villa in the 1902 2–2 draw was Bobby Templeton, winning his first cap, too. Bobby was to win three caps with United between March 1903 and April 1904 before moving on to Woolwich Arsenal and then Kilmarnock, where he would win the final six of his 11-cap total.

The England match at Crystal Palace in 1905 had four Newcastle players, including Andy Aitken, on show in the Scotland team, with one future Magpie as well.

Right-back Andy McCombie had actually been capped twice with Sunderland in 1903 and was also part of their 1901/02 title-winning side, before moving to local rivals Newcastle in 1904. He had already faced Wales in 1905 as a Newcastle player but the England match was to be his last. Andy was to win the 1904/05

and 1906/07 championships with the club.

Like McCombie, Peter McWilliam was born in Inverness and also played for Inverness Thistle. Peter joined Newcastle in 1902 and would win all three championships and the FA Cup with them. As for his Scotland career he would play eight times and captained his side on the last occasion, against Wales in Cardiff in March 1911. Unfortunately, a serious knee injury sustained in this match would see an end to his playing career. Peter would, however, go on to manage Tottenham Hotspur to an FA Cup win in 1921.

Striker James Howie played in that 1905 England game, too, and was also a triple league and FA Cup winner with the Magpies. He was to win three caps, netting a double in the 2–1 win over England at Hampden in 1906. George Wilson, then of Hearts, in 1905 moved briefly to Everton before joining Newcastle in 1907, where he would win one title and the FA Cup. He won six caps in total: four at Hearts, one at Everton and a final one in 1909 with Newcastle – against England at the Crystal Palace.

The April 1910 match against England at Hampden Park saw Scotland win 2–0 and also had a flock of past, present and future Magpies. Sandy Higgins was making his second Scotland start having played against Ireland in Belfast the month before. Sandy would win three caps and with Newcastle, the FA Cup and the 1908/09 championship.

The aforementioned teammate Peter McWilliam was involved in the 1910 England game, as was Andy Aitken, then of Leicester Fosse, and Bobby Templeton of Kilmarnock. James Hay of Celtic was winning his sixth cap and he would move to Newcastle in 1911, missing out on the trophies from the previous years. Mind you, he had just won six consecutive Scottish titles with Celtic so perhaps wasn't that disappointed. He was to win three more caps with United, giving him 11 caps in total.

Goalkeeper Jimmy Lawrence joined Newcastle in 1904 and remained with the club until 1922, making a record number of appearances of 496 that he still holds today. He, of course, won all three championships and the FA Cup. His only Scotland appearance was against England at Goodison Park, Liverpool, in April 1911, which ended in a 1–1 draw. Messrs Aitken, Hay and Higgins were all playing that day too, as was centre-half Wilf Low, making his second start for Scotland. Low would win the FA Cup with Newcastle and five caps with Scotland with an eight-year gap and the Great War between his third and fourth caps.

The FA Cup would return to St James' Park in 1924 with five Scots in the Newcastle line-up, but only two were to be capped and for one solitary cap each. A fortnight before the final, Billy Cowan and Neil Harris were picked to play against England in April 1924 for the first international to be held at the newly built Wembley Stadium. The match ended 1–1 with Cowan netting for Scotland, but two weeks later it was Harris who opened the scoring for Newcastle in their 2–0 victory over Aston Villa.

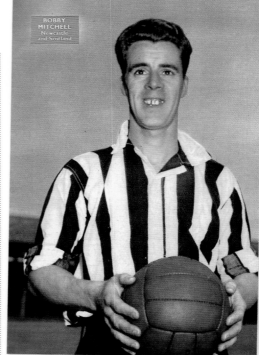
Bobby Mitchell

Hughie Gallacher arrived on Tyneside from Airdrie in December 1925 and by the end of the 1925/26 season he was the club's top goalscorer with 23 goals in 19 games. Hughie was made captain the following season and led Newcastle from the front to the league title, with 36 goals in 38 games, still

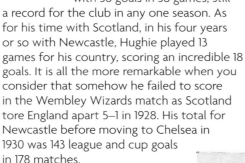
Hughie Gallacher

a record for the club in any one season. As for his time with Scotland, in his four years or so with Newcastle, Hughie played 13 games for his country, scoring an incredible 18 goals. It is all the more remarkable when you consider that somehow he failed to score in the Wembley Wizards match as Scotland tore England apart 5–1 in 1928. His total for Newcastle before moving to Chelsea in 1930 was 143 league and cup goals in 178 matches.

The FA Cup was won once more in 1932 and the side contained a few Scots, but only Jimmy Boyd was capped a few months later in a 2–1 defeat to Ireland at Celtic Park in September 1933. However, the cup was lofted up high by captain Jimmy Nelson, who was one of the Wembley Wizards during his time at Cardiff City.

Centre-half Frank Brennan would win the FA Cup in 1951 and 1952 with Newcastle. Frank was first capped with Airdrie in 1946 and his next two came later that year as a Magpie. It was to

Frank Brennan

be six years before Frank was capped again, playing in another five games. He played the last couple of games alongside Jimmy Scoular of Portsmouth, who won all his nine caps with the Hampshire club but was to go on to captain Newcastle in their 1955 FA Cup success.

Winger Bobby 'Dazzler' Mitchell actually won more FA Cups than Scottish caps, serving the Tyneside club well from 1946 to 1961 and scoring in the 1955 final. His two caps came in May 1951 as Scotland beat Denmark and then France in friendly internationals in the space of five days, but he was up against Billy Liddell for the coveted left-wing position and even though he scored on his debut he was always going to be second best behind the Liverpool legend. Of course, one player from the 1952 and 1955 FA Cup successes would not be capped until 1967 – goalkeeper, Olympian and Lisbon Lion, Ronnie Simpson.

The 1955 FA Cup was to be Newcastle's last major domestic trophy. However, long-serving captain Bobby Moncur would help them lift the Inter-Cities Fairs Cup in 1968/69. Moncur joined Newcastle in 1962 and would play for the Magpies until 1974. Not known for his goalscoring, central defender Moncur netted three goals in the two-leg final against

BOBBY MONCUR Newcastle Utd.

Bobby Moncur

JIMMY SMITH Newcastle Utd.

Ujpesti Dozsa of Hungary, as Newcastle ran out 6–2 winners.

Bobby was first picked by Bobby Brown to play for Scotland in May 1968 versus the Netherlands; however, he wasn't fully established until the start of the 1970 Home Internationals and for the following two years was a regular pick. Even with players such as Billy Bremner and John Greig, Bobby would captain Scotland in seven of his 16 matches.

Two players that were dearly loved on Tyneside, despite both their careers being cut short due to injury, were Tony Green and Jimmy Smith. Inside-forward Green had been first capped at Blackpool before moving to Newcastle in 1971. Tony was a slightly built, fast-flowing forward with a great touch and although he would only play 33 games for the Magpies he is remembered fondly and is a cult hero to many. He was to add two caps to his four won at Bloomfield Road.

Winger Jimmy Smith already had one cap under his belt when he moved to Newcastle from Aberdeen in 1969 for £80,000. Jimmy was one of those wingers who could amaze and delight fans as well as frustrate the hell out of them all in the same game. You never quite knew what you were getting and neither did Scotland manager Willie Ormond.

Willie gave Jimmy another three caps in the build-up to the 1974 World Cup but Jimmy was dropped by Ormond from the named pool of 22 for West Germany apparently for turning up late for the squad meet prior to the Home Internationals without offering any explanation. Persistent knee injuries would see Jimmy's career peter out by 1975.

Sometimes you do forget that Roy Aitken played for Newcastle United, albeit for just over a season, but the six caps (out of his tally of 57) that he won at St James' Park included his three matches at Italia 90.

Kevin Gallacher was to sign for Newcastle in 1999 and spent a couple of years there, winning the last nine of his 53 caps, including playing in the first Euro 2000 play-off match against England at Hampden that year.

Steven Caldwell, Brian Kerr, Grant Hanley and Matt Ritchie have all won caps with the Tyneside club since then but haven't impacted the club or country in the way that some of the previous players had.

41

■ **Roy Aitken**

■ ● ★ **31**

■ **Newcastle U (E)**

250,000

NOTTINGHAM FOREST

Nottingham Forest were formed in 1865 and had their first FA Cup success in 1898, and although there were a number of Scots in the side, none were to be capped for their country. However, full-back Archie Ritchie had actually been capped as an East Stirling player in March 1891 as Scotland beat Wales 4–3 at the Racecourse, Wrexham. John McPherson was to grab the third goal in the 3–1 cup final win over Derby County. John had also won his solitary cap in 1891 as a Hearts player, a month after Archie, facing England at Ewood Park, Blackburn – a match Scotland would lose 2–1.

It would be 61 years before Forest were to win the FA Cup again and once more there were a few Scots on show as Nottingham beat Luton Town 2–1, with one of the team having already been capped for Scotland. They say timing in football is everything and for Stewart Imlach that couldn't have been truer. Once Scotland had qualified for the 1958 World Cup finals, the Scottish selection committee had begun to tinker with the line-ups and a number of new players were given their chance to book a place at the finals in Sweden. Outside-left Tommy Ewing of Partick Thistle was given his chance in the Wales and England matches of the 1957/58 British Championships, but a crushing 4–0 defeat at Hampden to the latter saw major changes to the side and Stewart was brought in to fill the position a month later versus Hungary in a World Cup warm-up at home.

At the finals, Stewart was to play in the opening draw against Yugoslavia, although not fully fit, and by the time of the second match he was replaced by Willie Fernie of Celtic. Scotland went down 3–2 to Paraguay but Fernie was dropped due to an ineffective display and again the not fully fit Imlach was back in the side. Scotland would lose 2–1 to France in the final match and exited the World Cup, as did Stewart's Scotland career.

Centre-half Bob McKinlay played alongside Stewart at Wembley that day and despite his long service for the club in the top English flight he was never considered for a Scotland cap. Just as he was hanging up his boots Peter Cormack arrived at the City Ground from Hibernian in March 1970 for the sum of £85,000.

Midfielder Peter had already won four caps by this point and was to add another five in his time with Forest, including the 3–1 defeat at Wembley in 1971. Tommy Docherty

PETER CORMACK
Nottingham Forest and Scotland

would pick Peter for a friendly versus the Netherlands in late 1971 but this was to be his last appearance for Scotland. Peter's most successful club period was to follow when he joined Liverpool in 1972, but he would win no more caps.

Brian Clough took over as manager of Nottingham Forest in 1975 and was to preside over the greatest period in their history, with a league title, four League Cups and two European Cups won. Clough would sign a number of Scots that had been successful with him during his time with Derby County, not least captain John McGovern. McGovern had been signed by Clough on four occasions, initially at Hartlepool (or Hartlepools United as they were known at the time), then at Derby, Leeds and finally Forest. It would be McGovern who would lift the European Cup twice as captain and yet would only ever appear for Scotland at under-23 level.

The unlikely hero of this Forest side was winger John Robertson, who although he looked overweight and scruffy knew how to get past a defender, hit the byline and hook over a pinpoint cross. Robertson was to do just such a thing in the 1979 European Cup Final versus Malmo, effortlessly (in his own cumbersome-looking way) going past two defenders, before planting the ball on Trevor Francis's head for the only goal of the game. A

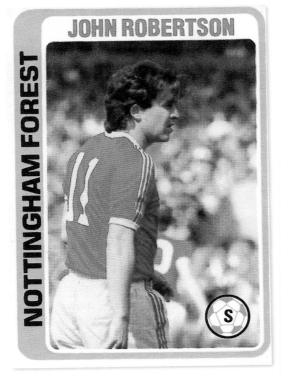

JOHN ROBERTSON

NOTTINGHAM FOREST

ARCHIE GEMMILL SCOTLAND

Club: Nottingham Forest.
Age: 31.
Height: 5ft 5ins.
Weight: 11st 2lbs.
Previous clubs: St. Mirren, Preston N.E. and Derby County.
Club Honours: Three League Championship medals, Third Division Championship medal.
International debut: February, 1971, v Belgium.
Birthplace: Paisley.
Highlight: Scoring against Holland in 1978 World Cup Finals.
Position: Midfield.
Last Transfer Fee: £130,000 from Derby County.

ARGUABLY the Scot who can look back on the 1978 World Cup Finals with most personal satisfaction. His superb individual goal against Holland was chosen as the Goal of the Tournament by El Grafico, the Argentinian magazine — praise, indeed. Archie did a first-class professional job against Liverpool in the European Cup, with close marking and unselfish running. He may be approaching the veteran stage, but Educated Archie has the sort of spirit that can make the difference between a winning and a losing side.

year later, a quick turn of pace and an almost ungainly but true finish saw him score the only goal to give Forest victory over Hamburger SV.

Robertson would gain 28 caps for Scotland, scoring eight goals, including the winning penalty at Wembley in 1981. John played in the Iran game at the World Cup in 1978 but was largely ineffective in what was only his third cap. He would play in all three Scotland games at Spain 82, scoring with a delightful free kick against New Zealand and would earn his last two caps at Derby County in late 1983. In the pantheon of great Scottish wingers Robertson is perhaps the most underrated but deserves to be ranked beside any others that could be named.

Playing in that Iran match in Argentina were two other Forest players. Kenny Burns had been capped during his Birmingham City days as far back as March 1974 in a friendly against that year's World Cup hosts West Germany. He had been a defender-cum-striker in his City days and had amassed eight caps but was still not considered a regular in the squad. Clough brought him to Forest, reinstated him to

KENNY BURNS

NOTTINGHAM FOREST

centre-half in 1977 and season 1977/78 saw the club win the First Division title and Kenny the Football Writers' Player of the Year award.

For Scotland, however, Kenny was still down the pecking order behind the likes of Martin Buchan, Gordon McQueen and Tom Forsyth. Injury to Buchan saw him come on early in the first match of the 1978 Home Internationals versus Northern Ireland, where he would be matched in alongside McQueen. This partnership didn't last long, though, as McQueen clattered the post in the next match, against Wales, and so Kenny found himself alongside Forsyth for the England game.

In Argentina, he started as full-back with Buchan and Forsyth through the middle. In the Iran game he played with Buchan until he was replaced by Forsyth early in the second half. Burns was one of the players among many cited for poor performances in Argentina but he was never really given a chance to establish himself in a Scotland XI. He would win 20 caps in total with his last few coming in the 1982 World Cup qualifiers, but by then younger players such as Willie Miller, Alex McLeish and Alan Hansen were becoming first choices.

Archie Gemmill had already played under Brian Clough during his days at Derby County and signed for Forest in September 1977. Gemmill was well established in the Scotland side having gained 22 caps at Derby when he arrived at the City Ground. He would help Forest claim the 1977/78 championship and was to score the 'Goal of the Season' too that year. No, not THAT ONE, but one against Arsenal in January 1978.

His time at Forest did include his three matches in Argentina and, of course, the greatest World Cup goal of all time ... perhaps ... no, only kidding – IT IS. Clough would drop Gemmill for the 1979 European Cup Final and their relationship became soured after that and he was soon on his way to Birmingham City. Archie won 11 caps at the City Ground and was to add ten more at Birmingham to give him a final total of 43.

Frank Gray was also to have a brief spell at Forest, joining in 1979, and was to take part in his second European Cup Final in 1980, having done so with Leeds United in 1975. The full-back was to add seven caps to his Scotland total before returning to Elland Road in 1981, where he was to win another 18 caps, ending up with 32 altogether.

Archie Gemmill's son Scot, or Scotland to give him his full name, was the next Forest player to be capped for Scotland almost 15 years on. Scot would become a regular for Forest in the early 90s and won his first cap for his country in the 1995 Kirin Cup match versus hosts Japan. He was to be included in

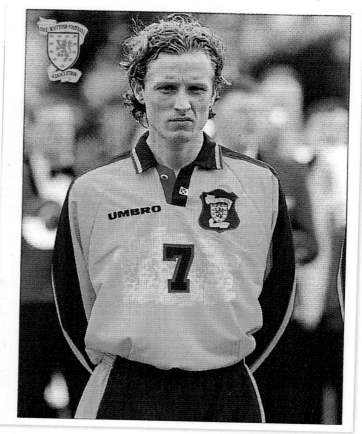

Scot Gemmill

both the 1996 Euro and 1998 World Cup finals squads but would be given no game time in either tournament. There was always a sense that Scot was a back-up guy rather than a stick-on starter for the national side. Scot was to move to Everton in 1999 and would add another 13 caps to his 13 won at Forest, before his final match for Scotland versus Austria in 2003.

A lot was hoped for when Gareth Williams was chosen for Scotland by Berti Vogts in 2002 and given five caps that year. Gareth was named Forest's Player of the Year for 2001/02 but injury would prevent him from reaching his true potential, despite moves to Leicester City and Watford.

Oliver Burke created a bit of a stir when he moved from Forest to RB Leipzig for a reported £13m after only 25 games or so, but by this time he had won two Scotland caps, with the first coming in a friendly match versus Denmark in 2016.

PARTICK THISTLE

Partick Thistle were formed in 1876 in the burgh of Partick, which was incorporated into Glasgow in 1912, and the Jags moved to their present location, Firhill Stadium in Maryhill, in 1909.

Willie Paul's name is writ large in the early history of Partick Thistle, playing for the side from 1884 to 1899, scoring 186 goals in 396 appearances officially, but perhaps a figure of well over 200 goals is closer to the mark. Willie gained three caps altogether, with all three coming against Wales – the first at Easter Road, Edinburgh, in March 1888, as Scotland won 5–1 and with Paul scoring one of the goals. A year later and the Welsh picked up their first ever point against Scotland in the Home International series with a 0–0 draw at the Racecourse, Wrexham. However, normal service resumed in March 1890 as Scotland won 5–0 at Underwood Park, Paisley, with Paul netting no less than four of the goals. It wasn't unusual at these times for different players to be used for differing games, nor for players to hit four goals and not play again. This was the case for Willie.

Thistle's (always Thistle never Partick) next internationalist was perhaps fittingly a goalkeeper, as a high proportion of their Scotland players are. John McCorkindale won his only cap against Wales in 1891. Scotland were to lose three goals, hitherto unheard of to a Welsh side, that day in Wrexham but would still come away with a 4–3 victory.

1905 would see three players being capped. First up, winning his solitary cap, was centre-forward Sam Kennedy, who was chosen to play against … Wales, of course, and at the Racecourse. Wales were to record their first ever victory over Scotland as they ran out 3–1 winners.

Just under a fortnight later and Scotland were to beat Ireland 4–0 at Celtic Park with two Jags in the line-up: goalkeeper Billy Howden and the gifted Neilly Gibson. Gibson had joined the Jags earlier that year after ten seasons with Rangers, where he had won four titles and three Scottish Cups. This was to be his 14th and final cap. His first cap had come in 1895 and the last one prior to this was in 1901. Neilly's son Jimmy was also to be capped with the Jags. Despite the clean sheet Howden would not play again either.

James McMullan, Partick Thistle

Partick Thistle were to win the Scottish Cup for the only time, so far, in 1921 and a number of the side were to be capped for Scotland. Goalkeeper (what else!) Kenny Campbell had moved from junior football to Liverpool in 1911. Kenny was picked for Scotland for the first two matches of the 1920 Home International series versus Wales and Ireland and then signed for Thistle two days before the game against England at Wembley in 1920. Kenny was to win six caps with the Thistle and he captained Scotland to a 2–1 victory over Wales at Pittodrie, Aberdeen, in 1921.

Defender Joe Harris played alongside Campbell in the matches versus Wales and Ireland in February 1921, two months before the cup final. Joe was to go on to play for Middlesbrough and then Newcastle United, taking part in their championship-winning season of 1926/27.

Jimmy McMullan is reckoned to have been one of the best wing-halves of his day and joined Thistle from Third Lanark. He was to remain at Firhill until 1926. Jimmy had been first capped on the same day that Kenny Campbell made his debut versus Wales in March 1920 in Cardiff, as Scotland drew 1–1. He gained his fourth cap against England on 9 April 1921, as Scotland ran out 3–0 winners at Hampden. Jimmy was to be injured in this game and a week later, on Thistle's greatest day, he was to miss the cup final victory over Rangers. He was to win a further four caps at Firhill before leaving in 1926 for Manchester City, where greater glory awaited him as the captain of the Wembley Wizards in 1928. Jimmy captained Scotland on six occasions and won 16 caps in total.

Inside-right Jimmy Kinloch was to win his only cap a year after the cup success against Ireland at Celtic Park, with Scotland winning 2–1.

Jimmy Gibson, the son of the aforementioned Neilly, joined the Jags the season after the cup success and quickly established himself in the side. Jimmy lined up for Scotland at right-half against England in April 1926 for his debut. His former clubmate Jimmy McMullan, then of Man City, occupied the wing-half position of the left side as Scotland won 1–0 at Old Trafford. Jimmy was to win

J. Gibson, Partick Thistle.

three more caps with the Jags before moving to Aston Villa for a then record fee of £7,500. He was to win four more caps and would line up with McMullan again for the 5–1 thrashing of England in 1928.

Another goalie was to be capped in Scotland's May 1931 tour of Europe. John Jackson had joined Thistle in the 1926/27 season and was to play over 300 times for the Maryhill club before moving to Chelsea in 1933. John's opening games for Scotland did not augur well for his career it would seem, as the Scots lost 5–0 in Austria and 3–0 in Italy, before recording a 3–2 win in Switzerland. However, in his final Scotland game as a Jag he was part of the 1933 side that won 2–1 against England at Hampden.

John was to win four more caps with Chelsea, including the 2–0 post-war victory over England in 1935 at Hampden, where tough-tackling left-back and former Firhill teammate George Cummings made his debut. George played a number of seasons with Thistle and won two more caps that year before joining the Jags diaspora in England to sign for Aston Villa, whom he was to remain with until his retirement in 1949. George won nine caps in total with the last coming in the final match before the outbreak of the war in September 1939, as Scotland lost 2–1 to England at Hampden in April of that fateful year. Thistle winger Alec McSpadyen was to win his second cap that day, as a crowd of 149,269 looked on.

GEORGE CUMMINGS,
Partick Thistle F.C.   TOPICAL TIMES.

George Cumming

The Victory Internationals would see Hugh Brown and long-serving Jackie Husband win three and two caps respectively. Except for a brief spell as manager of Queen of the South, Jackie served the Jags in many capacities up until his death in 1992. The Jackie Husband Stand, opened in 1994, is so named in his memory. Right-back Jimmy McGowan would also win a cap in the first 'counted' Victory International versus Belgium in January 1946.

The 1950s would not see the Jags win any major trophies; however, they would reach the League Cup Final on three occasions. During this era they were seen as an exciting,

JIMMY DAVIDSON
Partick Thistle and Scotland

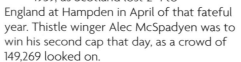

Timely header by Scotland's Mackenzie outwits Austria's Halla at Zurich. Scotland put up a great fight but were beaten 1–0.

Johnny MacKenzie

attacking side and a number of players were capped.

Johnny MacKenzie, aka the Firhill Flyer, was first picked for the Home International/World Cup qualifier versus Wales in November 1953 as Scotland drew 3–3 at Hampden. Centre-half Jimmy Davidson was to join him in the Scotland set-up in May 1954 in a 1–0 victory over Norway at Hampden and as Scotland geared towards the 1954 World Cup, left-half Dave Mathers was brought in for Scotland's final pre-World Cup friendly in Helsinki, as they defeated Finland 2–1.

The SFA, in their bungling ways that still pervade today, decided in their wisdom to take only 13 players to Switzerland, so Mathers would find himself on standby as one of the original 22-man squad and destined never to play for Scotland again. MacKenzie and Davidson, however, did find themselves at the World Cup finals and played in both of Scotland's games, although the searing heat of Basle, matched with heavy-duty Scotland shirts, meant the second game versus Uruguay passed most of the team by as they got skelped 7–0 by the South Americans. Scotland lost their first game 1–0 to Austria in Zurich.

Johnny and Jimmy, however, continued to be picked for Scotland and indeed Davidson scored direct from a free kick against Northern

Tommy Ewing, Partick Thistle's new star outside-left Versatile Andy Kerr, Scotland and Partick Thistle

Ireland in late 1954. The Hungarian legend Ferenc Puskas came to Hampden with his great national side in December 1954 and soundly beat Scotland 4–2; however, Puskas compleiented MacKenzie on his great wing play after the match.

For Davidson and MacKenzie it was all over after they won their eighth cap each, with Scotland losing 7–2 at Wembley to England in April 1955, although both would serve Thistle well for a number of years after this.

Tommy Ewing and Andy Kerr would also win a couple of caps in this period.

After the three losing finals of the 1950s, there was perhaps some trepidation when the Jags faced the all-conquering Celtic side at Hampden in the League Cup Final of 1971. However, David McParland's brash young side took it all in their stride and put four past Celtic before half-time to shock the nation. Of course, many a Jags fan was fearing a second half onslaught but all Celtic could muster was a solitary goal by Kenny Dalglish.

Five of the young Jags from that famous day (Saturday, 23 October) were to be capped. Scotland manager Tommy Docherty, the following month, in only his second game in charge, brought right-back John Hansen on as a late sub in the Euro qualifier versus Belgium up at Pittodrie. John is, of course, the older brother to Alan, who also started out at Firhill. John was only to be capped on one more occasion, making a second half appearance against Yugoslavia in the Brazilian Independence Cup in June 1972, replacing teammate Alex Forsyth in Belo Horizonte.

Forsyth could switch sides at full-back and was to play right-back in the two other games in Brazil, the first against Czechoslovakia in Porto Alegre and the match versus the hosts in the Estadio Maracana. He was also to play in Scotland's first 1974 World Cup qualifier against Denmark in Copenhagen,

before moving to Manchester United as one of Docherty's first signings. Alex would win ten caps in total.

Jimmy Bone also saw action in the Yugoslavian match but by this time he had moved to Norwich City and although he was to score in the aforementioned qualifier versus Denmark, he was only to win the two caps.

Almost five years after the League Cup Final, Alan Rough was handed his debut for Scotland versus Switzerland in April 1976. Docherty had actually included him in his squad versus Belgium way back in 1971. There has been much criticism over the years of Rough and many detractors would cite some poor goals conceded. However, in the 1978 and 1982 World Cup qualifiers Rough produced many a fine save to ensure Scotland would progress towards the finals. Who can forget his save from Wales's John Toshack at Anfield in 1977, or fail to appreciate the clean sheets he kept in those vital away matches against Sweden (1980), and Israel and Northern Ireland (both 1981)? Alan would win 53 caps with Thistle, playing at the 1978 and 1982 World Cup finals, and then a further two with Hibernian.

JOHN HANSEN

For Ronnie Glavin, it only took five and a half years after the cup final to win his cap, playing in a friendly match against Sweden in April 1977. By this time Glavin was a Celtic player and was only to ever have 58 minutes of international football. Still, it could have been worse, as Joe Craig, an ex-Jag also playing for Celtic at that time, came on against Sweden with just 14 minutes remaining, scored with his very first touch and never played for his country again either.

It would be a long while after Rough's departure before Thistle saw another player represent Scotland and, of course, it was a goalkeeper. Nicky Walker had performed heroics for the Jags in season 1995/96 and was given a second cap, three years after his first, versus the USA in the States in May 1996 as Scotland prepared for that year's Euros. He may have only played eight minutes but it still counts and he was also included in the squad for the 1996 finals.

Since then, goalkeepers Kenny Arthur and Scott Fox have both been included in Scotland squads but were given no game time. Shame ...

Alan Rough

RANGERS

Rangers were formed in 1872 and it was to be one of their founding fathers, the unlikely named Moses McLay McNeil, who was the first to don the dark blue of Scotland in March 1876, as Scotland beat Wales 4–0 at the West of Scotland Cricket Ground in Glasgow. Peter Campbell, another one of the four founding fathers, became the first Rangers player to score for Scotland, netting a double in a 9–0 thrashing of Wales at the First Hampden Park in 1878. Peter gained a second cap against Wales the following year and netted in that 3–0 match, too.

In 1886 Charles Heggie hit four goals in a 7–2 demolition of Ireland in Belfast but even this was not enough to secure him a second cap, a not too unfamiliar tale of these early pioneer days of international football.

Rangers were to win their first league title in 1891 (shared with Dumbarton) and would become more dominant towards the end of the century. Already having won a cap, Jock Drummond joined from Falkirk in 1892 and would win five league titles and four Scottish Cups with the Ibrox side and gain a further 13 caps. Jock is generally thought of as the last known outfield football player to wear a cap whilst playing in first class football.

Neilly Gibson was reckoned to be one of the most gifted players around the turn of the century and was to spend his whole career in Scotland, joining Rangers in 1894 and winning four consecutive titles at the turn of the century. Neilly was to win 13 caps with the Gers before moving to Partick Thistle in 1904, where he was to pick up a final one. His son Neil was also to play for Thistle and Scotland.

Rolling up from the Ayrshire village of Darvel to Ibrox was first full-back Nicol Smith and then, upon his recommendation, winger Alex Smith (no relation). Nicol won 12 caps from 1897 to 1902 and captained Scotland twice. Tragically, in 1905, aged 31, he and his wife were to die from illness caused by drinking infected household water.

Alan Morton

Winger Alex would remain with Rangers for 21 years, winning seven titles and three Scottish Cups, playing in well over 600 games. Alex would play 20 times for Scotland (scoring three goals) from April 1898, when they lost 3–1 to England at Celtic Park, until the 1–1 draw with England at Goodison Park, Liverpool, in 1911.

Playing around the same time was another multiple winner with Rangers and indeed their top goalscorer for nine consecutive seasons – Elgin-born Bob Hamilton. He would gain 11 Scotland caps, with his first coming against Wales as Scotland routed the Welsh 6–0 at the Racecourse, Wrexham, in 1899. This was to be one of the few occasions Hamilton was not to score, as he was to hit 15 goals in 11 games, including four against Ireland in Scotland's record win of 11-0 at Celtic Park in 1901. His last cap came whilst with Dundee, when he also hit his final two goals in a 2–2 draw with Wales in 1911. His tally of 15 leaves him currently seventh on the all-time top scorers' list. Bob finished his playing career where it began, with Elgin City.

The legendary Alan Morton had already won his first two caps at Queen's Park before becoming Bill Struth's first signing for the Ibrox club. Just like any great Scottish winger Morton stood at only 5ft 4in and was nicknamed 'The Wee Blue Devil'. He would win nine league titles with the Gers and the Scottish Cup three times. Between April 1921 and May 1932 he was to win 29 caps with Rangers, playing against England on 11 occasions and winning six of those encounters. The most famous win was, of course, as one of the Wembley Wizards as they defeated England 5–1 in 1928.

Winning 12 championships around this time was centre-back Davie Meiklejohn, whose Rangers career lasted from 1919 to 1936. Davie was first capped in February 1922 versus Wales and although his Scotland career was almost the same length as Morton's he only amassed 15 caps, with four coming against

A Good Hold on The Cup

A happy picture of Dave Meiklejohn (*right*), Rangers' skipper, and Bob M'Phail, with the Scottish Cup after their 1–0 victory over Third Lanark at Hampden. Ibrox had long innings of non-success from 1903 to 1928, but they've won the Trophy five times since then, and three times off the reel—1934–5–6.

Bob McPhail and Davie Meiklejohn

GEORGE YOUNG
Rangers and Scotland

England. Davie was to captain Scotland on six occasions and scored two goals.

Second only to Ally McCoist as Rangers's all-time top league goalscorer is Bob McPhail. Bob was to score 230 goals in 354 league appearances from 1927 to 1940. Inside-forward McPhail already had a Scotland cap and a Scottish Cup winners' medal, both won with Airdrie, when he joined Rangers for £5,000. He was to add another six Scottish Cup medals and a further 16 caps with the Ibrox club. Bob was to score seven goals for his country, with the pinnacle being the double he hit against England at Hampden in April 1937. Scotland won 3–1 in front of a record crowd of 149,547 but after this, it would be a long wait before Scotland again beat England at home in an official international.

Among the more notable players at this time were goalkeeper Jerry Dawson and centre-half Jimmy Simpson, both of whom were to make their debuts in October 1934 against Ireland in Belfast, as Scotland lost 2–1. Both were to win 14 caps and this initial match was the only one that Simpson would not be captain. Jimmy's son Ronnie was to go on to win the European Cup with fierce Glasgow rivals Celtic.

The first 20 post-war years in Scotland would see a variety of clubs win the Scottish League but Rangers would be the default club – not dominating like they had before but still winning ten league championships between 1945 and 1965. Much of the success was down to the 'Iron Curtain' defence of the time. Generally, this referred to keeper Bobby Brown, full-backs George Young and Jock Shaw, along with the half-back line of Ian McColl, Willie Woodburn and Sammy Cox.

Keeper Brown would only win a handful of caps but Jimmy Cowan of Morton was among his contemporaries. He would, of course, go on to manage Scotland from 1967 to 1971, starting his reign with the 3–2 win over England at Wembley in April 1967.

Jock Shaw was to win his six caps in the immediate post-war era and was to captain the side in all of his matches, playing alongside his brother David of Hibernian in one match.

Big George Young still holds the record for captaining the national side. He did so on 48 out of his 54 caps. However, in terms of World Cups he must rate as one of the unluckiest players ever. In 1950 the SFA had already decreed that Scotland would only travel to Brazil if British champions. Despite a perfect start to their campaign, including an 8–2 victory over Ireland in Belfast, Scotland were to lose to England at Hampden 1–0 and so were not to travel to the World Cup.

Scotland did, however, qualify for the 1954 World Cup finals as a poor second to England in the British Championship that year. The World Cup, though, was still not thought of as a big deal by the home nations and so Young along with other Rangers players such as Sammy Cox and Willie Waddell were allowed to travel with their club on a tour of North America instead. His last two Scotland caps were to come in May 1957 in qualifiers for the 1958 World Cup.

Waddell (Rangers)

Willie Waddell

Willie Woodburn won his first cap in April 1947 against England in a 1–1 draw at Wembley and would go on to play in the 1949 and 1951 victories in London. Woodburn, however, was to have his career prematurely ended when, following a series of violent incidents, he was banned from the game for life in 1954. Although this was rescinded three years later, by this time Woodburn was 37 and effectively his career was over. Willie won 24 caps in total.

Sammy Cox, who like Nicol and Alex Smith before him came from the Ayrshire village of Darvel, was to win 25 caps, making his international bow in May 1948, as Scotland went down 3–0 to France in Paris. Confusion has often surrounded this match as apparently forward Charlie Cox of Hearts was chosen for the original squad but he dropped out and had his place taken up by Eddie Turnbull of Hibernian. Sammy Cox played instead of Billy Campbell of Morton who also dropped out. Cox like Young played in the qualifiers for the 1950 and 1954 World Cups, with his last match being the 4–2 defeat at Hampden to England in the latter year. This would be the only occasion he was to captain the side.

Last but not least of the resolute defenders was Ian McColl. Ian joined Rangers in 1946 and played with them until 1960, winning seven league championships and four Scottish Cups. His first caps came in a spurt of five in 1950/51 and his last nine came from late 1956 to April 1958, when Scotland went down 4–0 to England at Hampden. McColl would travel to the World Cup finals in 1958

Willie Thornton

but was not selected. Five months after his final game for Rangers in May 1960, McColl was to find himself installed as the Scotland manager. McColl's tenure was quite successful, winning the 1962 and 1963 British Home International Championships, but he was 'bumped' from his post as Scotland began their attempt to qualify for England 1966. Resigned, coerced or sacked? To this day it is still not overly clear as to which was the most accurate description.

Of course, in this era, Rangers must have had some flair players and in winger Willie Waddell they certainly had one. Willie had joined Rangers in the pre-war years, winning his first championship in season 1938/39. He would remain with the club until 1952, winning four league titles and two Scottish Cups. Willie's first cap came in May 1946 as Scotland lined up to play Switzerland with teammates Bobby Brown, George Young and Willie Woodburn also making their 'official' international bows. Willie was to win 18 caps over an eight-year period but was perhaps up against some of the strongest competition any Scotland player has ever faced, in players such as Jimmy Delaney of Manchester United, Gordon Smith of Hibernian and Billy Liddell of Liverpool among others, for the coveted outside-right spot. Willie would, of course, go on to win the league as Kilmarnock manager in 1964/65, before achieving European success with Rangers in the Cup Winners' Cup Final in 1972.

As said, Ian McColl was selected for the 1958 World Cup but did not play and neither would winger Alex Scott. However, Sammy Baird was to play the last of his seven Scotland games in the third match, versus France in Orebro. Playing in all three games in Sweden, however, was a player who was known as 'Mr Consistency', both for club and country: Eric Caldow. Caldow had joined Rangers in 1952 and was to win five championships and three Scottish Cups. His first cap was won in April 1957 as Scotland lost 2–1 away to England. After that Eric was to only miss two games out of 42, captaining the side on 15 occasions. By 1960, he had also acquired the role of penalty taker for Scotland and scored four out of four for the national side.

Jim Baxter

Scotland's long-awaited post-war win at Hampden (against England) occurred in April 1962, with Eric netting the second from the penalty spot to seal the 2–0 victory. Tragedy, though, would strike a year later for Eric as he suffered a triple leg break following a tackle by England's Bobby Smith at Wembley Stadium. It would take a while for Eric to recover from this and regain his place in the Rangers team, but sadly he was never to grace the dark blue of Scotland again.

The 60s would bring a lot of flamboyant players to the Scottish football scene, and none more so than Jim Baxter. The Glaswegian term 'gallus' probably describes Jim best – a man of swagger, confidence and in this case a sublime left foot. Baxter had joined Rangers in June 1960 from Raith Rovers and was quite quickly ensconced as a favourite at Ibrox and was to win three championships and three Scottish Cups in his first five years there. Jim debuted for Scotland in November 1960, as they beat Northern Ireland 5–2 at home. Fortunately for Jim he would miss Scotland's next game as they were hammered at Wembley in 1961. However, he would face England three times whilst at Ibrox and come out a winner every time. Although Wembley 1967 is often talked about as a big part of the Baxter legacy, his double in the match of

1963 to give Scotland a 2–1 victory in London was perhaps his finest moment for the national side.

Outside-left and perhaps one of the forgotten Scotland heroes of the 60s was Davie Wilson. Davie joined Rangers from Baillieston Juniors in 1956. He had been capped the month before Baxter, as the Scots went down 2–0 to Wales in Cardiff. Davie would net a double in the 9–3 defeat at Wembley in 1961, although one of the goals is often credited to Motherwell's Pat Quinn. He was to open the scoring in the 2–0 win over England the following year at Hampden and was to play in the two Auld Enemy victories that followed. Davie gained a total of 22 caps, scoring ten goals, including one in his final match as Scotland beat Finland in Helsinki in a World Cup qualifier in 1965.

Forward Ralph Brand was given eight caps in an 18-month period from November 1960 to May 1962 and scored a remarkable eight goals, but any forward was an automatic second choice to Denis Law in this era.

Wee Willie Henderson is all too often compared to Jimmy Johnstone and is looked upon as second-best but it was Henderson who was first to burst on to the international scene in October 1962 and was to gain the greater number of caps. He had a blistering start, playing in a 3–2 victory away to Wales and scoring one of the goals. This was followed up with a 5–1 rout of Northern Ireland at Hampden, with Willie again netting, and then he starred in the April 1963 2–1 victory at Wembley. Willie was to win 29 caps and score five goals, playing his final match in April 1971 as Scotland lost 2–0 away to Portugal.

Willie Henderson

One of the players that would readily have fitted into the 'Iron Curtain' side of the 50s would have to be John Greig. Often cited as Rangers's greatest player ever, Greig gave everything for his club and indeed his country. He would win not only championships in the early 60s, but also captain Rangers to three in the 70s, as well as their European Cup Winners' Cup triumph in 1972.

For Scotland, John was first capped in April 1964 as they beat England at Hampden

John Greig

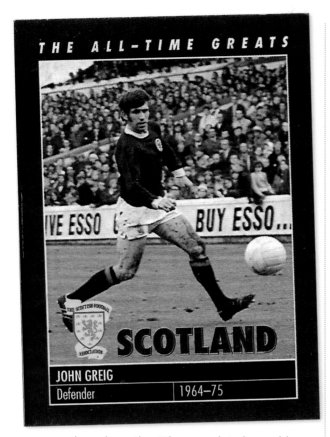

THE ALL-TIME GREATS

SCOTLAND

JOHN GREIG
Defender   1964-75

Davie Wilson started to lose his place in the Rangers line-up with the emergence of Willie 'Bud' Johnston and likewise in the Scotland set-up. Like Henderson, Johnston was first capped at 18 years old – in a World Cup qualifier against Poland at Hampden in 1965. Winger Johnston had blistering pace and a very quick temper to match. Willie would win nine caps at Ibrox and was to score two goals for Rangers in their European Cup Winners' Cup victory over Moscow Dynamo in Barcelona. His best and perhaps worst moments for Scotland came at West Brom, where he was to win 13 caps.

Also scoring in the 1972 final was striker Colin Stein. Colin moved to Rangers from Hibs in 1968 and shortly after made his Scotland debut versus Denmark in October 1968. He was to win 17 of his 21 caps in his time with Rangers and would score ten goals. His ten goals were to come between matches two and seven for him. He holds the record alongside Bob Hamilton of Rangers for scoring in consecutive matches for Scotland, with six games. He is also the last player to score four in a match for Scotland, achieving this feat in a World Cup qualifier versus Cyprus in May 1969. Coincidentally, like Hamilton, Stein would finish his playing days with Elgin City.

Ronnie McKinnon was to suffer a leg break playing for Rangers in the early rounds of the 1972 triumph and so missed the final – he had been with the club since 1961. Ronnie was to win 28 caps for Scotland from 1965 to 1971 and although not a spectacular player, he was seen as a very steady, dependable centre-half around this time and played in that game at Wembley in 1967.

RANGERS

SANDY JARDINE

through an Alan Gilzean goal. As he could play at full-back, central defence and in midfield, John was utilised in many ways for Scotland and he played 21 games in a row. He was to score in the 88th minute to give Scotland, thus far, our only victory over Italy, in a World Cup qualifier in November 1965. The last of his 21 games was the 3–2 victory at Wembley in 1967. The game he was to miss was the friendly against the USSR in May 1967, as Rangers requested that none of their players be selected for this match due to their upcoming European Cup Winners' Cup Final versus Bayern Munich later that month.

By May 1971 John had amassed 43 caps, having captained the side on 14 occasions, scoring three goals; however, there was to be one last swansong. In October 1975 as Scotland fans were still reeling from the lifetime ban handed out to Billy Bremner and others following a ruckus in Copenhagen the month before, manager Willie Ormond announced Greig's return to the set-up. Ticket sales doubled and so 48,021 saw Greig take to the field as Scotland captain for a final time as they disposed of Denmark 3–1 in a Euro qualifier at Hampden.

Among the young players in the 1972 final were Sandy Jardine and Derek Johnstone. The 70s and indeed the early 80s wouldn't see many Gers players gain a number of caps like before; however, Jardine is fondly remembered by fans of that era for his defensive partnership with Celtic's Danny McGrain.

Sandy was first capped in the Bobby Brown era in November 1970 as Scotland ground out a one-nil Euro qualifier victory over Denmark at home. On his fifth cap he was to play right-back to McGrain's left, as Scotland lost 1–0 to England at Wembley in May 1973. He and Danny were to play 20 matches together and although Scotland didn't win them all, they went hand in hand and were the pairing for the 1974 World Cup finals, both overlapping freely and becoming the template for Scottish full-backs ever since. Sandy also appeared in the finals in Argentina 78, against Iran, and played in a late flurry of games under Jock Stein in 1979, winning a total of 39 caps and captaining the side on nine occasions.

Derek Johnstone's Scotland career began in May 1973 in Willie Ormond's second game in charge. His first few caps came as a centre-half but his only goal in this position was sadly to give Brazil victory at Hampden in the May 1973 centenary celebration match. As Scotland hurtled towards Argentina under Ally MacLeod, Johnstone was in great form as a striker, scoring 38 goals in 1977/78. At the Home Internationals prior to World Cup 78, Johnstone netted a couple of goals in draws against Northern Ireland and Wales and was perhaps the only real positive to take from these matches. However, he was not chosen to play in South America and was only to win one more cap beyond that.

As Scotland romped through the 1976 Home International season, winning all three games, it is sometimes forgotten that not one but two Rangers players were our central defensive partnership. Colin Jackson was to play eight games for Scotland and was never beaten. Starting off in May 1975 with a draw in Sweden, Colin played a few other games before being injured for the match versus England at Wembley in 1975, unlike his Rangers teammate, goalkeeper Stewart Kennedy! He then came back for the 1976 Home Internationals and was perhaps unlucky that the 2–1 win over England at Hampden was his final match.

Against England in 1976, Jackson's clubmate Tom Forsyth was playing in his fifth Scotland game as a Ranger, having won his first cap at Motherwell way back in 1971. However, one particular moment in that match is forever embedded in the hearts and minds of many a Scotland fan. With Scotland winning 2–1 and only a few minutes to go, Mick Channon looked as though he was about to net the equaliser, only for Forsyth to time his tackle to perfection and clear the ball away. Tom was to gain 21 caps at Ibrox and was only to suffer four defeats in that time, including the loss to Peru in Cordoba. His last match was to be the 3–2 victory over Holland in Mendoza.

Rangers were quite a poor side in the early 80s and would have no players in the 1982 World Cup finals squad. Davie Cooper had actually travelled to South America for the tour of 1977; however, he didn't make his debut until September 1979 in a friendly versus Peru at Hampden, which was followed by an appearance against Austria the following month. It was to be five years before he was to receive his third cap. However, he was a regular for the side in the following years and played in most of the 1986 World Cup qualifiers, proving pivotal in Scotland qualifying for Mexico. Davie was to take the penalty against Wales at Ninian Park, Cardiff, to give Scotland the draw required to

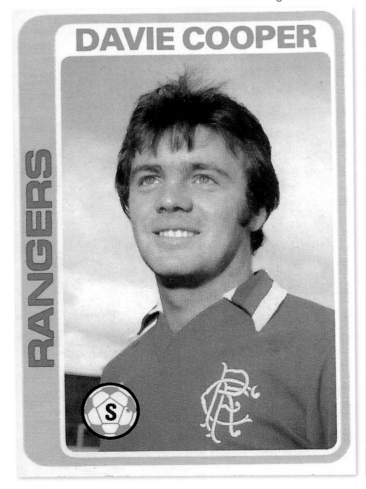

DAVIE COOPER

RANGERS

reach the play-offs. This, of course, was sadly the night Jock Stein was to pass.

Cooper was to produce one of those sublime moments that he was so capable of in the first leg of the play-offs against Australia as he netted direct from a free kick to give Scotland the lead. However, he was only to appear as a sub in two games in Mexico and was not to feature much after that. Davie was to win two caps with Motherwell for a total of 22. Injury kept him out of Italia 90.

1986 was a watershed moment for Rangers and indeed Scottish football, as by the time of the World Cup finals in Mexico, Graeme Souness had agreed to become Rangers player-manager.

Ally McCoist had been capped just before the 1986 World Cup and began making headway into the side afterwards. It was to take until his seventh match before he was to open his scoring account with a double over Hungary in a friendly in September 1987, which he followed up with a goal in a rare victory over Belgium in a Euro qualifier. He was only to net twice in the qualifiers for Italia 90 and was a sub in the first two matches versus Costa Rica and Sweden, but was given a start in the Brazil game.

McCoist's goals in qualifying for the Euros were vital, scoring the winner against Romania in 1990 and a late equaliser away to Switzerland in 1991. Ally would start all three matches at Sweden 92 but failed to score. Scotland had a poor qualifying campaign for USA 94 and the nadir was reached as they were hammered 5–0 in Lisbon. To make matters worse Ally suffered a leg break that would keep him out of the Scotland set-up for over two years.

Typical of McCoist, he was brought on as a sub in the 71st minute against Greece on his return in August 1995 with Scotland desperate to make a breakthrough and by the 73rd minute he had literally nosed us in front. Just as typical was on his 50th cap he was given the captaincy and, of course, scored the only goal versus Australia in March 1996. At the Euros in England, McCoist made an appearance in the second game against the hosts as a substitute, as Scotland sought an equaliser. However, teammate Paul Gascoigne put paid to all thoughts of a draw shortly after. McCoist would, however, strike a classic goal at Villa Park against Switzerland in the final group game to give Scotland victory, but once more

Ally McCoist

it was not to be enough. McCoist stands as Rangers' most capped player with 59 caps and also top goalscorer with 19. He was to win two more caps (with Kilarnock) after the World Cup finals in France 98, a tournament that he perhaps should have graced, even if just from the bench.

Rangers under Souness and then Walter Smith would dominate Scottish football from the late 1980s and a number of Scotland players would be on their books.

Richard Gough would be bought from Tottenham Hotspur and gain 27 more caps during his time at Ibrox. His two goals against Cyprus in February 1989 were vital in our qualifying for Italia 90. However, Richard carried an injury into the first match of the finals, had to be taken off at half-time and would play no further part in the tournament.

He captained the side at the 1992 Euros in all three games but would only play two games in the qualifying for USA 94. The first, versus Switzerland in Berne, saw him sent off for handball, as the ball bounced high over him after hitting a sprinkler apparently. The other match was the aforementioned heavy defeat to Portugal, which would prove to be his last game for Scotland. He became critical of the Scottish management team around this point and was never picked again.

Mo Johnston was only to play ten Scotland matches as a Rangers player which included the 2–1 victory over Sweden at Italia 90 in which he scored, but after this tournament he drifted from the Scotland scene.

Andy Goram and Stuart McCall both signed for Rangers in the summer of 1991. Goram would be an excellent signing for the Ibrox club and had by this time established himself as Scotland's number one goalie. He had been in imperious form in the 1992 Euro qualifiers and also at the finals. Knee surgery would keep him out of the Scotland side for over a year after our failure to qualify for the 1994 World Cup and Jim Leighton once more established himself as first choice. Jim was to play in the majority of the matches for Euro 96 but surprisingly Craig Brown was to turn to Andy as first choice for the finals. Andy once again had a great tournament, keeping clean sheets against the Netherlands and Switzerland.

However, Leighton once more took charge between the sticks as Scotland geared towards France 98. Brown announced that it would be Leighton who would be first choice in the finals and with 15 days to go before the tournament, Goram withdrew from the squad. Andy won 28 caps at Ibrox, gaining an overall total of 43, and for many he is the best Scotland goalkeeper ever.

McCall would continue to be an important part of the Scotland set-up having broken through to the team just before the World Cup in Italy. He was to play in both the 1992

and 1996 Euros whilst with Rangers, adding 29 caps to the 11 earned at Everton.

The 1998 World Cup would only see one Rangers player chosen for the squad and that would be Gordon Durie. Durie had joined Rangers in 1993 from Tottenham and started in all three games at the 96 Euros. Gordon also played in all three matches at France 98 and is the only Scotland player to have appeared in all four tournaments that Scotland qualified for in the 90s.

Since then, Scotland have all too often been 'nearly men' and some decent players have played for Rangers and done their bit for the Scotland cause, with Barry Ferguson perhaps being the best. Barry strutted his stuff in the play-off games against England for the 2000 Euros and captained the side in the two wins against France in 2006/2007 and indeed throughout that heartbreaking Euro 2008 campaign. However, Barry was part of the 'Boozegate' mess that typified George Burley's time in charge of Scotland and had his international career ended prematurely. Barry won 35 of his 45 Scotland caps at Ibrox.

Many other Gers have served Scotland well in the last 20 years or so, with the likes of Billy Dodds, Lee McCulloch, Kenny Miller and Steven Naismith winning caps. Some like Ferguson have come through the ranks with Ibrox as their starting point, including Alan Hutton, Charlie Adam and goalkeeper Alan McGregor, who was always a sure pair of hands for Scotland, and indeed in the recent Euro Nations League made several great saves which proved invaluable.

Throughout the years, many great Scotland sides have benefited from having Rangers players among their ranks and if Rangers and Scotland are to reach the heights of previous years, one suspects this will have to become true once more.

Alan McGregor

ST MIRREN

St Mirren were formed in Paisley in 1877 and were one of the founding teams of the Scottish Football League.

A number of players were capped towards the end of the 19th century and the beginning of the 20th. Centre-half Andrew Brown and winger James Dunlop were both capped for Scotland versus Wales in March 1890 at Underwood Park, Paisley, the home of local rivals Abercorn. Brown was to gain a further cap also against Wales a year later down at the Racecourse, Wrexham. Sadly Dunlop was to pass away after a match involving Abercorn, where he was to fall on a piece of broken glass and died from tetanus ten days later, still only 21.

Full-back Richard Hunter was to be capped the week after Brown and Dunlop in the match versus Ireland at Ballynafeigh Park, Belfast, as Scotland ran out 4–1 winners. David Crawford, Edward McBain, John Taylor and Hugh Morgan would play against Wales or Ireland over the next few years; however, goalkeeper John Patrick's second and final cap was to come in the 2–1 victory over England at Crystal Palace in 1897.

Into the new century and David Lindsay was capped in the 2–0 defeat to Ireland at Celtic Park in March 1903. David would go on to play for West Ham United but this was to be his only cap. Full-back Thomas Jackson was to win six caps from 1904 to 1907 and was to captain the side on one occasion as Scotland lost 3–1 to Wales at the Racecourse, Wrexham, in 1905. Thomas was killed in action during the First World War in 1916. Left-back Jock Cameron would play alongside Jackson in the 1904 match versus Ireland as the sides drew 1–1 at Dalymount Park, Dublin. Jock would go on to play for Chelsea and win another cap against England in 1909 at Crystal Palace.

The Roaring Twenties would see a number of Buddies capped as well as their first Scottish Cup success. Charlie Pringle would play against Wales at Pittodrie in 1921 in a 2–1 win. Pringle would move on to Manchester City, where he was to be a losing FA Cup finalist in 1926, a fortnight after the Saints' success in Scotland.

Denis Lawson would win a solitary cap versus England as Scotland drew 2–2 at Hampden Park in April 1923. Jimmy Hamilton was to win his only cap in a 2–0 victory over Ireland at Celtic Park in 1924.

John Miller

St Mirren had lost the 1908 Scottish Cup Final to Celtic, but in the 1926 version they were to beat the Glasgow side 2–0 at Hampden Park on 10 April. Four of the players involved in this match were to gain international honours, including goalscorers Davie McCrae and Jimmy Howieson. A week after the cup final, centre-half Willie Summers won his only cap in a 1–0 victory over England at Old Trafford.

Willie Summers

The following February inside-forward Howieson was to play against Ireland at Windsor Park, with Alan Morton of Rangers netting a double in the 2–0 win. April that year saw right-half Tom Morrison face England at Hampden. Scotland lost 2–1, with Everton legend Dixie Dean netting a double. Morrison would go on to play for Liverpool and then Sunderland, where he was to be part of the 1935/36 league championship-winning team. Last to be capped was David McCrae. McCrae is St Mirren's all-time top scorer with 222 goals in 251 games, in all competitions.

Scotland's first ever matches against overseas opposition (and away from home at that) took place at the end of May and the beginning of June 1929. The squad was made up of players from only home-based teams, so players from unfancied clubs like St Johnstone, Hamilton and Ayr United were to be capped alongside McCrae and Bobby Rankin of St Mirren.

Scotland won the opening match 7–3 against Norway, with Rankin among the goals. Both were to play in the drawn match with Germany before a 2–0 victory over the Netherlands in Amsterdam. Rankin would play in this match and score but McCrae was dropped for the final game. Both players were to be discarded after these

Robert Rankin

Scottish Cup Winners 1926

groundbreaking matches. Rankin would serve St Mirren as a director and then manager before his untimely death in 1954 at the age of 49.

However, there would be more forays abroad for a pair of Buddies around this time. Centre-half George Walker played in Scotland's first match away to France in May 1930 as the Scots won 2–0 thanks to a brace from Newcastle's Hughie Gallacher. George was the nephew of Hearts great Bobby Walker and he would play away to Ireland, Austria and then Switzerland, before bowing out of the Scotland scene.

Left-half John Miller had already won his first cap against England at Hampden in March 1931, with Scotland winning 2–0, before going on the overseas tour that year with Walker. He was to miss the 5–0 thrashing by Austria but played in the 3–0 defeat to Italy, before being picked alongside Walker for the 3–2 victory over Switzerland.

Miller once again got out the passport to play France in Paris in 1932, as Scotland ran out 3–1 winners thanks to a hat-trick by Neil Dewar of Third Lanark. His fifth and final cap came in the 3–0 defeat at Wembley in 1934.

Inside-forward Johnny Deakin was one of those players whose one and only Scotland cap is often overlooked as it came in the

January 1946 Victory International against Belgium. Some reference books will neglect this fixture but the SFA and the Belgian FA do include it. Inside-forward Johnny had joined the Paisley club in 1937 and did actually play in some unofficial war matches, too, and left the club in 1950 for Clyde.

Centre-half Willie Telfer joined St Mirren in 1943 and was to play over 300 games for the club, before moving to Rangers in 1957. Willie had taken part in Scotland's tour of the US and Canada in the summer of 1949 as they played clubs from the American Soccer League; however, it was to be four years later in 1953 when he was to win his only cap, against Wales in a 3–3 draw at Hampden.

Willie Telfer

The Scottish Cup would return to Love Street, Paisley, once more in April 1959 as St Mirren beat Aberdeen 3–1 at Hampden Park. The Saints had already demolished Celtic 4–0 in the semi-final. Inside-forward Tommy Gemmell had played with the club since 1951 and would rack up over 250 appearances by the time he left in 1961. He was to be the only member of the cup-winning side to win honours with Scotland, gaining two friendly match caps in May 1955. The first was in

IAIN MUNRO (St. Mirren)

remained as back-up. Billy was to win seven caps from 1980 to 1983, including World Cup qualifiers against Northern Ireland and Portugal.

Alex Ferguson had signed winger Peter Weir for the club shortly before his departure to Aberdeen, where Peter would also eventually move to. It is perhaps surprising that Peter, who was to only win six caps (although he was competing against the likes of John Robertson of Nottingham Forest and Davie Cooper of Rangers), would win the majority of his caps at St Mirren. Peter was given a run of games at the end of the 1979/80 season as Scotland competed in the Home Internationals and then tour games in Poland and Hungary in the space of 15 days, with Peter missing out on the match against England that year.

St Mirren were to win the Scottish Cup once more in 1987 with a goal from Ian Ferguson. Both he and Paul Lambert would go on from this success to play for either side of the Old Firm, where Ranger Ferguson was to win nine caps and Lambert 40 with Motherwell, Borussia Dortmund and Celtic.

Neither were capped at St Mirren, however, and only one more player has been capped since. Roy Aitken joined St Mirren for a season after a spell at Newcastle United and was given his 57th and final cap for Scotland in October 1991 as his country lost a Euro

Roy Aitken

qualifier 1–0 to Romania in Bucharest.

Young Lewis Morgan was snapped up by Celtic in January 2018 but was immediately loaned back to St Mirren for the remainder of the 2017/18 season, and although he had never played for Celtic before he appeared for Scotland against Peru and Mexico in the summer of 2018, both caps count as being won whilst at the Glasgow club.

the 3–0 victory over Portugal at Hampden, followed by an appearance versus Yugoslavia in Belgrade in May 1955, which ended 2–2.

The 1960s would pass without a Buddie being capped, as would most of the 70s, until full-back Iain Munro was picked by Jock Stein to face Argentina and a young Maradona in the Hampden sunshine in May 1979. Munro like the rest of the side had a torrid time trying to contain the young superstar as Scotland lost 3–1, but he held on to his place and was to win seven caps altogether, with his last being in the 2–0 defeat at home to England in 1980.

Goalkeeper Billy Thomson had spent the early part of his career as understudy to Alan Rough at Partick Thistle, before moving to the Saints in August 1978 for £50,000. His Scotland career would follow a similar pattern with him deputising for Rough, before Jim Leighton became first choice and Billy

Billy Thomson

TOTTENHAM HOTSPUR

Tottenham Hotspur were formed in London in 1882, and although no players were to win honours with Scotland until 1959, their first two FA Cup successes had a number of Scots in their sides.

Spurs's first FA Cup was won in 1901 when they were still a non-league team, beating Sheffield United 3–1 in a replay after a 2–2 draw in the first match. Beith-born Sandy Brown was to score 15 goals in Tottenham's FA Cup run, including the two goals in the drawn final, before also netting in the winning game. Sandy would win his only cap in 1906 during his time with Middlesbrough.

Forward John Cameron had won his only cap in 1896 as a Queen's Park player in a 3–3 draw with Ireland and would play for Everton before ending up with the dual role of Spurs player-manager. John was to score the equaliser against Sheffield United in the final. In 1907, after leaving Spurs, John was to take up a managing role at Dresdner SC in Germany. Unfortunately John was still there in 1914 when the First World War broke out and he found himself a prisoner at Ruhleban internment camp until 1918. Three other Scots took part in the final: full-backs Harry Erentz and Sandy Tait and forward David Copeland.

Tottenham won the FA Cup again in 1921, with the only Scottish players in their ranks being goalkeeper Alex Hunter and defender Bob MacDonald. Neither were to be capped for their country. Fast forward to 1959, however, and the reign of the legendary Bill Nicholson. Spurs were to become the first side in the 20th century to complete the English League and FA Cup double, with three Scots prominent in that side of season 1960/61.

Left-half Dave Mackay was the first one to arrive at White Hart Lane having signed from Hearts in March 1959. By this time he had won the league and both the Scottish and Scottish League (twice) cups with Hearts, as well as having played at the 1958 World Cup finals for Scotland, captaining the side in his last two caps.

Dave was to win 18 caps at Tottenham, which would give him a final tally of 22. The first 11 came right up until the 9–3 defeat to England in April 1961, after which he and Denis Law were dropped from the side, as towards

John Cameron

DAVE MACKAY

the end of the match they were deemed to have almost kicked anything that moved, such was their frustration that day.

Mackay was to be recalled two years later as Scotland beat England 2–1 at Wembley and captained the side for a number of games after this. Dave would have won more caps in this period but for a leg break in December 1963 that was broken again during his recovery period, and so he missed almost a year and a half of football. He would go on to play and manage Derby County, winning the league in both roles.

Goalkeeper Bill Brown had also played in the 1958 World Cup finals, winning his first cap in Scotland's third match, against France. By the time of his move to White Hart Lane, he had played over 200 times for Dundee. Injury would see Bill miss some important, but ultimately heartbreaking, games for Scotland, such as the 9–3 defeat at Wembley, as well as the 4–2 World Cup play-off loss to Czechoslovakia. He was, however, to rack up 24 caps at Spurs, adding to his four won at Dundee, and played in the 1962 and 1963 wins over England. His final match was the 1–0 World Cup qualifier win over Italy at Hampden in 1965.

Bill Brown

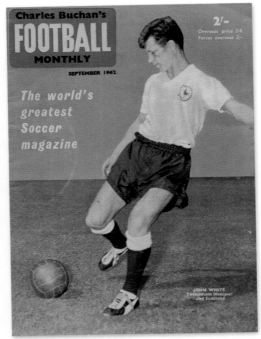
John White

And then there was John White. Inside-forward John had started out at Alloa before moving to Falkirk for a season and then to Tottenham in October 1959. John was to be an ever-present in the double-winning side, adding his share of goals, too. He was renowned for his ability to find space and with his timely runs into the penalty area unseen, he was nicknamed 'The Ghost' by the Tottenham faithful. John played in the hat-trick of victories over England in the early 60s to add 18 caps to the four won with Falkirk. Sadly, he was struck down by lightning in July 1964 at the age of 27. A great loss to Tottenham, Scotland and to the football world in general.

For the Scotland versus England match in April 1960 manager Bill Nicholson refused to release Brown, Mackay and White, as Spurs were very much in contention for the league that season. He later regretted this, saying that the three players seemed to lose a spark in their play that he put down to them missing the match against the 'old enemy'. Spurs lost the title to Burnley by two points and Nicholson always released his players after this.

Jimmy Robertson was one of the forgotten Spurs players of this era. Signed by Nicholson in 1964 from St Mirren, Jimmy would open the scoring in the 1967 FA Cup Final win over Chelsea and played over 150 times for the White Hart Lane club before moving to North London rivals Arsenal in 1968. Jimmy would win one cap as Scotland lost to Wales 3–2 at Ninian Park, Cardiff, in October

1964. Primarily a right-winger, Jimmy made his debut on the same day as one of the guys who would make sure he never got a run in the team made his international bow: Jimmy Johnstone. Between Jinky and Willie Henderson and a plethora of great wingers at the time, it is perhaps not surprising Jimmy only won the one cap.

Despite not being part of the double-winning side, Alan Gilzean is synonymous with the Spurs teams of the 60s and early 70s. Having hit 169 goals in 190 games for Dundee, it does make you wonder why he never ended up in England earlier than December 1964 when Nicholson laid out £72,500. Gilly had already won five caps at this point, scoring the winner versus England at Hampden in April 1964.

Gilzean was well known for his heading power and deft touch, setting up many a goal for fellow striking partners Jimmy Greaves and then Martin Chivers. He was to win the FA Cup, two League Cups and the UEFA Cup whilst at White Hart Lane. He was also to win 17 Scotland caps whilst with the Lilywhites and was to score 12 goals in total. Gilzean was a pivotal player in Scotland's ultimately unsuccessful attempt to reach the Mexico 70 World Cup finals and scored against West Germany in Hamburg as Scotland lost 3–2. Had he and Denis Law managed to strike up a partnership in the way Gilzean had

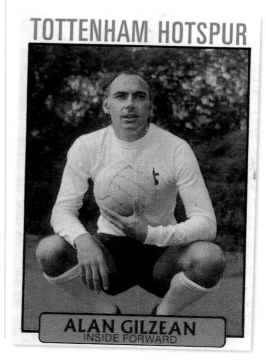
TOTTENHAM HOTSPUR
ALAN GILZEAN
INSIDE FORWARD

with Greaves and Chivers, who knows what Scotland could have achieved. As it was, they only played together nine times, losing just twice.

Alfie Conn was to be the last player Bill Nicholson signed for Spurs, joining the club from Rangers. His father had been one of the Hearts 'Terrible Trio' forward line of the 1950s and who, remarkably, was only capped once.

Midfielder Alfie, complete with cavalier hairstyle, suffered from injury during his time with Spurs, but he was dubbed the 'King of White Hart Lane' at the time, such was his standing with the fans. He would only play twice for Scotland, the second coming in the 5–1 defeat to England at Wembley in 1975. To be fair, Alfie was one of the decent players on view that day and perhaps should have won more caps. He was to return to Scotland to play for Celtic, of all teams, and was also to have spells in the USA.

Steve Archibald joined Spurs in 1980, just after Aberdeen had won the first of their three titles under Alex Ferguson, for £800,000. He was to win the FA Cup twice with the club as well as the UEFA Cup. Having made his Scotland debut (with Aberdeen) against Portugal in March 1980 (and scoring in a 4–1 win), Steve would go on to win a further 22 caps over the next four years with Spurs. However, like a lot of Scotland strikers at the time, he never seemed able to bring his club game to the international side.

Steve featured in the majority of games in qualifying for the 1982 World Cup but did not contribute any goals, although he was to score in the World Cup finals opener versus New Zealand in Malaga and was indeed pivotal in Joe Jordan's goal versus USSR in Scotland's third match in the tournament. Archibald would move to Barcelona in 1984/85 and was to win La Liga with them in that season and would make one appearance at Mexico 1986.

Richard Gough would play at centre-half with Spurs for just over one season, moving from Dundee United in 1986 for £750,000. He would captain the London club in the FA Cup Final defeat to Coventry City in 1987, before moving back to Scotland with Rangers for £1m the following season. He would win eight of his 61 caps in his time at White Hart Lane, mostly in Scotland's poor Euro 1988 campaign.

Striker Gordon Durie was another who spent a couple of seasons at White Hart Lane, moving from Chelsea in 1991. Gordon

had already played at the 1990 World Cup for Scotland whilst at Stamford Bridge, but during his time at Spurs would play in the 1992 Euro qualifiers and finals. Gordon scored one of the important qualifying goals as Scotland fought back from 2–0 down to draw 2–2 with Switzerland in the Wankdorf Stadium, Berne. This was his first as a player at Tottenham, where he would gain 13 of his 43 caps, scoring two of his seven goals before moving to Scotland with Rangers. As an Ibrox player, Gordon was to appear at the 1996 Euros and the World Cup in France 98, as would Spurs player Colin Calderwood.

Calderwood was 30 years of age by the time of his first cap in March 1995, as Scotland grafted to a 0–0 draw with Russia in Moscow in their pursuit of a place at England 96. By the time Colin had signed for Spurs in 1993 he had already racked up 100 games with Mansfield and a further 300 with Swindon. With Scotland he was immediately teamed up with Colin Hendry and between them they formed a formidable partnership in central defence that was to see Scotland reach those Euro finals. Calderwood played with Hendry in 26 of his 32 Scotland appearances. His last four caps came with Aston Villa, after a move there in March 1999.

Steve Archibald

Neil Sullivan had been part of the 1998 World Cup squad as second-choice keeper behind Jim Leighton. He had won 15 caps at Wimbledon by the time of his move to Spurs in 2000. Neil was Scotland's first choice for the 2002 World Cup qualifiers, however, playing in all eight matches. He would find himself out of favour at White Hart Lane by the end of his second season there and moved on to Chelsea in the 2003/04 season, but by then Berti Vogts had called time on his Scotland career.

Alan Hutton had made himself Scotland's first choice right-back with some great performances against the likes of France, Ukraine and Italy in qualifiers for Euro 2008 and moved to Spurs in January 2009 for a reported fee of £9m. Hutton's time at White Hart Lane seemed to blow hot and cold, though, as he often found himself out of favour. However, for Scotland he racked up 13 caps before a permanent move to Aston Villa in 2011. Hutton gained 50 caps altogether and remains as the last Lilywhite to play for Scotland.

Vauxhall International Challenge Match

Scotland v Costa Rica

Friday, 23 March 2018

Hampden Park, Glasgow | Kick-off 7.45pm

Official matchday programme £3

SCOTLAND

v URUGUAY

SCOTTISH FOOTBALL ASSOCIAT
OFFICIAL PROGRAMME

SCOTLAND v AUSTRALIA

International Challenge Match • Wednesday 27th March 199

v. NORW

SCOTLAN

HAMPDEN
GLASGO

WEDNESD
NOVEMBER 6t

KONING BOUDEWIJNSTADION
STADE ROI BAUDOUIN
BRUXELLES - BRUSSEL
16/10/2012 20:45

BELGIUM   SCOTLAND

VERELST   belgacom   BMW   BURRDA SPORT

Coca-Cola   ERGO   GLS   ING

Jupiler   pwc   RTL sport   sporza

Tribune   Blok-Bloc   Rij-Rang   Plaats-Place
2   A   37   4

30.00 EUR

SCOTTISH FA   18658174

Verantwoordelijkheid van de toeschouwers: zie keerzijde en reglement van inwendige orde.
Responsabilité des spectateurs: voir verso et règlement d'ordre intérieur.

Proud to sponsor Scottish National Football

LAND

A

FILA

Safeway

THE SAFEWAY INTERNATIONAL
CHALLENGE MATCH

SCOTLAND
V
NIGERIA

AFRICAN OPPONENTS

The Confederation of African Football (CAF) (which was formed in 1957) has more than 50 member associations, but as of June 2019, Scotland have played just five of them – Egypt, Morocco, Nigeria, South Africa and Zaire (now the Democratic Republic of Congo). Indeed, Scotland had been playing international football for 102 years before we first faced opposition from Africa, and all of our three home games arranged have been played at Aberdeen's Pittodrie Stadium. That apparent 'Take them as far north as possible' approach has only produced one victory, by the way. Furthermore, we have still to actually visit the so-called 'dark continent'. So come on SFA – arrange a wee tour – we can reach Morocco by EasyJet now …

When Scotland faced Zaire (nicknamed 'The Leopards') in 1974 and Nigeria in 2014 they were up against the reigning African Cup of Nations champions, with the latter side fielding Efe Ambrose of Glasgow Celtic and Ejike Uzoenyi of Enugu Rangers. Andy Robertson, then of Dundee United, made his first international start against the 'Super Eagles' at Craven Cottage.

When Egypt (known colloquially as 'The Pharaohs') visited Pittodrie in May 1990 in

Year	Opponent	Competition	Venue	Result	Attendance
1974	Zaire	World Cup finals	Westfalen Stadion, Dortmund	2-0	25,800
1990	Egypt	Friendly	Pittodrie Stadium, Aberdeen	1-3	23,000
1998	Morocco	World Cup finals	Stade Geoffroy-Guichard, St Etienne	0-3	35,500
2002	Nigeria	Friendly	Pittodrie Stadium, Aberdeen	1-2	20,465
2002	South Africa	Reunification Cup	Mong Kok Stadium, Hong Kong	0-2	3,007
2007	South Africa	Friendly	Pittodrie Stadium, Aberdeen	1-0	13,723
2014	Nigeria	Friendly	Craven Cottage, London	2-2	20,156

Scotland v South Africa, Pittodire Stadium, 22 August 2007

preparation for the World Cup finals in Italy, where they would face England, their manager was Mohammed El Gohary, an ex-army colonel. Scotland's manager at the time was Andy Roxburgh, a former primary school teacher.

Scotland midfielder Craig Burley of Celtic was the 90th player to be sent off in World Cup finals history, when he got a 'straight red' in the 54th minute versus Morocco (aka 'Lions of the Atlas') at France 98. Most supporters agree, however, that he should have been booked right at the start for his shocking peroxide-blond hairstyle that day.

Scotland's match against South Africa ('Bafana Bafana') in 2002 – which saw the international debut of Motherwell's James McFadden – was a 'semi-final' of the second edition of the Reunification Cup, which marked the fifth anniversary of the reunification of Hong Kong with China, thus ending colonial rule by the UK. South Africa then defeated Turkey in the 'final'.

Although Scotland have so far been 21st century World Cup flops, Egypt and Morocco appeared at Russia 2018, whilst Nigeria made it to the big stage in 2002, 2010, 2014 and 2018. South Africa hosted the finals in 2010 and also appeared at the 2002 finals. Incidentally, Morocco have made a record number of five unsuccessful bids to host the World Cup finals – 1994, 1998, 2006, 2010 and 2026. I blame Bob Hope, Bing Crosby and Dorothy Lamour.

ASIAN OPPONENTS

The Asian Football Confederation (AFC) was founded in May 1954 (it predates UEFA by about five weeks) and has almost 50 members. Scotland have played five members – Iran, Japan, Qatar, Saudi Arabia and South Korea. Scotland have also played a Hong Kong XI but this is not recognised by FIFA.

Israel was a member of the AFC from 1954 to 1974; however, from 1974 to 1992 it was not affiliated to any confederation. In 1992 Israel was formally admitted to UEFA. To muddy the geographical waters further, Australia left the Oceania Football Confederation to join the AFC in 2006. And if you want to be pedantic, about 95 per cent of the land mass of Turkey is in Asia, but ... ach, forget it.

When Scotland lined up against Iran at the 1978 World Cup finals we were facing the then holders of the AFC Asian Cup; indeed, Iran had won their continental championship three times in a row – 1968, 1972 and 1976.

Against Saudi Arabia in 1988, Andy Roxburgh's Scotland started the match with eight home Scots and

Year	Opponent	Competition	Venue	Result	Attendance
1978	Iran	World Cup finals	Estadio Chateau Carreras, Cordoba	1-1	7,938
1988	Saudi Arabia	Friendly	King Fahd Stadium, Riyadh	2-2	35,000
1995	Japan	Kirin Cup	Big Arch Stadium, Hiroshima	0-0	24,566
2002	South Korea	Friendly	Asiad Main Stadium, Busan	1-4	52,384
2002	Hong Kong	Reunification Cup	Hong Kong Stadium, HK	4-0	8,000
2006	Japan	Kirin Cup	Saitama Stadium, Saitama	0-0	58,648
2009	Japan	Friendly	Nissan Stadium, Yokohama	0-2	61,500
2015	Qatar	Qatar Airways Cup	Easter Road, Edinburgh	1-0	14,270

Scotland v Qatar, Easter Road, 5 June 2015

finished it with nine. Debut caps were awarded to John Collins (Hibernian), Henry Smith (Hearts) and John Colquhoun (Hearts).

A total of five Scotland players made their international debuts against Japan in 1995 – Brian Martin (Motherwell), Scot Gemmill (Nottingham Forest), Paul Lambert (Motherwell), Craig Burley (Chelsea) and Paul Bernard (Oldham Athletic).

In 2002, Hong Kong had been part of China for five years so it is hard to see how that match could constitute an international. I mean to say, it's not like they're Wales, Northern Ireland or Scotland! Scotland's scorers in the 'training exercise' were Kevin Kyle (Sunderland), Steven Thompson (Dundee United), Christian Dailly (West Ham United) and Scot Gemmill (Everton).

In 2015 when Qatar became the first Asian nation to visit Scotland (Israel's and Australia's claims notwithstanding), they were welcomed to Edinburgh with a demonstration (outside the stadium) against their hosting of the 2022 World Cup finals. On the pitch, they also had to endure a male streaker, plus a goal from Bournemouth's Matt Ritchie.

In the current millennium, Iran have appeared at the finals of three World Cups (2006, 2014 and 2018) and Saudi Arabia also at three (2002, 2006 and 2018), whilst Japan and South Korea have appeared at all five.

AWARDS, HONOURS, ETC.

To date no Scotland player has won the 'Golden Boot' award at the World Cup finals – however, I live in hope. That said, when it comes to international recognition we can look to 'The Lawman' – Denis Law, then of Manchester United, who won the European Footballer of the Year award in 1964. Near misses include Celtic's Jimmy Johnstone, who was placed third in 1967, whilst Liverpool's Kenny Dalglish finished runner-up to Michel Platini in 1983.

Scottish success in a 'foreign land' was achieved, however, in the shape of the English League Player of the

Year awards: Bobby Collins (1965, Leeds United), Dave Mackay (1969, Derby County), Billy Bremner (1970, Leeds United), Frank McLintock (1971, Arsenal), Kenny Burns (1978, Nottingham Forest), Kenny Dalglish (1979 and 1983, Liverpool), Steve Nicol (1989, Liverpool) and Gordon Strachan (1991, Leeds United). Meanwhile, back in Scotland, Rangers's Scottish internationalist Ally McCoist won the European Golden Shoe award in 1991/92 and 1992/93 for his 34 league goals scored in both seasons.

Staying at home, and in 2004 there was initiated the Scottish Football Hall of Fame. Located within the Scottish Football Museum, inductions are made on an annual basis and also include some great footballers from outside Scotland who have graced the game within these shores, e.g. Denmark's Brian Laudrup and Sweden's Henrik Larsson. There have been well over 100 inductions, mostly of the more 'obvious' Scottish players and managers (e.g. Jim Baxter, Billy Bremner, Dave Mackay, Danny McGrain, Graeme Souness, Lawrie Reilly, Willie Bauld, Alan Hansen, Ian St John, Alan Gilzean, Paul McStay, Alan Rough and Ally MacLeod).

Special mentions, however, for Rose Reilly (a pioneering and multi-medal-winning women's internationalist who represented both Scotland and Italy in the 1970s and 1980s) and the referee Tom 'Tiny' Wharton (he was 6ft 4in tall and matches he officiated included Scottish and European competition cup finals, as well as 16 international games during the 1960s).

For players who have won 25 or more caps, the SFA now presents them with a commemorative medal. The SFA also maintains a 'Roll of Honour' for players who have won at least 50 caps, and specially commissioned paintings of these footballers are also on display within the Scottish Football Museum. More than 30 players are currently on the list – Rangers defender George Young was the first player to hit the 50-cap landmark (versus Yugoslavia in 1956), whilst a recent

addition was Celtic keeper Craig Gordon, who got his half-century versus Slovakia in 2017. Kenny Dalglish (Celtic and Liverpool) is our only 'soccer centurion', having won 102 caps between 1971 and 1986. By comparison, the Scotland Women's International Roll of Honour includes more than a dozen players who have won 100 or more caps.

Modern-day man of the match awards may be ten a penny, as well as being formulaic in design. In May 1954, however, when Scotland visited the Olympic Stadium, Helsinki, for what was our final warm-up match before heading to Switzerland for the World Cup finals in June, Scotland beat Finland 2–1, and after the match the hosts presented Dundee's Doug Cowie with a cup after judging him to be Scotland's best player, whilst Bobby Johnstone of Hibernian received a clock after being voted second-best. It's nice when a wee bit of thought goes into a gift ...

In terms of UK establishment gongs etc., there have been knighthoods for Matt Busby (1968), Alex Ferguson (1999) and Kenny Dalglish (2018). Meanwhile, there were CBEs for the likes of Jock Stein, Craig Brown, Denis Law and Ernie Walker, whilst Willie Ormond, Andy Roxburgh, Bill Shankly, Walter Smith, Gordon Strachan and Tommy Walker all picked up OBEs. Some MBE recipients include Barry Ferguson, John Greig, Jim Leighton, Ally McCoist, Billy McNeill, Willie Miller and David Narey.

A World Cup or European Championship award would still be nice, though...

B BADGES OF VALOUR

This particular facet of football-associated collecting always makes me think of Mel Brookes's spoof Western movie *Blazing Saddles* and that scene when the Mexican bandit exclaims 'Badges! Badges! I don't need no steenkin badges!' Well, some of us *do* need them, amigo.

For some supporters the wearing of badges is a desire to show their allegiance to their country, whilst others prefer to keep their prized collection under wraps and refuse to expose them to the elements and/or put them at risk from the lustful, grasping hands of foreign maidens.

There is also the artistic merit of the products to be admired – the designs, the colours and the variety can be particularly attractive to the magpie in us all. Indeed there is something about the likes of lions (passant, guardant or rampant), as well as dragons, griffins, unicorns, hammers, sickles and large cocks that can be a bit of a turn-on, or is, er, appealing in a 'decorative art' sort of way.

It used to be that national Football Association badges of those countries which Scotland have actually played against were the big 'foreign' attractions, especially badges for nations no longer in existence (e.g. Yugoslavia and the USSR). Relatively recent 'new arrivals' such as San Marino, the Faroe Islands, the Baltic states and even Georgia have helped bolster many a collection, whilst the 2019 Euro qualifiers against Kazakhstan (which borders China!) have caused salivation of Pavlov puppy farm proportions. Meanwhile, we still eagerly await being drawn against the likes of Andorra, Armenia, Azerbaijan, Kosovo, Montenegro or Turkey.

A welcome addition, however, are those badges commemorating specific matches, be they friendlies or World Cup/Euro Championship qualifiers. Usually the badges are either of the split-flag design (i.e. a saltire plus that of the opposition) or include the two opposing football association crests, together with the date(s) of the fixture(s). These tend to be worn with the pride of campaign medals on hats, scarves and jackets – sometimes to an excess that would rival 'Pearly Kings and Queens' in the gaudily dressed stakes.

Then there are the badges depicting the World Cup and Euro Championship tournament logos and mascots, although for some reason *World Cup Willie* (circa 1066 – sorry, I mean 1966) was not a bestseller in Scotland. *Footix*, the mostly blue and red cockerel from France 98, was a personal favourite, however.

Staying on the campaign trail, and for a while I went through a phase of attaching to my saltire flag sew-on badges of coats of arms of European cities visited on national service, until some smart alec suggested that was the kind of nerdy activity Girl Guides or Boy Scouts would do. Yet another thing I can no longer air in public – the list is growing.

Back to the advantages of 'metallica' then, and unlike match programmes, it's perfectly acceptable to produce a match badge years after the game took place. Indeed the demand for souvenirs of past glories sometimes increases as time goes by; for instance, the 50th anniversary of Wembley 67 and the faintly ludicrous claim that Scotland were 'unofficial world champions'.

As per usual it's a case of you pays your money and you makes your choice. All I'll say is that be it metal, enamel or cloth, it's time for us badge-kissers of the world to unite – we have nothing to lose but our lip salve!

BEER & SPIRIT LABELS

Labology (beer label collecting, and which must never be confused with labiology) tends to play second fiddle to tegestology (beer mat collecting). As such, when it comes to obtaining Scotland souvenir labels, the range available is more limited than those of drip mats, but interesting nonetheless.

The Edinburgh brewer Robert Deucher Limited (which closed circa 1961) produced a *Hampden Roar* malt ale, the label for which comprised largely of a drawn crowd scene, which can be interpreted as being the view from atop the old west terracing at Hampden Park. Goalscoring celebrations on the old 'dust bowl' sections of the stadium quite often necessitated a liquid refreshment in order to prevent choking!

Much more recently, The Clockwork Beer Company, a microbrewery and bar (less than a mile from Hampden Park itself) brews on-site its version of *Hampden Roar* – a loud, dark ale with a six per cent abv and admittedly tasty at that, but for me the roaring lion's head which dominates the label should have been replaced with something much more appropriate – like a bellowing James McFaddennnn!

Back in 1998 and because I was a dogmatic Export/heavy/bitter drinker, I foolishly missed out on Co-op-produced bottles of lager which commemorated the 20th anniversary of 'Archie's Golden Goal'. By 2016, however, my collecting habits dictated to my taste buds and so I didn't lose out when Tennent's brewers brought out their limited edition 'Legendary' label for their lager bottles, which featured a combined image of legends Denis Law, Kenny Dalglish and Archie Gemmill in goalscoring celebratory poses. So why not create a whole new series of individual Scottish football legends adorning bottles and cans in the way that the (much-missed) 'Lager Lovelies' did between 1965 and 1991?

I also wish some alcohol (or soft drink) producer in Scotland would follow the example of the Italian brewers *Peroni*, who in 2006 produced lager labels depicting the six Italy teams which had finished in the top four at World Cup competitions between 1934 and 1994 – the last of which had helped eliminate Scotland at the qualifying stages en route to a runners-up spot in the USA. A Scottish version

of this type of collectable could, of course, show images of the squads which travelled to eight World Cup finals between 1954 and 1998 – with the unbeaten squad of 1974 being allocated a special shiny, gold-trimmed label. I digress.

Extend our label hunt into whisky, however, and we discover, for example, that the Rutherglen Scotch Whisky Company produced a *Flower of Scotland* single Highland malt collection (5cl miniatures), which included a label featuring Rangers and Scotland skipper George Young (53 caps between 1946 and 1957). Meanwhile a separate *Football Legends* miniatures collection includes the likes of Billy McNeill (29 caps, 3 goals), Jimmy Johnstone (23 caps, 4 goals) and Jock Stein (Scotland manager from 1978 to 1985), plus Jim Baxter (34 caps, 3 goals), Davie Cooper (22 caps, 6 goals) and Ally McCoist (61 caps, 19 goals), albeit in their 'Old Firm' attire.

Going full circle, there was also a Hampden Roar Scotch whisky – a single Highland malt which was bottled to commemorate BT Scotland's sponsorship of the National Football Stadium in the early years of the new millennium – available in 70cl and miniature bottles. *Findlaters* also produced a celebratory blended whisky for Italia 90 in a football-shaped bottle.

Back in 1967 there was a commemorative blend produced (by Independence Scotland) in celebration of Scotland's historic 3–2 win at Wembley that year. The attractive-looking labels featured the 3–2 scoreline, as well as match details and today the 70cl bottle is available for around £150.

Another collectable bottle which came on the market in late 2018 was *Bohemian Brands*'s official licensed Scotland National Team Vodka, complete with crystal SFA logo. Looking to the future and perhaps Scotland's burgeoning gin industry will also produce something special to commemorate Scotland's qualification for Euro 2020 – with the emphasis on using *renaissance*-herb botanicals.

And finally, the shameful bit – I'm a Scotsman who doesn't actually like the taste of whisky (or vodka or gin) – I much more prefer rum, so I guess I belong on the roof over the Popular Side at the old Ninian Park, Cardiff alongside the advert for Captain Morgan's finest ... and some of Alan Rough's clearances.

CALENDAR BOYS

Some dates are more meaningful than others – e.g. 1314 ahead of 1066, 1666 or 1966, although the latter is still very important for on 27 June of that year Glasgow airport was officially opened. Here are some other important dates to ponder.

St Valentine's day
For Al Capone read Alf Ramsey, as 'Dourface' and his mob from south of the border dished out a 5–0 St Valentine's Day Massacre to Scotland at Hampden Park as part of our centenary celebrations, with our very own hotshot, Peter Lorimer of Leeds United, scoring an own goal after only six minutes. 48,470 witnessed the crime of the century but unbelievably, no one got the jail for it!

On St Valentine's Day in 1925, however, Tynecastle felt the love as Scotland defeated Wales 3–1 in a British Championship match.

St. David's Day
Just to be nice, Scotland lost 3–2 to Wales in a British Championship match played at Wrexham on St David's Day 1909. Apparently, the Scots' defence 'leeked' three goals in a 14-minute spell in the first half. Sorry.

St Patrick's Day
On St Patrick's Day in 1888 an Irish referee called Sinclair 'allowed' England to beat Scotland 5–0 in a British Championship match at First Hampden. The Scotland team comprised of players from Queen's Park, Dumbarton, Renton, Vale of Leven, Third Lanark and Battlefield, whilst our skipper was debutant David Gow of Rangers. Where were all those great Celtic players when we needed them? Oops, sorry – Celtic didn't play their first game until May 1888.

On Ireland's big day in 1906, however, Scotland travelled to Dalymount Park, Dublin, and won 1–0.

St George's Day
Scotland, having won the inaugural Rous Cup in 1985, failed to retain it the following year when we lost 2–1 to England at Wembley on St George's Day. Incidentally, our good friends Georgia have two St George's Days – the additional one being 10 November.

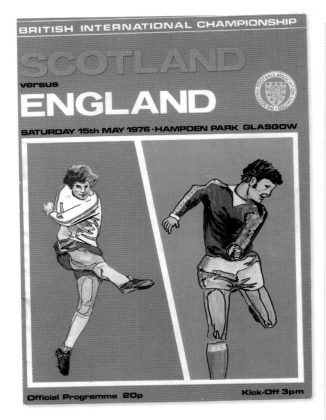

 Scotland have played more internationals on this date (12) than on any other date in the calendar. The trend started as recently as 1989 when we lost 3–0 to France in Paris in a World Cup qualifier (Scotland still made it to Italia 90, though). In 1997 it was a good day all round, however, as Scotland defeated Latvia 2–0 at Celtic Park to clinch qualification for the France 98 World Cup finals.

 St Jude's Day – Patron Saint of desperate cases and lost causes Appropriately enough, centre-forward Lawrie 'Last Minute' Reilly was born on this day in 1928. An apparent 'lost cause' was Wembley 1953, until the Hibs man scored his second equaliser of the day in the dying seconds of the game against England. 2–2 it finished.

31 OCT Scotland have played and won three games on Halloween – all away. 1925 (3–0 versus Wales), 1931 (3–2 versus Wales) and 1936 (3–1 versus Northern Ireland). Trick or treat?

 St Andrew's Day The world's first ever official international football match was played on this day in 1872, when Scotland and England drew 0–0 at the West of Scotland Cricket Ground in Partick, Glasgow. Scottish internationalists born on St Andrew's Day include George (?) Graham (1944), Andy (that's more like it) Gray (1955), Brian McAllister (1970), Robbie Stockdale (1979) and Alan Hutton (1984).

 Gary McAllister came into this world on Christmas Day 1964. Now I know he's not the Messiah but he had most of Scotland exclaiming 'Jesus Christ!' when he missed that penalty at Euro 96. Sorry Gary, but it still hurts.

 Two excellent Scottish internationalists were born on New Year's Eve: overlapping full-back Sandy Jardine (1948) and goalkeeper Craig Gordon (1982) – so every Hogmanay, remember to raise a glass to both of them. I suppose I should also mention **15 May** (aka **National Nutmeg Day**). This special day of celebration was initiated by Kenny Dalglish at Hampden in 1976, although to be fair England keeper Ray Clemence also had an important role to play.

Going off on a tangent now, and for one reason or another Scotland tend not to play matches in the height of either winter or summer. Indeed, up to and including 2019, Scotland have played only two matches at full international level in the month of January and two in July.

On 26 January 1884 Scotland visited Ballynafeigh Park, Belfast, and won 5–0 in front of a crowd of around 2,000. It was the first ever match in the British Championships, which Scotland won that year by being victorious in all three matches against the home nations.

There was then a wait of over 100 years, until 28 January 1986 when Scotland travelled to Tel Aviv for a friendly fixture against Israel

in the Ramat Gan Stadium. It was Scotland's first fixture after caretaker manager Alex Ferguson had safely steered us through a two-leg play-off against Australia and into the Mexico 86 World Cup finals. A crowd of 7,000 saw the visitors grind out a victory thanks to Celtic's Paul McStay scoring the only goal of the game in the 57th minute.

Scotland also played out a 2–2 draw with Belgium at Hampden on 23 January 1946; however, many record books list this post-Second World War 'Victory' International as being unofficial. 46,000 paying customers turned up to see it anyway.

Both of Scotland's July matches took place in the southern hemisphere, when Brazil chose their winter of 1972 to host a tournament in celebration of the 150th anniversary of their independence from Portugal. Following a 2–2 draw with Yugoslavia in Belo Horizonte on 29 June, Tommy Docherty's Scotland drew 0–0 with Czechoslovakia in Porto Alegre on 2 July, and then three days later we lost 1–0 to the host nation in Rio de Janeiro.

It should be both desirable as well as relatively easy to increase these paltry figures. For January, all the SFA has to do is to arrange some away friendlies in warmer climes such as Cuba, the Cape Verde Islands or the Maldives and the Tartan Army will follow in support. For July, all Scotland have to do is reach the latter stages (probably the quarter-finals) of the World Cup or European Championships, or alternatively organise our own summer independence tournament if we ever vote **Yes.** Simples.

C COLLECTING FOOTBALL SOUVENIRS
– INTERESTING HOBBY OR BEHAVIOURAL PROBLEM?

Some writers have suggested that it is supposed flaws or inadequacies that drive us to do what we do. Sexual sublimation is given prominence in that it is suggested that collecting is a substitute/compensation for the sex life you are not having. Personally speaking, I don't see why you can't enjoy **both** of these pleasurable experiences. It's all to do with time management – I mean to say, the sex usually only takes about two minutes out of my day, leaving me with hours to spend on my collecting ...

Moving swiftly along, and other pains of collecting include the argument that it's expensive, that the time could be better spent with family and friends, and that it promotes excessive pride, vanity, greed and selfishness. Academic studies are quoted as suggesting that collecting can lead to obsessive or deviant behaviour and that ultimately the whole exercise is pointless.

I much prefer to concentrate on the suggested positives of the hobby, such as gaining knowledge, escapism, the excitement of the chase, the joys of possessing and/or completion, and a social life involving like-minded individuals. A pie, a pint and a programme fair – a threesome that I can still enjoy without the need for an oxygen mask.

Other suggested benefits of collecting, however, are that it's a modern-day extension of the hunter-gatherer role, that it's perfect for people who live alone, that there are possible investment opportunities, and that it facilitates an improvement to an individual's

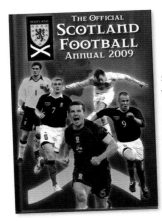

sense of identity or self-worth. The academics also suggest, however, that we may be anally retentive. My arse!

One big pain in the posterior, however, is the storage problem; e.g. matchday programmes are now bigger and bulkier than ever before, although that shouldn't be an issue for today's super-wealthy players, who could afford to build their own mini-museums. All of which begs the question – do footballers collect? Do they treasure what we treasure? Do they get a buzz out of reading about themselves in programmes, match reports and annuals? Do they get a thrill out of inserting stickers of themselves into Panini albums?

More specifically, does Paul McStay have the space to display all 76 of his Scotland caps at the one time, never mind the many medals he won whilst playing for Celtic? And what about all those traditional souvenirs Ally McCoist received for scoring hat-tricks for Rangers – did Super Ally hold on to his balls? Did Denis Law retain a copy of Scotland's 1974 World Cup vinyl album in which his vocals feature? Does Davie Weir have a fridge magnet of himself like what I do? Never mind 'What is the meaning of life?' – these are the really important questions which need answering.

My own conclusion to the academic debate? Collecting is fun, it's creative and by and large it's harmless. To my knowledge no country ever got invaded because of its abundant supply of trading cards or Corinthian figurines. Similarly, there has never been purges and mass executions of philatelists by football programme collectors because the latter group believe theirs is the one true hobby.

The world needs more collectors. Sermon over.

CONCACAF OPPOSITION

The Confederation of North, Central American and Caribbean Association Football (Concacaf) was founded in its current form in 1961. It has over 40 member associations of which Scotland have played just five.

Scotland's biggest victory against a Concacaf nation came about in a friendly match at Hampden Park, Glasgow, in 1952, when an incredible crowd of 107,765 saw the USA defeated 6–0, with Hibs's Lawrie Reilly grabbing a first-half hat-trick. The visiting side included six of the players who two years previous had sensationally defeated England 1–0 at the World Cup finals in Brazil.

Conversely, the USA dished out Scotland's worst defeat against Concacaf opponents, when Jurgen Klinsmann's team stuffed Craig Levein's side 5–1 in a friendly at EverBank Field, Jacksonville, Florida, in 2012. 44,428 saw

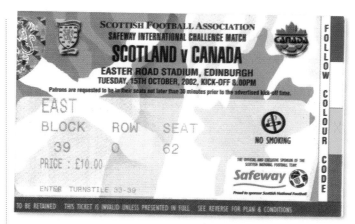

Everton's Landon Donovan hit a hat-trick, whilst Scotland's sole reply was an own goal. Clucking bell! Furthermore, the USA have appeared at ten World Cup finals – two more than Scotland. Clucking bell, again.

Opponent	Played	Won	Drew	Lost	Goals for	Goals Against	%
Canada	6	5	1	0	14	3	92
Costa Rica	2	0	0	2	0	2	0
Mexico	1	0	0	1	0	1	0
Trinidad & Tobago	1	1	0	0	4	1	100
USA	7	2	3	2	10	8	50
TOTAL	**17**	**8**	**4**	**5**	**28**	**15**	**59**

Scotland's first three matches/victories against Canada were played over an eight-day period in June 1983, as Jock Stein's boys traversed the dominion, starting at the Empire Stadium, Vancouver (2–0 in front of 14,942), then the Commonwealth Stadium, Edmonton (3–0 – 12,358), and finally the Varsity Stadium, Toronto (2–0 – 15,500). Canada have appeared at just the one World Cup finals, Mexico 86; however, in 2026 the Canucks will co-host the finals along with Mexico and the USA.

In 2004 when Scotland managed a rare friendly match victory with Berti Vogts at the helm, by defeating Trinidad and Tobago 4–1 at Easter Road Stadium, Edinburgh, the visitors' defensive line-up included Brent Sancho of Dundee, plus Livingston's 'Marvellous' Marvin Andrews. A crowd of 16,187 also witnessed Gary Caldwell net the first of his two goals for his country.

When Trinidad and Tobago appeared at their one World Cup finals at Germany 2006, Scotland travelled with them – Jason Scotland

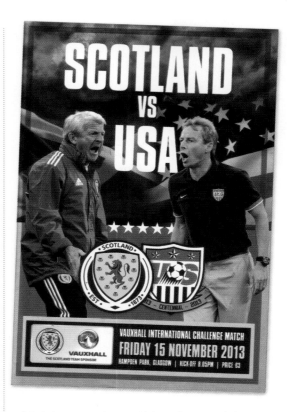

of St Johnstone that is. Although Jason didn't see any playing time in Germany, his Scottish colleagues Kelvin Jackson (Dundee), Russell Latapy and Densill Theobald (both Falkirk) did – to varying degrees.

When Costa Rica's completely home-based team defeated Scotland 1–0 in front of 30,867 mostly disbelieving supporters at Genoa's Luigi Ferraris Stadium at Italia 90, the Central Americans were making their debut at a World Cup finals – they have appeared at a further four finals since – 2002, 2006, 2014 (when they reached the quarter-finals) and 2018. Meanwhile, instead of starting with the recognised (and successful) striking partnership of Mo Johnston and Ally McCoist, Scotland manager Andy Roxburgh chose to drop the latter in favour of Bayern Munich's Alan 'Rambo' McInally. Richard Gough won his 50th cap that day, whilst Alex McLeish was awarded his 70th. Rambo never played for Scotland again, but it would be another year before Scotland dropped those hellish-looking white jerseys with the navy-blue and yellow horizontal bands that had failed to dazzle Costa Rica.

D

DIMINUTIVE DYNAMOS
– MINIATURE FOOTBALLER COLLECTABLES

By miniature footballers, I don't mean the likes of Jinky Johnstone or Willie Henderson – diminutive geniuses that they were – no, I'm mostly talking about the *Corinthian* 7cm 'high' footballer figurine collectables. Corinthian first launched its Prostars collection in 1995 and within a year more than 3,500 shops in the UK stocked the collectable 'bighead' footballers. In 2001 Corinthian then launched their Microstars collection – slightly smaller 5cm high footballers/managers – which were available inside hollow chocolate spheres.

With such a wide variety and large number of figurines available, you just had to specialise. For me that meant the big household names in their national team colours, *plus* Scotland players such as Colin Hendry, Don Hutchison and Barry Ferguson – the latter two of which were acquired as part of the McDonald's Happy Meal series.

As the years progress and the grey matter struggles to differentiate between different tournaments, the Corinthian figures also serve as an 'aide-memoire' as to who were the main players – literally – at each passing World Cup or European Championship.

For example, Portugal's Luis Figo along with Stelios Giannakopoulos of Greece remind me of Euro 2004, whilst Bastian Schweinsteiger of Germany and Spain's Fernando Torres evoke memories of Euro 2008, etc., etc. I have allowed myself but one player from Scotland's regular nemesis, Belgium – Gilles de Bilde (from Euro 2000); however, he is hidden well away just in case he upends my Paul Lambert whilst I am asleep.

Incidentally, the missus considers my collection to be something of an eyesore – that the colouring is all wrong, with the yellow shirts of Brazil and Sweden clashing with the red and white chessboard of Croatia and the brilliant orange of the Dutch – but Donatella Versace I'm not!

Anyway, as well as contemporary or 'current at the time' footballers, Corinthian also produced figures of star players from the past, and so in

their national team strips I can have Denis Law and Kenny Dalglish going hand-painted eyeball to hand-painted eyeball with Gerd Muller and Johan Cruyff.

Of course, some of these figures are more lifelike than others. For example, I've had Gary McAllister in Scotland colours (it's always our home strip mercifully) for about 15 years now and not once has he ventured over the halfway line. Similarly, my plastic miniature of goalkeeper Rab Douglas has yet to come out for a cross. That seems pretty lifelike to me. I also have a number of overrated England internationalists, who have yet to **disappear** or **self-destruct** when a World Cup or Euro finals takes place; however, I remain confident that they will in the fullness of time.

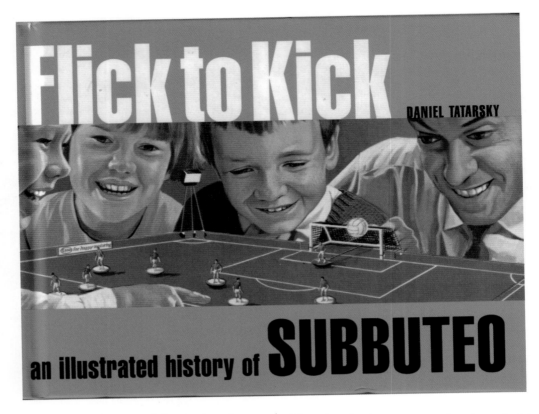

Flick to Kick

DANIEL TATARSKY

an illustrated history of **SUBBUTEO**

In 2013 SoccerStarz and the SFA (so often the home of small men syndrome) got together to produce a batch of around 20 5cm Scotland internationalists, such as Scott Brown, Gary Caldwell, Darren Fletcher, Kenny Miller and Steven Naismith. Sadly all of them have failed to make it into a World Cup or Euro finals special collection.

To date I have managed to resist the temptation to snap the head off any of my players in anger or frustration, although a Chris Iwelumo figure would have been a strong contender. Similarly, any thoughts about using my collection as voodoo dolls have been banished for the time being.

By way of a comparison, my football-hating son has a collection of 8cm high figurines of heroes and villains from the Marvel comics. However, no matter how shapely and alluring heroines the likes of Elektra, Storm and Black Cat may be, they just don't excite me in the same way that mini Rivaldos and Maradonas or even Neil McCanns do. Sad but true.

Arguably, the ultimate miniature footballers are to be found in the table football game *Subbuteo*. Founded in 1946, the title is derived from the neo-Latin scientific name 'Falco Subbuteo' (a bird of prey commonly known as the 'Eurasian Hobby'). Whilst the OO-scale players can look great in the colours of Argentina, Brazil, the Netherlands or Scotland, a regular criticism was their uniformity – the same pose, size and blank facial expressions,

although to be fair, some weird and wonderful hairstyles and dodgy moustaches did feature in the 1978 and 1982 Scotland retro collections. Those standard-issue boxes, however, which contained only Soviet-bloc style automatons cried out for diminutive wingers (Tommy Hutchison excepted), towering centre-halves, snarling midfielders and toothless strikers (in both senses of the word), for some much-needed added realism.

Talking of realism or 'ray-alism', a 1988 TV mini-series, entitled *Playing for Real*, told the story of a fictional Subbuteo team called Real Falkirk and starred Edinburgh-born Patricia Kerrigan as its player-manager. Back in the real (pronounced 'reel') world and 1970 saw London host the first ever Subbuteo World Cup, with Scotland being one of the 13 competing nations.

The 1986 Subbuteo World Cup was held in Greece, and in the seniors event Scotland's John McGiffen lost the third place play-off 4–3, after extra time, to Bruno Goset of Belgium. In the 1980 Subbuteo European Championships team event Scotland lost 3–0 in the semi-finals to ... Belgium. In 2001, Aberdeen hosted the World Sports Table Football Masters competition, which was won by David Ruelle of Belgium. The runner-up was Gil Delogne, also of Belgium.

Belgium and Scotland (life-size or miniature) ... there's a joke in there somewhere about Walloons and Balloons.

E
EIGHTY-TWO REMEMBERED

'Will we ever see their likes again? If not, and we must always hope that we will, then any record of this golden age must be preserved with the same diligence as that applied to the Dead Sea Scrolls.'

(*Adventures in the Golden Age: Scotland in the World Cup Finals 1974–1998* by Archie MacPherson, 2018.)

I was still at secondary school when Scotland performed magnificently at the 1974 World Cup finals in West Germany, and although I was in employment by the time Argentina 78 came around, I just couldn't afford to travel to South America. In 1982, however, Spain was accessible and relatively inexpensive, and as such it became my first (and my favourite) major. Problem was all of my mates were seriously 'loved up' at the time, so I 'shanghaied' Allan, my punk rocker of a wee brother, into joining me on my expedition to the south of Spain.

I was able to plunder my Abbey National savings account (because *I wasn't* seriously loved up, although I did have a bit of a crush on John Wark) and paid A.T. Mays the princely sum of £340 for a fortnight's half board

for two in a three-star hotel 50 yards from Torremolinos beach. With my hand luggage containing a precious cargo of two two-litre bottles of Irn Bru, we departed Glasgow Central railway station on 13 June – Allan's 17th birthday, Alan Hansen's 27th and the day the tournament opened with Belgium defeating Argentina 1–0 in Barcelona. The train (which, quite rightly, was in public ownership) took us to Manchester where we would catch a late-night flight to Malaga.

The plane was, of course, chock-full of Scotland supporters, mostly well-oiled Scotland supporters. For company we had several officers from the Greater Manchester Constabulary, but their presence wasn't required for there was no trouble whatsoever, although the English police had to endure several choruses of 'Where did you get that hat?' There were also a few drunken renditions of the official World Cup song 'We have a dream' that actually had you pining for an appearance by the lead singer-songwriter B.A. Robertson.

New Zealand v Scotland, Malaga, 15 June 1982

Top left: Seville [v Brazil] and above, Malaga [v USSR], June 1982

Spain 82 was Scotland's third successive World Cup finals and under Jock Stein's guidance, we had got there by topping a group that included Billy Bingham's Northern Ireland, Sweden, Portugal and Israel. Four well-attended Hampden matches produced an average crowd of 70,550, with tickets for the uncovered North Enclosure costing £2.50/£3.00.

Our first full day in Spain, Monday 14 June (which, somewhat surreally, coincided with the end of the 74-day long Falklands conflict with Argentina), centred around a short (17-mile) bus trip to central Malaga, then a hike to the Estadio La Rosaleda (Field of Rosebushes) in pursuit of match tickets. The 45,000-capacity stadium is situated next to the River Guadalmedina (which was completely dry in June) and its World Cup revamp included the construction of new upper tiers, the erection of floodlights on high gantries above each side and the digging of a moat – dry, of course.

Malaga

Allan then got badly sunburned queueing for the briefs, wearing nothing much more than his own briefs. The deal was that you had to purchase tickets for all three group matches which Malaga would host – Scotland versus New Zealand and the USSR, plus New Zealand versus the USSR, all for 900 pesetas (about £4.75!). £20 to a locally based Scottish 'entrepreneur' got us a coach trip to Seville and a ticket for the Brazil game. All four matches would kick off at 9pm local time – when it was still uncomfortably warm for most peely-wally Scots.

All the tournament group matches were geographically clustered – thus keeping travel costs and time to a minimum. FIFA have not been so considerate in many of the subsequent tournaments, although in 2022, Qatar – which is only 100 miles by 40 miles in size (and as hilly as Holland) – could be a welcome return to logistical common sense.

In the tournament programme there was a 'Hello' from King Juan Carlos I of Spain, who was still busy helping his country with the transition to democracy following the death of the country's ultra-conservative military dictator General Franco seven years previous. Meanwhile the section on Scotland was headed 'Time for Dalglish and co to make it third-time lucky'.

On Tuesday, 15 June, 'Scotland the Brave' replaced 'God Save the Queen' as our (football) national anthem for the first time and we then proceeded to score five goals in a World Cup finals match (my 'heart-throb' hitting a double, plus strikes from Kenny Dalglish, John Robertson and Steve Archibald) – I love it when a plan comes together! Unfortunately our opponents, New Zealand, netted twice and that would ultimately prove costly. Gordon Strachan was man of the match and seven goals represented excellent value for money, so we departed the stadium in buoyant mood. I seem to recall that in the vicinity of the stadium, there appeared to be an abundance of rather attractive-looking 'ladies of the night'. I wonder what General Franco would have had to say about that. As I had my wee brother in tow I chose to play it safe and so I bought some souvenir World Cup badges instead.

A most welcome contact from home were the special World Cup editions of the *Daily Record* newspaper, which were flown out to the Costa del Sol on a specially chartered Burnthills Aviation freight plane. 'Glorious Gordon Steals Show!' exclaimed Alex Cameron in reference to the win against New Zealand. Reading the match report sitting by the swimming pool in glorious sunshine with a glass of Irn Bru in hand – absolute bliss ...

On Friday, 18 June, the Torremolinos Tartan Army supporters' bus headed 125 miles over the mountains and through the beautiful 'bandit town' of Ronda (where Ernest Hemingway and Orson Welles used to hang out) to Seville – the capital of Andalusia and future 'home' to former Rangers manager Jock Wallace at Sevilla FC in 1986/87 and an estimated 80,000 Celtic supporters in 2003 for the UEFA Cup Final.

The 50,000-capacity Estadio Benito Villamarin, home to club side Real Betis, is situated about three kilometres from the historic city centre – too far to walk in that heat and besides, time was against us, so it became a question of locating the nearest bar and joining the queue. It was all very picturesque, however, with orange trees

everywhere reinforcing the emblematic image of Naranjito, the endearing World Cup mascot.

From our position on the uncovered north-west terracing, I was somewhat surprised to see that the Brazilian supporters actually outnumbered the Scots. I was also surprised, though absolutely delighted, when David Narey's 'toe-poke' flew into the back of the Brazilian net, to give Scotland the lead after 18 minutes and me the belief that we would go on and win the cup. Four excellent goals from Brazil in reply said 'Don't be so bloody stupid!'

After the game our journey back to Malaga was delayed, whilst jubilant Brazil supporters did the conga/samba/highland fling around the coach park – to the victors, the spoils. 'Masters Shoot Us Down' said the *Daily Record*'s Alex Cameron the following day.

On Saturday, 19 June, it was back into Malaga to lend our support to our 'Kiwi Cousins' in their match against 'Brezhnev's Boys'. The Soviets, however, recorded a comfortable 3–0 win, with two of the goals coming from Ukrainian legends Oleg Blokhin and Sergei Baltacha. I recall seeing several red flags, complete with hammers and sickles, being waved by members of the local Communist Party in support of the USSR. Again, I couldn't help but wonder what General Franco would have had to say about it all.

Tuesday, 22 June brought us our fourth game in seven days – Scotland versus the USSR, or Alcoholism versus Communism as some unkind foreign journalist put it. Once again, we stood on the terracing behind the north goal, and from there we were able to see the sun set on Scotland's time at Spain 82.

It's still painful so I'll keep it short. Scotland required a victory to stay in the competition, along with Brazil. After 15 minutes Joe Jordan scored at his third consecutive World Cup finals to give Scotland a half-time lead. In the second half, however, two Georgians scored for the Soviets, the first a mishit fluke, the second as a result of two Scots colliding (Willie Miller and Alan Hansen), before skipper Graeme Souness equalised at the death. Just for good measure we also had two good penalty claims rejected by the Romanian referee. So once again we exited the World Cup due to an inferior goal difference.

Although I didn't know it at the time, Danny McGrain and Joe Jordan had just played their last games for Scotland, finishing on 62 and 52 caps respectively.

'LOOKING BACK IN ANGER!' bemoaned my 'pen pal' Alex Cameron.

Back in 82 the technological advancement I would have welcomed most would have been a decent camera – my *Kodak Ektralite 10* was okay for parties and beach photographs but it struggled to keep up with the pace of the likes of Falcao, Socrates, Zico or even Alan Brazil. As such my souvenir snapshots are somewhat hazy.

Two days after the completion of all the group matches (which included a magnificent and much-envied victory for Northern Ireland over hosts Spain), we flew back to Manchester and an awaiting rail strike (privatisation, that's what's needed) which helped ensure that the postcards were home before us.

As we didn't buy our first video recorder – a Betamax – until later that year there was no taped TV coverage of Scotland's matches for me to review. However, I stuck with the tournament and cheered on Ron Greenwood's England (yes, really), as well as ITV's main man in Spain, former Scotland striker Ian St John (21 caps and nine goals between 1959 and 1965). I watched gobsmacked, however, as somehow Enzo Bearzot's Italy (with Paolo Rossi starring and scoring, and Marco Tardelli scoring and screaming) overcame both Argentina and Brazil en route to beating West Germany in the final. To help ease the pain I made a special effort to complete a Panini stickers album for the first time – those demi-gods Alan Rough, Kevin Keegan and Martin O'Neill have never looked so good.

Spain 82 – a great country, a great trip and a great tournament. Muchas gracias!

EURO CHAMPIONSHIPS EVOLUTION & QUALIFICATION - 1960 TO 2020
PART ONE: TOURNAMENT EVOLUTION

Year	No. of entrants [finalists]	Host nations [no. of venues]	Factoids	Winners
1960	17 [4]	France [2]	Eire were the sole entry from the 'British Isles'.	**USSR**
1964	29 [4]	Spain [2]	Scotland, Cyprus, Finland, & West Germany did not compete.	**SPAIN**
1968	31 [4]	Italy [3]	Two British Championships doubled as qualifying group 8. Iceland & Malta did not compete.	**ITALY**
1972	32 [4]	Belgium [4]	Iceland did not compete.	**WEST GERMANY**
1976	32 [4]	Yugoslavia [2]	Albania did not compete.	**CZECHOSLOVAKIA**
1980	32 [8]	Italy [4]	Albania did not compete.	**WEST GERMANY**
1984	33 [8]	France [7]	All UEFA members competed for the first time.	**FRANCE**
1988	33 [8]	West Germany [8]	Last Euros for East Germany & West Germany.	**NETHERLANDS**
1992	34 [8]	Sweden [4]	Last Euros for Czechoslovakia and USSR. New entrants: Faroe Islands, Germany [unified] and San Marino.	**DENMARK**
1996	48 [16]	England [8]	New entrants: Armenia, Azerbaijan, Belarus, Croatia, Czech Republic, Estonia, Georgia, Israel, Latvia, Liechtenstein, Lithuania, Macedonia, Moldova, Russia, Slovakia, Slovenia & Ukraine.	**GERMANY**
2000	51 [16]	Belgium & Netherlands [8]	Last Euros for Yugoslavia. New entrants: Andorra & Bosnia-Herzegovina.	**FRANCE**
2004	51 [16]	Portugal [8]	New entrant: Serbia & Montenegro.	**GREECE**
2008	52 [16]	Austria & Switzerland [8]	New entrants: Kazakhstan and Serbia.	**SPAIN**
2012	53 [16]	Poland & Ukraine [8]	New entrant: Montenegro.	**SPAIN**
2016	54 [24]	France [10]	New entrant: Gibraltar.	**PORTUGAL**
2020	55 [24]	Azerbaijan, Denmark, England, Germany, Hungary, Ireland, Italy, Netherlands, Romania, Russia, Scotland, Spain [12]	New entrant: Kosovo.	**SCOTLAND?**

UEFA WOMEN'S EURO 2017 THE NETHERLANDS

LET'S CELEBRATE! EK VROUWEN
Komende zomer in Nederland!

16 juli – 6 augustus 2017

Kicky

ROYAL MAIL GLASGOW

12 OCT '10

EURO2012
POLAND-UKRAINE

SCOTLAND 1
SWITZERLAND 0

18.6.96

GROUP A

ERLANDS   SCOTLAND

ROAD TO
UEFA EURO 2020™

UEFA NATIONS LEAGUE
FINALS
PORTUGAL 2019

ADRENALYN XL™
OFFICIAL COLLECTOR'S ALBUM

FFF
www.fff.fr

ICATION
21H00

SSE
19H00

BLEU HAUT
PLACE
107
45654720

Euro 2004 Play-off, 1st Leg

Scotland   v   The Netherlands

SCOTLAND

Hampden Park
Glasgow

KNVB

Saturday
15th November 2003
Kick off 3.00pm

ROYAL MAIL GLASGOW

15 NOV '03

Match Result
Scotland - 1   The Netherlands - 0
McFadden

EURO CHAMPIONSHIPS EVOLUTION & QUALIFICATION - 1960 TO 2020
PART TWO: SCOTLAND'S QUALIFYING CAMPAIGNS SUMMARY

Year	No./names of opposition teams	No. of qualifying matches/Final position
1960	Did not participate	
1964	Did not participate	
1968	3: England, Wales & N. Ireland	6 / 2nd / Failed to qualify
1972	3: Belgium, Denmark, Portugal	6 / 3rd / Failed to qualify
1976	3: Denmark, Spain & Romania	6 / 3rd / Failed to qualify
1980	4: Austria, Belgium, Norway & Portugal	8 / 4th / Failed to qualify
1984	3: Belgium, East Germany & Switzerland	6 / 4th / Failed to qualify
1988	4: Belgium, Bulgaria, Luxembourg & ROI	8 / 4th / Failed to qualify
1992	4: Bulgaria, Romania, San Marino & Switzerland	8 / 1st / Qualified
1996	5: Faroes, Finland, Greece, Russia & San Marino	10 / 2nd / Qualified
2000	5: Bosnia-Herzegovina, Czech Republic, Estonia, Faroes & Lithuania [plus England in two-leg play-off]	10+2 / 2nd / Scotland lost play-off and failed to qualify
2004	4: Germany, Faroes, Iceland & Lithuania [plus Netherlands in two-leg play-off]	8+2 / 2nd / Scotland lost play-off and failed to qualify
2008	6: Faroes, France, Georgia, Italy, Lithuania & Ukraine	12 / 3rd / Failed to qualify
2012	4: Czech Republic, Liechtenstein, Lithuania & Spain	8 / 3rd / Failed to qualify
2016	5: Georgia, Germany, Gibraltar, Poland, & Republic of Ireland	10 / 4th / Failed to qualify

Up to and including the 2016 event, Scotland have participated in 13 of the 15 competitions, successfully qualifying for the finals on just two occasions – 1992 and 1996. Rubbish innit?

Furthermore, sandwiched between two successful World Cup qualifying campaigns in 1982 and 1986, Jock Stein's multi-talented Scotland team somehow contrived to win only one match out of six in the qualifying campaign for Euro 84

– our opening match against East Germany at Hampden!

In the Euro qualifiers proper (i.e. excluding the Nations League) Scotland have faced a total of 34 different nations, with Hungary, Sweden and Turkey being notable omissions. Conversely, we have been drawn against Belgium five times (1972, 1980, 1984, 1988 and 2020), with the 'Red Devils' topping the qualifying group on the first three occasions.

EURO 92 & 96 CHAMPIONSHIPS FINALS MATCHES

Between 1960 and 2016 there have been 15 European Football Championships and Scotland have qualified for the finals on just two occasions – Sweden 1992 (when there were a mere eight finalists) and England 1996 (when there were 16 finalists). Euro 2020 will comprise of 24 finalists.

Scotland's matches at the finals

Date	Opponents	Venue	Result	Attendance
12 June 1992	Netherlands	Ullevi Stadion, Gothenburg	0-1	35,720
15 June 1992	Germany	Idrottsparken, Norrkoping	0-2	17,638
18 June 1992	CIS	Idrottsparken, Norrkoping	3-0	14,660
10 June 1996	Netherlands	Villa Park, Birmingham	0-0	34,363
15 June 1996	England	Wembley Stadium, London	0-2	76,864
18 June 1996	Switzerland	Villa Park, Birmingham	1-0	34,926

In total Scotland have played six matches, won two, drawn one and lost three. We have only managed to hit the net in two of those fixtures, with our total goals for being four, with goals against five. Our goalscorers were Paul McStay (Celtic), Brian McClair (Manchester United) and Gary McAllister (Leeds United) (versus the CIS in 1992), and Ally McCoist (Rangers) (versus Switzerland in 1996).

In 1992 the third match, against the Commonwealth of Independent States (CIS), was a dead rubber for Andy Roxburgh's Scotland; however, if the former USSR had won the game then they and not Berti Vogts's Germany would have reached the semi-finals. In 1996, with Craig Brown as manager, Scotland lost out to the Netherlands for a place in the quarter-finals by virtue of fewer goals scored.

To date, only 25 footballers (from 11 clubs) have represented Scotland at the Euro Championship finals. If our current squad do the business, here's the illustrious list they'd be seeking to join.

Aberdeen [2 players, 7 caps]
Stewart McKimmie
1992: Netherlands, Germany & CIS
1996: Netherlands & England

Scott Booth
1996: Netherland & Switzerland (sub)

Blackburn Rovers [3 players, 5 caps]
Kevin Gallacher
1996: Netherlands

Colin Hendry
1996: Netherlands, England & Switzerland

Billy McKinlay
1996: Netherlands (sub)

Celtic [4 players, 12 caps]
Tommy Boyd
1992: CIS
1996: Netherlands, England & Switzerland

Paul McStay
1992: Netherlands, Germany & CIS

John Collins
1996: Netherlands, England & Switzerland

Tosh McKinlay
1996: England & Switzerland

Chelsea [2 players, 6 caps]
John Spencer
1996: Netherlands (sub), England & Switzerland (sub)

Craig Burley
1996: Netherlands (sub), England (sub) & Switzerland

Coventry City [2 players, 4 caps]
Kevin Gallacher
1992: Netherlands (sub), Germany (sub) & CIS
Eoin Jess
1996: England (sub)

Dundee United [3 players, 4 caps]
Duncan Ferguson
1992: Netherlands (sub)
Jim McInally
1992: CIS (sub)
Maurice Malpas
1992: Netherlands & Germany

Everton [1 player, 2 caps]
Pat Nevin
1992: Germany (sub) & CIS (sub)

Leeds United [1 player, 6 caps]
Gary McAllister
1992: Netherlands, Germany & CIS
1996: Netherlands, England & Switzerland

Manchester United [1 player, 3 caps]
Brian McClair
1992: Netherlands, Germany & CIS

Rangers [6 players, 26 caps]
Andy Goram
1992: Netherlands, Germany & CIS
1996: Netherlands, England & Switzerland
Richard Gough
1992: Netherlands, Germany & CIS
Stuart McCall
1992: Netherlands, Germany & CIS
1996: Netherlands, England & Switzerland
Ally McCoist
1992: Netherlands, Germany & CIS
1996: England (sub) & Switzerland
Dave McPherson
1992: Netherlands, Germany & CIS
Gordon Durie
1996: Netherlands, England & Switzerland

Tottenham Hotspur [2 players, 5 caps]
Gordon Durie
1992: Netherlands & Germany
Colin Calderwood
1996: Netherlands, England & Switzerland

Rangers goalkeeper Andy Goram and midfield clubmate Stuart McCall plus the often, but unfairly maligned Gary McAllister of Leeds United are the only players to have appeared in all six Euro 92/96 finals matches for Scotland.

EURO CHAMPIONSHIPS SCOTTISH MATCH OFFICIALS

Despite finishing third in our qualifying group, 'Scotland' made it through to the last four in the 1972 European Championships. Well, actually it was referee William J. Mullan, who went to Antwerp to take charge of the semi-final between host nation Belgium and West Germany. The Germans won 2–1 and went on to claim the first of their three Euro crowns to date.

Eight years later and Brian McGinlay officiated at a finals that now comprised of eight teams. Euro 80 suffered from hooliganism and poor attendances, however, and there was a crowd of under 14,000 in Turin's Stadio Comunale to watch Mr McGinlay stifle yawns as Greece and West Germany played out a goalless draw, which would

take our Teutonic friends through to a final where they would defeat Belgium to win their second European title.

Following on from his 'successes' at the Spain 82 World Cup, Bob Valentine was our man at the Euro finals of 1984 and 1988. In Nantes at France 84 he was the ref when the host nation hammered Belgium 5–0 in a group match with the aid of a Michel Platini hat-trick, although Bob did his bit by throwing in a penalty award. France, of course, went on to win the tournament – their first major title.

Four years later in Gelsenkirchen, West Germany, Valentine again officiated at a group match host victory as the Germans, managed by Franz Beckenbauer, beat Denmark 2–0,

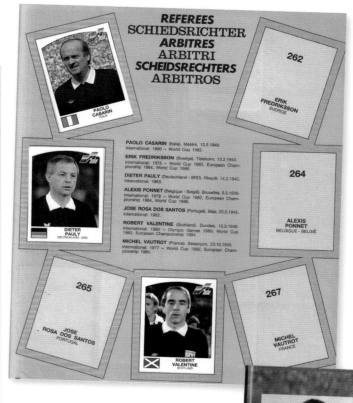

with goals from Jurgen Klinsmann and Olaf Thon. It would be the Dutch, however, who would go on to win the competition, their only major success to date.

Bob Valentine never refereed beyond the group stages of the European Championships, but consolation came in 1988 in the shape of being the only Scottish referee to make it into a Panini sticker album, alongside the likes of Michel Vautrot (France) and Erik Fredriksson (Sweden)!

The Scotland football team made it to Euro 92 in Sweden (hurrah!) but unlike Denmark (last-minute replacements for the disintegrating Yugoslavia) there would be no 11th hour call-up for any of our officials, and so our refs and linesmen remained on the beaches that summer.

Scotland has been represented by our match officials at the past six Euro finals in a row now (1996 to 2016 inclusive), although in 2004 and 2008 Stuart Dougal then Craig Thomson only travelled as 'fourth officials'.

At Euro 96 Les Mottram crossed the border mob-handed with assistants John Fleming and Robert Orr to take charge of a group game (Italy 2 Russia 1 at Anfield), plus a semi-final (Czech Republic versus France at Old Trafford, with the Czechs winning 6–5 on penalties following a goalless draw).

At Euro 2000 it was none other than the *Shugsterino*, Mr Hugh Dallas, who succeeded where Craig Brown and his boys had failed, and so off he went to the Low Countries to ref a couple of group matches (Italy 2 Turkey 1 in Arnhem, followed by Yugoslavia 1 Norway 0 in Liege, with 'Serbia and Montenegro in disguise' also 'winning' 4–2 on yellow cards). Arnhem was arguably 'a balls-up too far' for Dallas, who was offered police protection by UEFA after awarding Italy a controversial late penalty against the furious Turks.

At Euro 2012 the 'Scotland squad' comprised of referee Craig Thomson, assistants Alasdair Ross and Derek Rose, plus additional assistants William Collum and Euan Norris. Graham Chambers was listed as a standby.

'Five go Mad in Wroclaw' could have been the headline as Thomson (ably supported by his 'team') dished out eight yellow cards as the Czech Republic beat the co-hosts Poland 1–0 in Group A.

Three days earlier in Lviv, Ukraine, only four yellow cards were issued in the Group B game, which ended in a 3–2 win for Portugal against Denmark but which included one for Cristiano Ronaldo in the 92nd minute. Nice one Craig.

At Euro 2016 the 'Scotland squad' headed by referee William Collum also included John Beaton, Bobby Madden and Francis Conner. Wicked Willie 'reffed' the group games involving France and Albania in Marseille (2–0) plus the Czech Republic and Turkey in Lens (0–2) and dished out eight cautions over the two games. However, like Scotland teams before them, they went home before the knockout rounds commenced.

Time will tell as to which of our whistlers will get the prestigious Euro 2020 gig, including whether or not 'Oor Wullie' makes it three in a row.

EURO 2020 AND ALL THAT

Many of us were in denial for weeks but eventually we were forced to accept that Scotland had failed to qualify for the Russia 2018 World Cup finals – our tenth successive 'major' qualification failure. The pain appears to be never-ending, although the achievements of the Scotland Women's team, making it to the Euro 2017 finals and the 2019 World Cup finals, did alleviate some of the suffering.

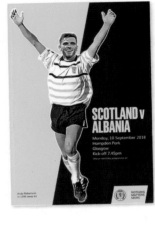

Looking ahead, though, to the 2020 European Football Championships, as Scotland are one of 12 co-hosts for the finals, it would be especially embarrassing if we failed to make it to our own party so to speak.

By way of assistance, UEFA (in conjuction with Mensa?) have created the Nations League, a new, fandangled competition designed to reduce the number of meaningless international friendlies, whilst at the same time offering the possibility of an additional route to qualification for Euro 2020, particularly for football's lesser lights, such as Belarus, Kosovo, Macedonia … and Scotland.

In the inaugural Nations League competition, Scotland were allocated a place in League C and then drawn in Group 1 with Albania and Israel. The plan is that the winners of the four groups in League C will play off in

March 2020 for a place at the finals – unless any of those four teams have qualified via the conventional route, which commenced in March 2019. I think. I'm sorry we don't have room for a flow chart to expand further, including explaining the promotion and relegation between the leagues.

Anyway, on Monday, 10 September 2018 Scotland duly played their first ever match against Albania and 17,455 came along to a rain-soaked Hampden Park to see fixture history being made, as well as Scotland win their first competitive match under the stewardship of Alex McLeish, the managerial successor to the marmite Gordon Strachan. Two second-half goals did the trick – an o.g. from Atalanta's Berat Gjimshiti and a looping header from Steven Naismith of Hearts.

On 11 October Scotland then turned up (sort of) in the 'Holy Land', where they gave a 'Holy shocking performance, Batman' against Israel at the Sammy Ofer Stadium in Haifa. (By the way, Mr Ofer was an Israeli shipping magnate and philanthropist.) Against the run of play, Scotland somehow managed to lead 1–0 at half-time thanks to a penalty converted by Blackburn Rovers's Charlie Mulgrew. In the second half, however, Scotland and their questionable formation were found out. Dor Peretz equalised in the 52nd minute, Hearts' John Souttar was sent off for a second bookable offence in the 61st minute and 13 minutes later Celtic's Kieran Tierney shanked the ball into his own goal. I can't speak for Jesus but I know the Tartan Army *wept* – as well as booed.

Into November and on Saturday the 17th, Scotland went behind the old 'Bamboo Curtain' to Shkoder and the Loro Borici Stadium (named after the celebrated Albanian international footballer and coach) to once again face Albania, a nation which at one time revered Norman Wisdom comedy films, for apparently to some communists they were a parable on the class war!

As it transpired, a largely makeshift Scotland team (hampered by nine call-offs) were a joy to watch as they comprehensively defeated their hosts 4–0. The scorers were Bournemouth's Ryan Fraser and Sheffield Wednesday's Steven Fletcher (penalty) in the first half, followed by a glorious double from James Forrest of Celtic in the second 45. Okay, so Albania were reduced to ten men in the 21st minute when Mergim Mavraj was red-carded for headbutting Ryan Christie, but Scotland were outstanding – yes, really. We can only speculate as to what Mr Grimsdale and Enver Hoxha would have made of it all?

Three days later on a cold, wet evening at a half-empty Hampden Park, Scotland got it right again by defeating Israel 3–2 to top the group, win promotion to League B, climb into the third pot for December's Euro draw and guarantee ourselves a March 2020 play-off spot should we bugger up the qualifiers proper!

Scotland's three goals came courtesy of James Forrest, the first Celtic player to hit a treble for his country since Jimmy Quinn put four past Ireland in 1908! It was far from straightforward, however – Israel took the lead in the ninth minute and it took an excellent save at the death from Rangers keeper Allan McGregor to prevent the visitors from making it 3–3 and giving *them* top spot and all that goes with it. It was just a pity that only 21,281 were inside the national stadium to savour the moment, but savour it we did. Yahoo!

The December 2018 draw in Dublin then pitted Scotland in qualifying Group I, along with Belgium (we beat them 5–0 in Brussels in 1951!), Russia (two draws on our way to Euro 96), Cyprus (played five, won five), San Marino (played six, won six) and Kazakhstan (a brand-new opponent for Scotland, which brought the worry that they could be Georgia Mark II).

Into March 2019 for the first of five double-header Euro qualifiers. On Thursday, 21 March, Scotland were in the Astana Arena in central Asia where another largely makeshift and inexperienced side – defenders Liam Palmer of Sheffield Wednesday won his first cap and Hamburg SV's David Bates collected his third – were stuffed 3–0 by Kazakhstan; indeed, we were 2–0 down after only ten minutes. Woeful Scottish defending combined with excellent Kazakh finishing enabled the home side, who were rated 77 places below Scotland in the FIFA rankings, to record a much-cherished competitive victory, having failed to win a single game in their last World Cup qualifying campaign.

It was quite possibly the worst meaningful result in the history of Scottish international football, for whilst we have suffered heavier defeats, they have been dished out by some of the world's elite footballing nations, in addition to friendly match gubbings from the likes of Wales and the USA.

On Sunday, 24 March, Scotland, with skipper Andy Robertson back in the team following absence due to an abscess, took to the field in Serravalle, San Marino, and this time collected the expected three points thanks to a 2–0 win. Scotland started well, taking the lead after only four minutes with Norwich City's Kenny McLean's header giving the Rutherglen-born midfielder his first international goal at full level. Scotland then laboured for another 70 minutes before Johnny Russell, of Sporting Kansas City, rifled in a shot straight down the middle to calm the nerves and quell the booing.

The stats confirmed that San Marino had now lost 150 of 155 competitive matches – whilst the SFA website pronounced 'Scotland back on track', totally ignoring the vocal and verbal dissatisfaction of much of the Scotland support.

The agreed Brexit date of 29 March 2019 was duly postponed (until 31 October 2019 at the latest) but Eckxit came on 18 April when Alex

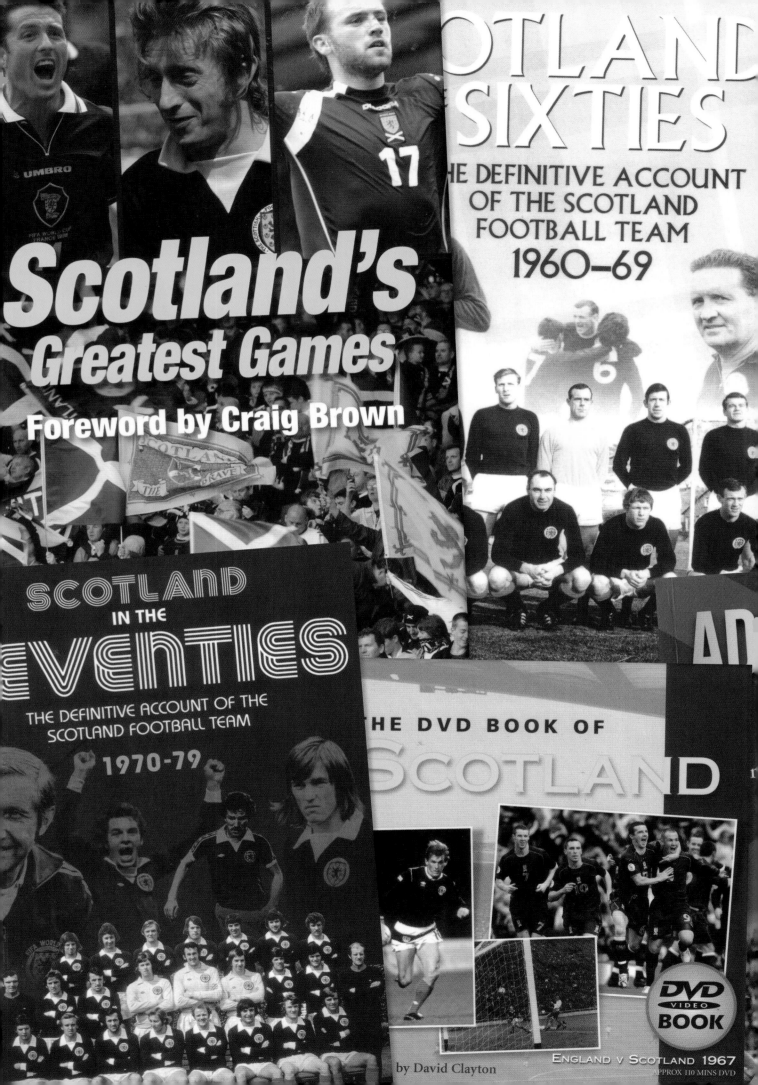

Scotland's Greatest Games

Foreword by Craig Brown

OTLAND SIXTIES

THE DEFINITIVE ACCOUNT OF THE SCOTLAND FOOTBALL TEAM 1960–69

SCOTLAND IN THE EVENTIES

THE DEFINITIVE ACCOUNT OF THE SCOTLAND FOOTBALL TEAM 1970–79

THE DVD BOOK OF SCOTLAND

DVD VIDEO BOOK

ENGLAND V SCOTLAND 1967
APPROX 110 MINS DVD

by David Clayton

DREAMLAND
SCOTTISH WORLD CUP SUCCESS STORY
GRAHAM McCOLL

"...are going to win the World Cup or I will want to know why not" **Billy Bremner**

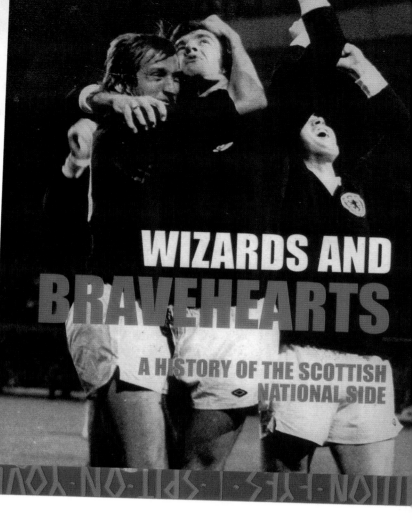

WIZARDS AND BRAVEHEARTS
A HISTORY OF THE SCOTTISH NATIONAL SIDE

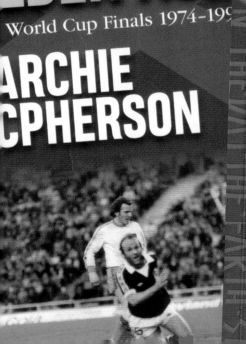

...NTURES IN ...LDEN AGE

World Cup Finals 1974–199...

ARCHIE ...CPHERSON

SEX AND SCANDAL IN SCOTTISH FOOTBALL

HAMPDEN BABYLON

by stuart cosgrove

THIS BOOK
BRINGS

McLeish's second term as Scotland manager came to an end after just 14 months. About five weeks later Big Eck was duly replaced by former Kilmarnock FC manager Steve Clarke.

The former St Mirren and Chelsea defender earned six Scotland caps between 1987 and 1994, and in his coaching career spanning 20 years, he has assisted Ruud Gullit at Newcastle United, Jose Mourinho at Chelsea, Gianfranco Zola at West Ham United and Sir Kenny Dalglish at Liverpool.

June 2019 brought the end of Theresa May's tenure as leader of the Conservative Party, in effect making her a temporary 'caretaker' UK Prime Minister, whilst Scotland's First Minister, Nicola Sturgeon, spent time in Brussels meeting with key EU figures in a bid to 'keep Scotland in Europe'. June also gave us Scotland Euro qualifiers against Cyprus at Hampden and Belgium in Brussels, as Steve Clarke attempted something similar to the Sturge's objective.

On Saturday, 8 June, and in front of a crowd of just over 31,000, a surprisingly pedestrian Scotland laboured to a 2–1 win over Cyprus. Just over an hour was played before Scotland took the lead thanks to a 25-yard rocket shot from Liverpool's left-back and recent Champions League hero, Andy Robertson. However, we had to rely on a strike from West Brom's on loan to Celtic Oliver Burke two minutes from time to earn the points when two minutes prior to that, some 'Oliver Hardy' defending had allowed the unmarked Cyprus right-back, Ioannis Kousoulos, to head an equaliser from a corner.

On Tuesday, 11 June, Scotland took to the field at the King Baudouin Stadium and then were simply outplayed and outclassed by a Belgium side which must be one of the favourites to win the competition. Skipper Andy Robertson missed the game due to a hamstring injury which allowed for Kilmarnock's Greg Taylor to make his debut, and hopefully he and his teammates all learned something from the experience of facing the side currently ranked number one in the world. Ironically, Belgium's three goals all came from Manchester, with United's Romelu Lukaku bagging a goal in each half before City's Kevin De Bruyne netted at the death. Five minutes from the end, however, Celtic's James Forrest squandered a great opportunity to pull it back to 2–1 ... and then who knows what might have happened.

At the end of June, and with four of the ten qualifying matches played, Belgium sat top of the group on 12 points with Russia next on nine. After them came Kazakhstan and Scotland on six points, Cyprus on three and San Marino set to lose their deposit again.

So can we fix it? YES, WE CAN! Four of our six remaining games are at home, where I would fancy Scotland against any team — and that's not the drink or my medicine talking. There's also the 'safety net' of the play-offs. Of course, it goes without saying that we are also quite capable of making a complete 'Roger Hunt' of it.

Come 2020, then, I'll either see you at the Euros ... or at the Care Home for Disillusioned Tartan Army Veterans. I'll either be partying with our overseas visitors in Glasgow's George Square and salivating over my collection of tournament merchandise OR I'll be gibbering 'what might have been' nonsense to fellow 'inmates'. Either way, 2020 is going to be a memorable year.

F FOOTBALL MEMORIES SCOTLAND

In August 2017 I went along to my local public library to take in an 'awareness day' organised by 'Football Memories Scotland' – which celebrates its tenth birthday in 2019. Over the past decade FMS (with Hibs and Scotland legend Lawrie Reilly as their first ambassador) have developed into Scotland's national football reminiscence project and is a partnership involving Alzheimer Scotland and the Scottish Football Museum. Old photographs and football memorabilia are used to trigger memories and improve peoples' lives. It is estimated that there are over 90,000 people living with dementia in Scotland, the equivalent of every spectator on an average Scottish football weekend.

Volunteers across Scotland have set up a network of local groups and people within these groups are encouraged to compile a hardback 'This is your football life' memories book, combining personal and family photographs with images from their time as players and/or supporters.

Another useful 'conversation-stimulating tool' is the specially created Football Memory Cards. These are sets of 60 laminated cards which include five players from each position from specific periods of time. The reverse of each card includes clues to assist recall and over time it is hoped to have a set for every Scottish club as well as international teams. Ironically, these memory-triggering cards will probably become collectors' items in themselves.

The FMS project continues to evolve, and seeks also to assist people living with mental health conditions or who are lonely and isolated. FMS would appreciate donations of old football books, programmes or memorabilia.

All of this got me thinking that as collectors of football memorabilia, we should therefore have some weapons already at our disposal for the battle against old age and memory loss. It's a side to our hobby that I hadn't really thought about before but will certainly shape things in the coming years.

It was the 1980s before I starting taking my own football photographs but these images, backed up with special match programmes, trading cards and a whole host of football souvenirs, should offer a considerable number of potential 'trigger' items. My only concern

For more information see
www.footballmemoriesscotland.co.uk

is that I have too many items, resulting in the possible threat of overload. Other positives from our hobby, however, are the programme shops and fairs, which also provide opportunities for social interaction and mental stimulation. It's not so sad this collecting malarkey after all then, is it?

Returning to that impressive awareness day at Rutherglen library, on the south-east outskirts of Glasgow, there was also offered up a photo opportunity of the towering Scottish Junior FA Cup trophy (as well as the smaller Scottish FA Cup), both of which were on display adjacent to the crime section, and, as many of the supporters might testify, this was highly appropriate as some of the tackling in Scottish junior football is truly criminal!

Seriously, though, I think FMS represents a rare double in Scottish football – a noble cause and a success story which has been tapped into by countries such as Brazil and the Netherlands. There are now over 6,000 digital photos/images contained within the FMS resource website at Hampden Park, which allow volunteers to personalise football memories sessions for individuals.

G GENDER EQUALITY?
WOMEN'S FOOTBALL

Women's football deserves a book all of its own, so anything confined to a page or a few paragraphs could come over as trite or patronising, which is not the intention. What is intended is a salute to achievements made in the face of adversity, apathy and good old sexist attitudes – of which I have been guilty in the past.

Portugal v Scotland, Rotterdam, 23 July 2017

Indeed, whilst it can be argued that for the men's team, the period of 1998 to 2019 represents an international footballing famine, much-needed aid has been provided in the shape of the Scotland women's team reaching the finals of the 2017 European Championships (16 finalists) and the 2019 World Cup finals (24 finalists) – topping a five-nation group to qualify for the latter. I travelled to both the Netherlands and France to cheer on the Scotland women at these finals – glory hunter that I am.

Scotland's women first played an *unofficial* international match in 1881 – we stuffed an England XI 3–0 so I think it should be made 100 per cent **official**, and maybe throw in a trophy as well! Unfortunately, however, women's football struggled for recognition and was eventually banned by the football authorities in 1921. I wouldn't be surprised if that was in retaliation for women getting the vote.

Women's football continued despite the ban, albeit on a piecemeal basis, until 1971 when UEFA instructed its members to take control of women's football. In a UEFA members' vote only the SFA had said **No**. (Have we ever voted *Yes* for anything? Ach, don't start me ...)

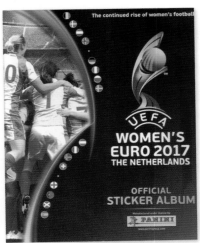

In recent years much progress has been made and prior to their Euro 2017 breakthrough the Scotland women's team reached the play-offs on four separate occasions – falling at the ultimate hurdle for the 1999 and 2015 World Cups, as well as the 2009 and 2013 European Championships.

At Euro 2017, Anna Signeul's Scotland, amazingly, had 11 players on 100-plus caps, including their goalkeeper Gemma Fay, who won her 200th cap just prior to the finals, but that didn't prevent us from being eliminated at the group stage on goal difference – just like the men often did when they reached tournament finals. Defeats against England (0–6 aaaargh!) and Portugal (1–2, with Chelsea's Erin Cuthbert netting Scotland's first ever goal at a finals) were followed by a 1–0 victory over Spain (Liverpool's Caroline Weir scoring the winner), but somehow it was the Spanish who progressed to the quarter-finals. Host nation the Netherlands defeated England in the semi-finals en route to winning the competition.

At the June 2019 World Cup finals Shelley Kerr's Scotland were again paired with the 'old enemy' and again lost their opening group match to them. This time, however, the scoreline was 2–1, and England were a tad fortunate to survive a second-half rally from Scotland in Nice, which saw Manchester City's Claire Emslie net her country's first ever goal at a World Cup finals. England were dominant in the first half but had to rely on a VAR decision to give them a soft penalty for the opener.

Five days later against Japan in Rennes, Scotland again gave the opposition two goals of a start before fighting back to lose 2–1. Once more, the opposition were the recipients of a soft penalty award and just for good measure Scotland were denied a stonewaller of a handball claim. The Scotland goal came two minutes from time and was a magnificent 25-yard strike from Fiorentina's Lana Clelland.

And so to the Parc des Princes on 19 June for the game against Argentina. I viewed this tie from the discomfort of the Francis Borelli Stand and months later, I still can't believe what I witnessed. Goals from Arsenal midfielder Kim Little (19 minutes), Man City defender Jen Beattie (49 minutes) and Chelsea striker Erin Cuthbert (69 minutes) meant Scotland were coasting it. Easy! Easy! Easy!

Argentina v Scotland, Paris, 19 June 2019

3–0 ahead with 20 minutes to go, Shelley's heroes were set to become history-makers (in a good way). And then Scotland did what Scotland do – we imploded. We blew a place in the last 16 by conceding three goals (in the 74th, 79th and 94th minutes) when even a one-goal victory would have allowed us to remain in the competition. The equaliser was particularly cruel – a penalty awarded via VAR was saved by Lee Alexander only for another VAR review resulting in the North Korean referee ordering a retake after the Glasgow City keeper was adjudged to have moved off her line. Florencia Bonsegundo made no mistake second time around. 3–3 it finished.

The closing stages of that match will haunt players, coaches and supporters for a long time to come. We were outplayed on the pitch and outsung off it, when suddenly it appeared that around 75 per cent of the crowd of over 28,000 were Argentina supporters. As sore ones go, the *Parc de Priceless* epic is right up there with putting a drunken ferret down the front of my trousers.

Just for the record, the USA defeated England in the semi-finals en route to winning the trophy for the fourth time out of the eight official tournaments played to date. Scotland's day will come, however ... mibees.

Snatching defeat from the jaws of victory at major tournaments notwithstanding, we're still a long way from full equality but one significant cultural/collectors' achievement is that women's tournaments now merit sticker albums of their own. I feel I must point out, however, that in the associated Panini album for Euro 2017 there was something strange and unnatural about the images of the England team players. They looked like computer-generated images, photofits with no teeth on show – call it sour grapes if you like but I think Scotland lost their opening match in Utrecht to a Stepford Wives XI!

And finally, whilst I know that men and women are different in many respects, I didn't know (until I started digging) that research by FIFA has suggested that female footballers are much more likely to suffer knee injuries because of physiological differences, such as generally wider hips which increases the leg's angle into the knee. There's a joke in there somewhere about Mark Yardley, Dean Windass, Charlie Miller and co.

HIGHBROW SCOTLAND
– MUSEUMS AND EXHIBITIONS

You can keep your Louvre, Guggenheim and Victoria and Albert – the museum most worthy of a visit is the Scottish Football Museum, which is located in the bowels of the Main (i.e. South) Stand at Hampden Park, Glasgow. More than 500,000 have visited the museum since it opened in May 2001 and in my humble opinion it is a much-underrated gem which amongst other things gives due recognition to a sport which remains hugely influential on the Scottish way of life, whether we like to admit it or not.

Whilst the museum endeavours to cover all aspects of Scottish football, the exhibits relating to international football and Hampden Park itself are my favourite treasures. Examples include some early turnstiles (no barcode machines in sight, just ornate wrought iron), part of the home dressing room from old Hampden and Harry Haddock's Arsenal-like Scotland jersey worn against Hungary in 1954, when the white sleeves were designed to help those early black and white TV viewers differentiate between the two sides. The life-size model recreation of Archie Gemmill's wonder goal at Argentina 78 also makes me smile.

Other popular exhibits include a ticket from the first international fitba match, which was played at the still in use West of Scotland Cricket Ground in Glasgow in 1872, and the Scottish FA Cup trophy which, dating from 1874, makes it the oldest existing national football trophy in the world. To give these exhibits some sort of historical perspective, they predate the founding of the Labour

Party and the Scottish National Party as well as the Battle of the Little Bighorn!

Of course, there is also action from numerous football matches to be savoured and forget about YouTube – watching SUCCESSFUL World Cup qualifying matches is much more enjoyable and atmospheric when viewed from within the confines of the National Stadium ... and no one thinks you're daft if you cheer out loud.

The museum is also an important research facility which houses an extensive archive and library and includes a great many original documents and published books relating to the game. I understand that a copy of the prequel to this book, namely *Scotland: Glory, Tears and Souvenirs*, is held on file. I just thought I would slip that one in there.

Sometimes the museum's exhibits go on tour, even if it is just to the other side of Glasgow. From 27 March to 18 August 2013 the Kelvingrove Art Gallery and Museum in Glasgow's west end hosted the somewhat self-congratulatory-sounding exhibition *More than a Game: How Scotland Shaped World Football*.

The truth is, however, that Scotland has indeed played a significant role in the growth of the game of football – from Scottish regiments in India to railway engineers and textile entrepreneurs in North and South America, the world game was significantly shaped by Scots and our short passing game of the late

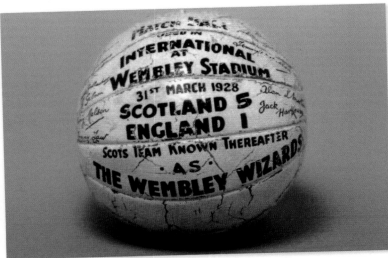

19th century, which makes it all the more galling that in recent years we seem to have lost our way completely.

The £5 entrance ticket incorporated a reproduction of the ticket from the aforementioned first ever (1872) *Scotland v. England International Foot-Ball Match*, complete with hyphen, which no doubt will cause some linguists to hyperventilate.

To accompany the exhibition there is a superb 48-page programme (priced £3.50) which has a front cover designed by the renowned football artist Paine Proffitt. A large chunk of the publication was devoted to the global pioneering work of the Scots footballers, coaches and administrators. For example, in 1893 Scottish schoolmaster Alexander Hutton became the first president of the Argentine Association Football League.

In association with the exhibition there were a number of football talks and displays taking place at various Glasgow Public Libraries, as well as football-inspired organ recitals and a couple of 'memorabilia road show' events.

The message was clear – try and forget the fact that in the 21st century, Scottish international football has been one disappointment followed by another, and instead share in, or allow yourself to wallow in, our former glories. And why not, for I expect the likes of Germany did something similar prior to 2014 when they were in the middle of their marathon 18-year wait for a major trophy!

And finally, it would be remiss not to mention that some of our clubs' museums contain excellent 'international' sections. For example, Hibernian display many interesting artefacts celebrating those footballers who have played for the Edinburgh club as well as their country, be it Scotland, the other home nations, European sides or the likes of Ecuador and Trinidad & Tobago. I also recall an occasion when an Edinburgh pub landlord was kind enough to let a few of us Weegie Thistle supporters view his highly impressive 'private museum' of Hearts and Scotland memorabilia that he had located in the attic above his hostelry. McEwan's Export plus souvenirs of the 'Terrible Trio', as well as John Robertson, Dave McPherson and Craig Levein, etc., made for an excellent day out.

I COULDA BEEN A CONTENDER
– SCOTLAND IN THE MOVIES

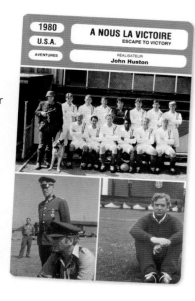

Generally speaking, the game of football tends not to translate well into the movies. That said, there are still some great 'footie films' out there where the beautiful game has been central to the plot; for example, *The Arsenal Stadium Mystery* (1939) and *Gregory's Girl* (1981). The latter cinematic tour de force did, of course, star Scots actor John Gordon Sinclair, whose vocals feature prominently on Scotland's 1982 official World Cup single 'We Have a Dream'.

Looking at the Scottish football internationalist moving pictures connection, who could forget the deliberately underplayed performance of Scotland and Ipswich Town midfielder John Wark as Private Arthur Hayes (wearing the number seven shirt) in the 1981 classic World War Two yarn *Escape to Victory*, which also starred Michael Caine, Sylvester Stallone, Bobby Moore and Pelé. Apparently, for some countries, Wark's two lines had to be dubbed for fear that his Glaswegian accent might not be understood by viewers ... and yet Sly has 'mumbled' his way through many a movie.

Incidentally, well-known German actor Anton Diffring played the chief football commentator and if you thought Arthur Montford's Scotland commentaries were a shade biased, you should listen to that from the man from Koblenz. Spoiler alert, the allied prisoner of war footballers (let's call them a World XI) manage to avoid defeat in an exhibition match against a German team, and then all escape at the end ...

Let's also not forget about that other great Scottish method actor, Ally McCoist (once of Rangers, Kilmarnock and Scotland), playing the role of ex-Celtic striker Jackie McQuillan in the 2002 blockbuster *A Shot at Glory* alongside the likes of Michael 'Batman' Keaton and Robert 'Apocalypse Now' Duvall. As Mr Duvall, who played the role of coach of fictional Highland League side Kilnockie FC, might have said, 'I love the smell of Ralgex in the morning'.

And then there was *The Damned United*, a 2009 film about Brian Clough's ill-fated, 44-day tenure as manager of Leeds United in 1974, with flashbacks to his time as manager of Derby County. As you would expect, a number of Scottish international footballers featured and at the forefront were Dave Mackay (Derby) and Billy Bremner (Leeds). Whilst in the central role of Clough, actor Michael Sheen looked and sounded the part, the portrayal of Scotland's 'dynamo duo' was unflattering and unconvincing – all aggression, sarcasm and backstabbing. They didn't even walk like footballers; indeed, they had the look and feel of a couple of renegades from Jonathan Watson's *Only an Excuse* TV comedy programme.

Despite its shortcomings and inaccuracies, the film is still fascinating to watch and concludes with the caption 'Brian Clough remains the greatest manager England never had'. I can remember a time when Clough was being touted by some as the next *Scotland* manager – 1986 it was – but ultimately the job went to Andy Roxburgh ... and quite right too!

As for movie turkeys I strongly recommend *Soccer Dog European Cup* (2004) – the plot of which is: 'In a laboratory in Scotland, a mad scientist (Dr Oddlike) conducts experiments on a dog which proves to be unusually adept at soccer. The dog subsequently escapes, then helps a lonely American kid find the father he has never known, as well as assist a struggling football team make it to the finals'. And I thought I could dream up a load of 'David Nish'!

The Scottish footballing oscar, however, goes to Cloughie and Scotland's midfield maestro Archie Gemmill, for his flawless, undistracted performance during the sex scene in the 1996 black comedy movie *Trainspotting*. Never mind the carnal antics of Ewan McGregor's character Renton, it's what wee Archie did to the Dutch in Mendoza 78 that viewers should focus upon. To quote the words of our other legendary football commentator, Archie MacPherson, 'Renton's orgasm was fictional. Mine was real'.

JEALOUSY AND SCHADENFREUDE

Jealousness of your neighbour's footballing achievements is a terrible thing. England winning the 1966 World Cup is the most obvious example. By that I mean the feelings of jealousness engendered by Bobby Moore and co is the terrible thing. I'm not saying the fact that Sir Alf Ramsey's wingless wonders won the competition was in itself a terrible thing. Then again ...

Anyway, *schadenfreude* (or cheering out loud and wetting yourself laughing when England are eliminated – sometimes unfairly – from a tournament) is something else we Scots should try and avoid, or am I getting too preachy here? Surely it is what *Scotland* does (or doesn't do) that matters. That said, there is a perverse humour in there to be savoured to varying degrees.

The names which adorn the 'legendary/infamous' Loony Alba (London Tartan Army) Scotland Players of the Year T-shirt say it all really. Here's a list of the winners, together with reminders of what they did to achieve such 'adulation'.

1986 Diego Maradona

For his two goals for Argentina against Bobby Robson's England in the Aztec Stadium in the quarter-finals of the Mexico World Cup. The first goal was 'Jordanesque' whilst the second was a real thing of beauty as the Napoli man weaved his way past five England players before slipping around Peter Shilton to score. Argentina, of course, went on to lift the trophy. At the 86 finals Scotland also lost out to South American opposition, in the shape of Uruguay. No 'Hand of God', however, just 22 (then reduced to 20) feet of Satan.

MATCH WORLD CUP WONDERS

No. 9 Diego Maradona (Argentina)

1988 Marco Van Basten

In their opening group match at the Euro finals England lost 1–0 in Stuttgart to the Republic of Ireland and, as the winning goal was scored by Glasgow-born Ray Houghton, he would have got my vote. However, in their second group match England faced the Netherlands in Dusseldorf with both sides requiring a victory to stay in the competition. A hat-trick from Marco Van Basten in a 3–1 win for the Dutch knocked the English Out! Out! Out! Sorry ... De Oranje eventually won the tournament.

1990 Stuart Pearce

The England versus West Germany World Cup semi-final in Turin finished 1–1 after extra time and duly went to penalties. The Germans won 4–3 but in fairness I think Olympic Marseille's Chris Waddle should have shared the POTY award with Nottingham Forest's Stuart Pearce, as both of them missed their penalties. Indeed, Pearce's effort at least hit the goalkeeper and not the nearby Alpine mountains. Yet again, England's conquerors went on to win the competition. Incidentally, there were four Glasgow Rangers players in England's 1990 World Cup squad.

1992 Tomas Brolin

1992 was the last Euro finals at which only eight teams competed – two of which were British. Hopes of a Scotland–England final were dashed, however, when (a) Scotland lost their opening two games against the Netherlands

and a now re-unified Germany, and (b) England lost their third group match 2–1 to tournament hosts Sweden in Solna. England led the Swedes 1–0 after four minutes but in the second half it all went horribly wrong for Graham Taylor's boys, culminating in conceding a goal to Tomas Brolin eight minutes from time. In later years Brolin went on to do some more 'damage' at Leeds United and Crystal Palace.

1993 Ronald Koeman

England failed to qualify for the 1994 World Cup finals in the USA thanks in part to the Netherlands and their skipper Ronald Koeman. (Scotland also failed to qualify, but we won't go into that ...) In England's penultimate qualifier in Rotterdam an away win was required; however, early in the second half, with the game goalless, a cynical foul by RK on David Platt 'merited' a red card and a penalty. The referee, however, said yellow card and free kick at the edge of the box. Minutes later Koeman, at the other end, netted the first goal in a 2–0 win for the Netherlands. Well, at least Jack Charlton made it to the United States – managing a Republic of Ireland side which contained Celtic keeper Packie Bonner and Motherwell striker Tommy Coyne.

1996 Gareth Southgate

England hosted the finals of Euro 96 and were many people's favourites to win the competition, particularly after they managed to defeat a classy Scotland side 2–0 at the group stage. Alas, England were eliminated at the semi-final stage by their old adversary Germany 6–5 on penalties. This time the English culprit was future England manager Gareth Southgate, whose penalty was saved by Andreas (let's call him Andrew) Kopke. Germany, managed by future Scotland coach Berti Vogts, then defeated the Czech Republic 2–1 in the final.

1998 David Batty/Paul Ince/David Beckham

At the France 98 World Cup England were eliminated at the round of 16 stage by Argentina – 4–3 on penalties after the match had finished 2–2. This time the penalty villains were Paul Ince (Liverpool) and David Batty (Newcastle United). England's hopes had been undermined early in the second half, however, when a naive/ petulant David Beckham got himself sent off (okay, so the Argentinians conned/ harassed the ref into showing a red card). Incidentally, seven days earlier, Scotland lost 3–0 to Morocco at the same Stade Geoffroy-Guichard stadium in St Etienne and have not been seen at a major finals since!

2000 Phil Neville

In their third group match, England were one minute away from a 2–2 draw with Romania in Charleroi and a place in the quarter-finals of Euro 2000. A clumsy and unnecessary challenge from Manchester United defender Phil Neville on Viorel Moldovan, however, resulted in a penalty, which Romania converted to send Kevin Keegan's England home. Incidentally, the penalty 'hero' was none other than future 'villain' Ionel Ganea, whose dreadful tackle against John Kennedy in an international friendly at Hampden in 2004 effectively ended the Celtic and Scotland defender's playing career.

2002 David Seaman

In the 2002 World Cup England reached the quarter-finals where they faced Brazil. In Shizuoka, Japan, England scored first but were pegged back on the stroke of half-time. In the 50th minute, however, Ronaldinho launched a forty-yard free kick which sailed over the head of the ponytailed Arse-nal keeper David Seaman (who was perhaps anticipating a cross) to make it 2–1 to Brazil, who went on to lift the trophy for a fifth time. At least the ponytail made Alan Rough's curly perm look good.

2004 Ricardo

England reached the quarter-finals of Euro 2004, where they came unstuck against hosts Portugal in Lisbon – in the usual manner – losing 6–5 on penalties. Although David Beckham missed the first penalty, the award went to the Portuguese goalkeeper Ricardo, firstly for saving Darius Vassell's penalty with his gloves off, and secondly for converting the winning penalty himself – beating fellow goalkeeping 'legend' David 'Calamity' James.

2006 Cristiano Ronaldo

The World Cup finals in Germany and again Luiz Felipe Scolari's Portugal stick it to Sven-Goran Eriksson's England at the quarter-final stage and on penalties. This time the Portuguese won 3–1 in Gelsenkirchen, with Cristiano Ronaldo converting the decisive penalty. Frank Lampard, Steven Gerrard and Jamie Garragher all missed for England, so you are in good company, Don Masson.

PORTUGAL
RONALDO

Known for their dazzling style of play, Portugal will be hoping to bring home the trophy after making the semi-final of the 2006 FIFA World Cup. Coach Carlos Queiroz once managed South Africa and he has a wealth of talent to call on such as Real Madrid, Hype, Chelsea's Deco and Ricardo Carvalho, and of course, Cristiano Ronaldo. Arguably the greatest player in the world, Ronaldo's skill on the ball and incredible goalscoring record will make Portugal one to watch this summer.

MILES FROM SOUTH AFRICA	5108
FINALS APPEARANCES	4
FANBASE (millions)	11
INTERNATIONAL TROPHIES	0
FIFA RANKING	5

2007 Mladen Petric

To reach the finals of Euro 2008, all Steve McClaren's England had to do was avoid defeat in their last qualifier, at home to Slaven Bilic's Croatia who had already qualified. At Wembley Stadium, Croatia led 2–0 at half-time, but second-half goals from Frank Lampard and Peter Crouch looked to have saved England's bacon. Thirteen minutes from time, however, substitute Mladen Petric netted the winner for Croatia and so England failed to reach Austria/Switzerland – Russia went in their place. A defeat from the jaws of victory performance which was positively Scotland-esque.

2010 Thomas Muller

At the World Cup finals in Bloemfontein, South Africa, England got their collective arses felt by Germany at the round of 16 stage. 4–1 it finished, with Thomas Muller netting the third and fourth goals on his way to winning the Golden Boot. Uruguayan referee Jorge Larrionda might have been a better recipient of the Scotland POTY award for somehow contriving to disallow an earlier 'equaliser' by Frank Lampard that was at least a foot over the goal line. I felt for England that day. Yes, really.

2012 Alessandro Diamanti

At the Euro Championship finals in Kiev, Roy Hodgson's England were eliminated by Italy in the quarter-finals, 4–2 on penalties. Both Ashley Young and Ashley Cole failed to convert their spot kicks, whilst Big Al (a former West Ham striker) slotted the decisive one home for the Italians.

2014 Bryan Ruiz

A bit convoluted this one, but basically, England were eliminated at the group stages of the World Cup finals in Brazil after just two matches because (a) England lost their first two matches, and (b) the consequential arithmetic of Costa Rica's surprise 1–0 victory over Italy in Recife rendered England's third match meaningless. The scorer for Costa Rica was, of course, Bryan Ruiz – an employee of Fulham FC who was on loan to PSV Eindhoven. I wonder what one-time Craven Cottage man Jimmy Hill thought about that.

2016 Kolbeinn Sigthorsson

At the round of 16 stage at the Euros in France, England came face to face with Iceland, who proved not to be minnows but Cod War Warriors. Wayne Rooney gave England the lead after only four minutes and so commentators, pundits, supporters, etc. started to think about who England could be playing in the next round. Fulham-bound Ragnar Sigurdsson equalised two minutes later, however, and then

we all got the Viking clap when 'Thor' hit the winner for Iceland in the 18th minute. As The Stranglers sometimes sing – it was so nice in Nice. Incidentally, it was a Scottish printer by the name of James Ferguson who is credited with having introduced football to Iceland in 1895. So there.

2018 Mario Mandzukic

As the World Cup finals in Russia progressed it looked increasingly likely that England could snatch the crown. However, Gareth Southgate's lucky blue waistcoat came apart at the seams at the semi-final stage thanks to an extra-time winner from Croatia's Super Mario. Incidentally, Mandzukic was also in the Croatia sides which lost both home and away to Scotland in the qualifiers for the 2014 World Cup. Just saying.

And finally, a quick mention for the A.B.E. T-shirts which have also proved popular. A.B.E.? Why, *Anyone But England*, of course. Caledonian churlishness I hear you say and you'd probably be right ... but it can still raise a titter or two.

K KITS – COOL CLASSICS v CRAP CONCOCTIONS

For many people, their favourite Dr Who(s) is/are the one(s) that they grew up with, and it has been argued that the same applies to many supporters' favourite Scotland kits. Now I 'grew up' with Patrick Troughton and Jon Pertwee in the late 1960s/early 1970s but

that doesn't mean I would have liked to have seen Scotland take to the field wearing tartan trousers, red velvet jackets and white frilly shirts. What it does mean is that my introduction to international haute couture was in the shape of the Umbro long-sleeved, dark-blue jersey with white crew neck and cuffs, as immortalised in the 3–2 victory over England at Wembley in 1967, when Scotland became unofficial world champions!

Puberty coincided with the appearance of the flamboyant white-wing collar and insert. The short-sleeved version looked super cool on Scotland's unbeaten 1974 World Cup finals squad – if only I had been allowed to wear it to the school disco. Come the 1978 World Cup finals, the blue jersey now came complete with Umbro's sexy diamond taping – West Brom's Willie Johnston: Dig it the Dancing Queen!

SANDY JARDINE (Rangers and Scotland)

In the early 1980s there were introduced attractive, red away tops which perhaps sought to mirror Liverpool FC's European Cup glory and the contributions made by super-Scots Kenny Dalglish, Graeme Souness, Alan Hansen and Steve Nicol. In 1985, however, came the white shorts with navy-blue horizontal panel, which tended to give Gordon Strachan and co the 'suspender belt' look. Not a pretty sight.

Another personal favourite of mine, however, was Umbro's rather sophisticated, dark-blue Italia 90 job. This was a landmark creation – it was the last medium-sized jersey that I fitted into – and it featured an updated crest design, an elegant shadow pinstripe and a button-down collar, plus a long placket with a hint of tartan. You can keep your Armani!

Returning to the Dr Who theme and whilst aficionados also tend to have a favourite villain, for Scotland supporters that translates as 'most hated kits'. In 1991 the away strip Daleks duly arrived in the shape of a design called 'The Hampden', which was a white jersey with purple and red paint splashed on to it – or so it looked. Caledonian Cybermen then appeared in 1994 sporting an abstract arrangement of green and purple angular geometric shapes on a white background. Holy art school atrocity, Batman.

At Euro 96 Scotland went for the 'Braveheart look' – an all-navy design featuring an SFA-commissioned green and purple tartan. Hmmm ... although to be fair, it looked good on Colin Hendry and Gary McAllister – penalty miss against England notwithstanding.

L

Sheer Magic

LUVVIE LAND
- SCOTLAND THEATRICALS

Many of the bigger club sides in the UK are big on theatricals – by that I mean they are often the subject of stage productions celebrating the history of the team and/or the exploits of their supporters. So what about productions relating to the national team? Only a couple of 'Scotland spectaculars' spring to mind – starting with *The Game*, which was written by Paul Pender and played the Glasgow Pavilion theatre in the summer of 1982.

The Game was set in a Glasgow living room against the background of the 1978 World Cup finals and was a tragicomedy in three acts (act 1: Peru, act 2: Iran and act 3: the Netherlands).

The author's notes suggest that football has become a surrogate religion for the working man, who needs the thought of the game on Saturday to get him through the rest of the week. In addition, he argues that the violence of Scots fans invading Wembley should be contrasted with the much more insidious violence of those who are transforming Scotland into Britain's nuclear dustbin. As such, *The Game* attempts to integrate politics with entertainment.

Lofty, noble ambitions or pretentious poo? You pays your money, you makes your choice. Anyway, *The Game* ran for 13 nights (which is longer than Scotland lasted at the 1978 World Cup – or **any** World Cup). Back then, a seat in the stalls at the Pavilion Theatre cost £2.50, whilst the 16-page programme, which makes for an unusual football collectable, was priced at 25 pence.

Fast-forward to 2017 when Glasgow's Webster Theatre hosted Jim Orr's black comedy play *Bend it like Baxter*, which celebrated the 50th anniversary of the football match that many Scots fans voted the greatest ever (i.e. the 1967 British Championship/ European Championships double-header versus England at Wembley).

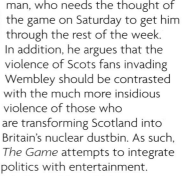

At the start of the new millennium, along came a new designer – the Italian sportswear company Fila, followed by Diadora in 2003, then Adidas in 2010, and new home, away and third strips came fast and furious. Most of the home jerseys worked for me, the exception being the 2002 effort in which the thick white pinstripe looked like something extrovert jazz singer George Melly would be more comfortable in, as opposed to the likes of Jackie McNamara or Barry Ferguson.

I was not a big fan of the away top which comprised a sky-blue saltire on a white background; however, its one redeeming feature was the fact that James McFadden was wearing it when his 40-yard wonder goal gave Scotland a 1–0 victory over France in Paris in a 2007 Euro qualifier.

In 2015, however, Adidas produced *The Master* (or should I say *Missy*) of bad jerseys – a neon pink, ClimaCool monstrosity which I'm totally convinced contributed to our 3–0 gubbing from England in a World Cup qualifier at Wembley in 2016.

As for the future, I'll take any dark-blue jersey that has the SFA crest and a Euro/ World Cup finals logo side by side.

Best team in the world, aye right! They needed to be put in their place so it's time to...

Bend it like Baxter

A play (rehearsed reading) by Jim Orr

19 November 2017
Kick Off 7:30pm
Tickets £10 (incl. Ticket admin fee)
Websters Theatre
416 Great Western Road,
Glasgow G4 9HZ

HOW TO BOOK
Online - www.webstersglasgow.com
email - boxoffice@cottiers.com
Phone - 0141-357-4000
In person - Websters Theatre Box Office

The plot revolves around the misadventures of two 1967 Wembley-bound Scotland supporters and how they get caught up with a Charlie Endell-type character, counterfeit money, strip clubs and murder. There is a happy ending, of course, as our two hapless heroes ultimately make it to the Empire Stadium to see Jim Baxter, Denis Law and co inflict on England their first defeat since becoming world champions the previous summer.

Anyway, the play, as well as being thoroughly enjoyable, also generated two collectable souvenirs in addition to the admission ticket. An A5-sized promotion flyer is dominated by a psychedelic image of the eponymous 'Slim Jim' almost being strangled by a pitch-invading Tartan Army,

many of whom wore suits, shirts and ties to the game. On the reverse side, the front cover of the match programme is reproduced and embellished with A and BC trading card images of the Scotland 11.

Then there was the A4-sized single sheet programme. It too was double-sided, with the front depicting souvenir images such as the match programme's associated community singing song sheet, newspaper headlines and match tickets. On the reverse page were iconic photographs from the match plus the unofficial football World Championships all-time table, which is topped by Scotland ahead of England, Argentina and the Netherlands.

You won't get gems like these on Broadway nor the likes of the 1982 *Official World Cup Touring Show* – a variety show which starred the likes of the singer Christian (who played in the same school team as future Scotland manager Andy Roxburgh), blues guitarist George 'Big George' Watt and Bert Coen – 'The unparalleled king of comedy mime in Scotland'. I kept the souvenir programme as it also contained photographs and pen pics of Jock Stein and his Spain 82 squad, including Willie Miller and Alan Hansen who would become an unintentional comedy double act on the Costa del Sol that summer.

Maybe Glasgow's role as a co-host of the Euro 2020 Football Championships will inspire something creative from 'Luvvieland'. Alternatively, let's look further ahead to 2023 and the 150th anniversary of the Scottish Football Association. Here's hoping that the SFA commission something 'special' to mark the occasion. There is certainly plenty of creativity in the Tartan Army for them to tap into.

M

MATCHDAY RITUALS

I'm not superstitious when it comes to supporting Scotland; for example, I don't have any lucky tartan underpants that I must wear, or a convoluted route to Hampden that I must travel – I just turn up and hope for the best. That said, there are plenty of 'ancilliary joys' to be had on home matchdays.

Fixed odds coupon

This is often uplifted purely for souvenir purposes – unless you end up doing something rash like regularly putting £10 on a Scotland player to score a hat-trick (pre-Gibraltar game). As a fussy collector, I prefer those coupons which include the flags or crests of the two competing nations. As Edvard 'The Scream' Munch would have said – symbolism is important.

Anyway, as well as being a reminder of who the squad players were at the time, it is also interesting to see what the odds were for the actual end result. Great for playing *What if ...*

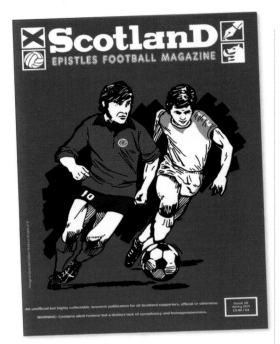

For example, what if I had put my mortgage on Scotland beating Gibraltar 6–1 at Hampden in 2015 at odds of 33/1? The answer to that is that Scotland would probably have done something stupid like score a seventh!

Pre-match refreshments

Until relatively recently (i.e. until Craig Levein seriously sickened numerous supporters and armchair fans alike), up to a dozen of us would meet in a Glasgow hostelry to debate the match we were about to attend and to discuss provisional arrangements for travelling to the finals should Scotland qualify.

Quite often this was the best part of the day – meeting up with friends to enjoy the craic, the camaraderie and the pina coladas. Other traditions include joining in the sing-songs (plus the occasional dancing on tables), checking my pocket umpteen times to make sure I've still got my match ticket and phoning the wife – sometimes from the salubrious privacy of a toilet cubicle – to tell her that I love her (but not quite in the same way that I love the Scotland football team).

Returning to the sing-songs, and whilst the Tartan Army don't do motivational team talks as such, a drunken rendition of Neil Diamond's 'Sweet Caroline' usually sends us off to the match in good cheer. Altogether now:
'Hands, touching hands
Reaching out, touching me, touching you ...'

Fanzine selling

Since 2014 we have been producing and selling the fanzine *Scotland Epistles*, and whilst it has been an educational as well as enjoyable experience, it has had an adverse effect on the pre-match refreshments ritual – as has my now sensitive bladder, but that is another story altogether.

If truth be told it's not always easy shifting fanzines in the great outdoors; indeed, it never fails to amaze/depress me that some people would rather spend their cash on heart-disease haute cuisine than on a literary masterpiece.

Actually, the competition to fanzines comes in all shapes and sizes – from nearby match programme and souvenir vendors to busking pipers, charity workers and kids (seemingly hundreds of them) collecting to raise funds for football strips and/or trips to tournaments in Blackpool. I think my worst pitch, however, was just outside Glasgow's Queen Street Station where two well-dressed Jehovah's Witnesses were attracting more interest than this half-jaiked seller of fanzines. As my wife often tells me, maybe I just have to work on my technique.

Photographs

Digital cameras are, of course, a godsend for taking snapshots at football matches. You can take as many photographs as your memory card and/or battery will allow, then delete all your 'non-requirements' later. It's not just the teams lining up and the match action which require snapping, but also the likes of pre-match singers and pyrotechnics, away supporter antics, scoreboard updates, sad-looking stewards sitting in the rain facing away from the pitch, and furry

mascots on motorcycles. The downside of all this is the consequential storage problem as I much prefer to print my photographs and insert them into albums. I now need a spare room that is Tardis-like.

Post-match refreshments

This is much more straightforward when there is an afternoon kick-off, thus ensuring plenty of drinking time available for post-mortems, playing the blame game or just having a right good greet! On the plus side, watching the match highlights on a big screen and cheering the Scotland goals as shown from various angles is also enjoyable, as well as therapeutic.

Newspaper clippings

Win, lose or draw, I try to keep a press report and/or a banner headline on how the game went. There was a time, in my alcohol-fuelled youth, when the newspaper report was essential reading purely to inform me, when I had sobered up, of what had actually happened the day previous.

At one time I also held on to a complete set of *Daily Record* newspapers covering the 1974, 1978 and 1982 World Cup finals, but they were all binned when I first got married in 1985. Wedlock can make you do silly things.

N NINETY-EIGHT REMEMBERED

1998 was, of course, the last time that Scotland appeared at the finals of a major tournament — not only was it in the previous century, it was in the previous millennium! A hell of a lot has changed since then.

Back in 98 Scotland's football comedy TV show *Only an Excuse* was actually quite humorous. In comparison, Tony Blair's 'Cool Britannia' Labour UK Government were

perhaps not so hilarious. Furthermore, a UK music chart dominated by the likes of the Spice Girls, Boyzone and Steps was no laughing matter either.

A devolved Scottish Parliament would eventually arrive in 1999 and the introduction of the Euro currency was four years away. Three-time European Footballer of the Year Michel Platini was the joint head of the FIFA World Cup Organising Committee, whilst the President of France was Jacques Chirac — or was it the other way round?

Technology-wise, we had still to reach the 'tipping point' for mass ownership of mobile phones, whilst the World Wide Web had yet to become ubiquitous. To paper-loving technophobes such as myself, it was the twilight of 'the good old days'.

Scotland (managed by Craig Brown) appeared at their eighth World Cup finals by virtue of being the best of the second-placed teams in the European qualifiers — finishing behind group winners Austria but ahead of Sweden, Latvia, Estonia and Belarus. Match-winning goals had come from the likes of John Collins (Monaco), Darren Jackson (Hibernian), John McGinlay (Bolton Wanderers), Tommy Boyd (Celtic), Kevin Gallacher (Blackburn Rovers), Gary McAllister (Coventry City), David Hopkin (Leeds United) and Gordon Durie (Rangers). Aberdeen keeper Jim Leighton chipped in with five shutouts, whilst Rangers goalie Andy Goram had three.

For the allocation of match tickets I seem to recall four of us applying to the SFA for all three games, then subsequently being advised that we had been successful for the Scotland versus Brazil game only. What a game, though, for whilst we have yet to see Scotland play in a World Cup *final* match, in 1998 we got to see our country face the defending champions in the *opening* game of the finals at the new, showpiece, 80,000-capacity Stade de France in St Denis on the northern outskirts of Paris. A global TV audience in the hundreds of millions also looked in.

The day before the Scotland–Brazil game, myself and two of my mates (Les and Steph) flew from Glasgow to Paris (Charles De Gaulle) Airport on British Midland flight number

BD2413 (I still have my paper flight ticket – priceless ephemera or just plain sad?) and then on to the Hotel de L'Exposition in the Place de la Republique (I kept their business card as well!). Not a fancy hotel but it was fit for purpose by having a roof, three single beds and an en-suite toilet that held its nerve.

Sightseeing was interspersed with refreshments ... and possibly food, although I can't be certain – I think Steph splashed out at one point and bought a large bag of crisps for us all to share. We also took part in a 30-a-side game of football in the shadow of the giant pylon (aka La Tour Eiffel, which, incidentally, was completed in 1889, the same year in which Scotland defeated England 3–2 at Kennington Oval to clinch the British (and World) Championship for the fourth time). The mass kickabout reminded me of many of the games I played at school in that I hardly got a touch of the bloody ball thanks to those big, rough boys! I sought solace in my own (small) supply of McEwan's Export – airport security was much more understanding in those days.

Zoe, a former work colleague now living in Paris, was our much-appreciated guide for the evening and she got us to the Auld Alliance pub (the unofficial HQ of the Tartan Army) in the fourth arrondissement just after an unsavoury, headline-making incident involving a well-known English Premiership footballer and an equally well-known Swedish television presenter. Let's just say the relationship between Stan and *Ollie* was a much more positive one than that of Stan and Ullie.

Wednesday, 10 June duly arrived and after meeting up with two friends (Keith and Richie), who now lived in exile in the south of England, we headed to the second most visited monument in Paris, the Sacre Coeur Basilica, for a touristy photoshoot and to

Brazil v Scotland, Paris, 10 June 1998

offer up some silent prayers for the boys in dark blue. Sacred Hearts, Bravehearts and broken hearts would sum up our day. Keith would be particularly disappointed as he remained ticketless and would watch the match on a giant screen within the official fanzone adjacent to the stadium, with only scantily-clad, attractive-looking female Brazil supporters helping him to keep a stiff upper lip.

We pub-crawled it from the Montmartre to the stadium – no ludicrous matchday alcohol ban like there was at Italia 90 – and made it through some decidedly dodgy territory to the lung-bursting middle tier in time to 'savour' an opening ceremony that screamed *pretentieux!* The Stade de France was transformed into a magical garden whereby fantastic and colourful 'insects' performed around and above giant buds that bloomed to reveal flowers that concealed giant footballs within their petals – or so the internet says. I was there and I couldn't understand any of it – being half-cut probably inhibited my existentialism or something like that. My personal pre-match highlight, however, was hearing that electronic masterpiece of a World Cup song, *Carnaval de Paris* by Dario G, which to this day still has the

Norway v Scotland, Bordeaux, 16 June 1998

ability to make the (now white) hairs on the back of my neck stand on end.

Whilst some of Scotland's qualifying matches seemed to last for an eternity, the Brazil match flew by. Cesar Sampaio headed the defending champions into the lead after only four minutes and we all braced ourselves for a damn good thrashing ... but it didn't happen. Somehow Scotland, skippered by Colin Hendry, held out, played their way back into the game, won a penalty and equalised in the 38th minute. John Collins was the super-cool dude who brought us level.

Rivaldo, Bebeto and the original Ronaldo were at their scary best but ultimately Scotland were undone when in the 73rd minute Jim Leighton blocked Cafu's shot but the rebound struck Tom Boyd and dribbled over the line. So two Scotsmen scored that day but it finished 2–1 to Brazil. As we departed the stadium a downpour of biblical proportions came upon us – I suspect that God was angry, frustrated and disappointed as well.

With work commitments adding to my logistical problems, the solution for travelling to Bordeaux on Tuesday, 16 June proved to be my first ever overseas football day trip. It was an expensive and at times surreal experience. My Scotland Travel Club criteria were only enough to get me a ticket for the opening match, but I got totally carried away with the whole occasion and so handed over £120 to an *English* Sports Travel company for a charter flight on Sabre Airlines, plus another £120 for a ticket for a seat behind the south goal for the game against Norway. The cover price on the ticket actually said 250 French francs (about £25), but what the hell – shelling out £70 a time for Neil Diamond tickets over a decade later was arguably a much more reckless thing to do.

The trip got a bit weird when I was 'befriended' in the, ahem, gents toilet at Glasgow airport by another lone-travelling supporter. Yes, I know how that sounds but he was just looking for someone to 'pal about' with in Bordeaux. Needless to say, since that day, he's never phoned, he's never written ...

We met up with the rest of the troops and then encamped in a café bar in a picturesque tree-lined square called *La Place de Victoire*, where we sat back and enjoyed/partook in the unfolding cabaret that was the Tartan Army meets Viking Valhalla, as we sang and danced,

BRAVE HEARTS

Daily Record

FRANCE '98

and blethered and bladdered the morning and afternoon away. The explosion of colours and the skirl of the bagpipes, the banter and the camaraderie, the array of cold meats and the wide selection of cheeses – it was all there that magical sunny afternoon in June.

And so to the footie and a Mardi Gras of a march to the Parc de Lescure – an oval-shaped, reinforced concrete masterpiece, which successfully fused neo-classicism with contemporary art deco. It was a stadium which had also hosted matches at the 1938 FIFA World Cup, as well as the 2007 Rugby World Cup. I was in *groundhopper* heaven. Add 30,236 colourful, noisy but friendly Scottish, Norwegian and French fans and it became *football* heaven, with another 5.30pm kick-off.

The first half ended goalless, however, but no matter, for the vino had made me somewhat laid back and so I was quite happy to wait. Indeed, I only had to wait for one minute after the restart to witness the opening goal. Unfortunately it was Norway who scored it when with the Scots defence napping (and my mates Richie and Keith still in a queue at the gents) the unmarked Havard Flo headed the ball past Jim Leighton – who incidentally was winning his 88th cap that day. It was a sucker-punch but we got up off of the canvas immediately and fought hard for an equaliser. It came 20 minutes later when a long ball from Davie Weir to the toothless terror that was Craig Burley resulted in the midfielder lofting the ball over the Norwegian goalie Frode Grodaas and into the net. Deep joy or as legendary commentator Archie MacPherson was wont to say, *absolute bedlam!*

Scotland, in their unfamiliar yellow jerseys, pushed hard for a winner and not for the first time I wished that our squad included Rangers's deadly striker and all-round jammy beggar Ally McCoist, who instead was

starring alongside 'Dishy' Desmond Lynam as part of the BBC TV World Cup team. The match ended all square, however, with both teams going into the final group game with everything to play for. On reflection, Scotland were the better, more attacking side and as such deserved to win, but hey-ho, Cliff Richard also deserved to win the Eurovision Song Contest and that didn't happen either!

Unfortunately I had time for only *one* post-match refreshment before heading to the airport where some of my fellow passengers were kind enough to provide entertainment by showing off their football skills via a five-a-side 'exhibition match' in the departure lounge.

I decided against travelling to France for the make or break game against Morocco on Tuesday, 23 June – I was holding back my cash for our second round match – probably against Italy or Chile. I also decided against splashing out £7.50 for a 'day ticket' at the Tartan Special Tent on Glasgow Green (which came complete with 'Big Vern 'n' the Shootahs') and opted instead for the Auctioneers pub near George Square, where they also had that 'new invention' – a big screen!

Big screen, big hopes, big let-down. In St Etienne's Stade Geoffroy-Guichard, 35,500 witnessed Scotland getting their collective arses felt by Morocco. It finished 3–0 to the north Africans, with a now peroxide-blonde Craig Burley getting his marching orders in the 53rd minute.

Even if Scotland had won the match, progress would have been beyond us thanks to Norway's coupon-busting 2–1 victory over Brazil in Marseille. Ach, not to worry, though. An exciting new millennium was just around the corner and in four years' time the Tartan Army would almost certainly be heading to the Far East for a World Cup finals in Japan and South Korea. Five Doctor Whos, four Prime Ministers and two Popes later …

OCEANIAN OPPONENTS

The Oceania Football Confederation (OFC) was formed in 1966 and the top dog (or dingo) tended to be Australia, until they did a runner to the Asian Football Confederation in 2006. To date, Scotland have only faced Australia and New Zealand at Association Football – we have still to match our rugby union counterparts and 'test' ourselves against the likes of Fiji, Samoa and Tonga.

In 1967 Scotland embarked on a world tour which included three victories against Australia in Sydney (1–0), Adelaide (2–1) and Melbourne (2–0), with Alex Ferguson (then of Dunfermline Athletic) netting all the goals in the first and third matches. Unfortunately the SFA deemed that all the matches played on the tour did not merit full international recognition. The seven official matches to date are:

Year	Opponent	Competition	Venue	Result	Attendance
1982	New Zealand	WC finals	Estadio La Rosaleda, Malaga	5-2	20,000
1985	Australia	WC play-off	Hampden Park, Glasgow	2-0	61,920
1985	Australia	WC play-off	Olympic Park, Melbourne	0-0	32,000
1996	Australia	Friendly	Hampden Park, Glasgow	1-0	20,608
2000	Australia	Friendly	Hampden Park, Glasgow	0-2	30,985
2003	New Zealand	Friendly	Tynecastle Stadium, Edinburgh	1-1	10,016
2012	Australia	Friendly	Easter Road Stadium, Edinburgh	3-1	11,110

Jock Stein's Scotland's 5–2 victory over New Zealand at Spain 82 represents our biggest World Cup finals win in 23 matches across eight tournaments. Celtic's Danny McGrain captained Scotland that evening for the tenth and last time, whilst Aston Villa defender Allan Evans won his fourth and final cap.

Under the caretaker management of Alex Ferguson, Graeme Souness (Sampdoria) won his 50th cap skippering Scotland against Australia in the World Cup play-off second leg in Melbourne in December 1985. Two weeks earlier Frank McAvennie (West Ham United) made his Scotland debut in the first leg at Hampden and scored the second goal in a 2–0 win for his country.

Ally McCoist won his 50th cap, captained his country and scored the only goal of the game against Australia in a friendly at Hampden in 1996. Celtic defender Brian O'Neil (who played in the 1989 World Youth Final at Hampden against Saudi Arabia) made his full debut that same evening. Craig Brown was the Scotland manager at the time.

Scotland's sole reverse against Antipodean opposition came about in a friendly against Australia at Hampden in 2000 – so we were undefeated in all of the previous millennium! That particular evening, manager Craig Brown gave a debut cap to Leeds United midfielder Dominic Matteo, who had previously won under-21 and B caps with England. Winning his second and final cap for Scotland was Celtic keeper Jonathan Gould, who would later undertake coaching roles in both Australia and New Zealand.

The game against New Zealand at Tynecastle in May 2003 (attendance: 10,016) was another one of Berti Vogts's infamous friendlies, which also served as a preparatory match for New Zealand who were on their way to the Confederations Cup competition in France where they would lose all three games and concede 11 goals in the process.

Towards the end of Scotland's 3–1 win against Australia at Easter Road in 2012, manager Craig Levein brought on midfielder and former Jambo Ian Black, who was then plying his trade with Rangers – a fourth-tier outfit due to 'financial mismanagement, etc.'. However, it had been previously suggested that Rangers's demotion to the Scottish Third Division would adversely affect the international career of Black's clubmate Lee Wallace. The point is Black was booed on to the pitch by a significant proportion of the crowd of 11,110 and never played for Scotland again. It was not a good

Scotland v New Zealand, Tynecastle Stadium, 27 May 2003

evening for the reputation of Mr Levein or the Tartan Army.

Since the commencement of Scotland's post-1998 wilderness years, Australia have appeared at four consecutive World Cup finals (2006–2018). New Zealand appeared at South Africa 2010 and were eliminated at the group stage – undefeated – after draws with Slovakia, Italy and Paraguay. Scotland (and England) both look as though we are light years away from appearing at a Confederations Cup competition, and yet in 2013 Tahiti managed to. It's all rather galling, isn't it?

PHILATELY GETS YOU EVERYWHERE

PIt's the UK's Royal Mail which determines what images will appear on our postage stamps, and unfortunately they seem to get more excited at the likes of birds, cats, wild flowers and lighthouses than they do with the game of football.

Our nearest and dearest neighbours, England, have staged two major international football championships (in 1966 and 1996) and in both cases the philatelic end result was pretty uninspiring. Against a backdrop of the swinging sixties we got three rather nondescript stamps featuring drawings of some rather nondescript footballers, all in somewhat contrived action scenes, whilst the first-day cover included images of an old-style brown leather football and the (now melted down?) Jules Rimet trophy. By way of 'celebration' the words 'England Winners' were overprinted on the stamps post-30 July. It would appear that back then at least, they didn't want to go overboard.

For Euro 96, again 15 other nations came to the party, so the Royal Mail in their wisdom produced a series of five stamps depicting now deceased British football greats, such as Bobby Moore and Danny Blanchflower. Insular or what? More appropriate productions came from Guernsey and Gibraltar, whose stamps featured matches from previous tournaments, as well as flags and jerseys of the competing nations – which, of course, included Craig Brown's Scotland.

In 1978, however, and just in case Scotland became world champions, two special celebratory stamps (9 pence and 11 pence)

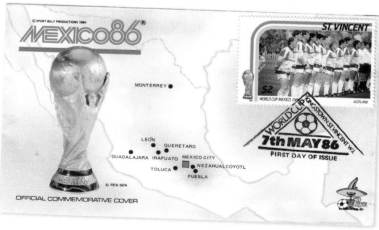

OLLOW THE **CAMPUS**
TARTAN ARMY

POST MATCH PARTY
HOSTED BY TAM COYLE - OFFICIAL TARTAN ARMY DJ

SCOTLAND v SLOVENIA
SUNDAY 26TH MARCH - KO 7.45PM

SCOTLAND v ENGLAND
SATURDAY 10TH JUNE - KO 5.00PM

MATCHES SHOWN LIVE ON THE CAMPUS BIG SCREEN

PINT FOSTERS PLUS CHEESE BURGER & CHIPS	2PT STEIN OF FOSTERS & A PIZZA	8 PINT CARLSB... BEER TOWER AND ANY SHARING PLATTER
ONLY £6	**ONLY £8**	**ONLY £32**

BOOK A BOOTH ON 0141 332 5388

SVEZIA '92
★ PLAY SAFE ★

Danimarca Inghilterra Svezia Germania
168 Francia Olanda ?

VÄSTERÅS

NING
LIN
RY

 nce to relive the Scotl

national team from

through to the

Worl

ut the Walkman with

otally awesome mi

n the Mark & Lard S

nderwall, Parklife,

r Life and Devils Ha

and put on your J

Pollo

DENIS LAW
Manchester United

Placed on the transfer list by United at the end of 1969-70, but no offers came and Denis trained throughout the summer to prove United were wrong. He was re-signed and finished last season with 15 League goals, only 3 behind top scorer Best. Began with Huddersfield and cost Manchester City £53,000 in March 1960, moved to Torino (Italy) for £100,000 in June, 1961 but returned to England in July, 1962 to sign for Manchester United for £115,000. Since then he has won two League title medals and an F.A. Cup winners medal. Denis has been capped 43 times by Scotland and is the top post-war scorer with 28 goals. He is also the leading F.A. Cup scorer (41) in post-war football.

BILLY LIDDELL
Liverpool

Only the war stopped Billy s up new appearance records. Busby tipped off Liverpool an signed him as a professional in 1939. A winger who was very with a terrific shot, he wo first cap for Scotland in April, He was 23 when League s resumed after the war and w League Championship medal i first peace-time season (1948 followed by a F.A. Cup runner medal v Arsenal in 1950. Playe 28 Scotland matches and score goals, and apart from Stan M thews, was the only player to in two Great Britain sides aga the Rest of Europe, in 1947 1955. Played in 492 League matc for Liverpool (216 goals).

ARCHIE MACAULAY
Arsenal

It was a pity World War Two cut into Archie Macaulay's career. If it had not been for the war he would have won many more caps for Scotland than the seven heended his playing days with. Archie played his first League game for Rangers in 1935 and it caused a surprise when they allowed him to join West Ham in 1937 for £6,000. Following the war, he signed for Brentford (£7,500) and although

DAVE MACKAY
Derby County

Starts the coming season wi Swindon Town, and like ole m river, Dave keeps rolling alon Now one of the all-time greats an still doing a grand job in his role sweeper. Has played over 50 League matches in a career whic has taken in Hearts, Spurs, Derb and now Swindon. Since signin professional with Hearts on his 17t birthday in November, 1952, he ha collected an amazing haul o medals: with Hearts – Scottish League Championship, Scottish Cup Winners and Scottish League Cup Winners : with Spurs – Football League Championship, three F.A. Cup winners medals and European Cup Winners Cup Winners medal: with Derby – Second Division Championship medal and skippered Derby to the Watney Cup victory. Capped as a Schoolboy, Under-23 plus 22 full caps. Footballer of the Year 1969.

Scotland 1   W. Germany 2
8th June 1986

promotion from the Second Division in 1963. Last season he recovered in turn from groin injuries, ligament trouble and an ankle injury, to win back his place.

LAURIE REILLY
Hibernians

Laurie Reilly only played for one club – Hibernians, but he is also remembered as the most capped centre-forward and had the honour of playing for Scotland no less than 38 times, in those games he scored 22 goals. He had joined Hibs as a youth of 16 in 1943 and played in the first post-war season of 1946-47. He was forced to retire from football in 1958 at the age of 29 owing to cartilage trouble. When he retired he had scored 185 League goals in only 253 matches for the famous Edinburgh club – including 50 in one season. He won two Scottish League championship medals and a Scottish League Cup runners-up medal.

SCOTLAND IRELAND'08

were designed a month prior to the Argentina finals commencing in June. Seriously. Sadly, the stamps were not required to be produced but the draft images, which are retained by the Postal Museum in central London, are things of real beauty which serve as a reminder that it wasn't just north of the border that got a bit carried away by it all.

Just to rub salt into Britain's postal wounds, a number of other (lesser footballing) nations would appear to commemorate the World Cup and Euro Championship finals on a more regular and much more attractive basis than we do. A couple of colourful examples include St Vincent and the Grenadines (a territory in the Caribbean Sea), who produced an excellent set of stamps and first-day covers for Mexico 86 (with the Scotland line-up stamp looking particularly attractive), and Tuvalu (which consists of nine coral atolls in the South Pacific Ocean) but who produced a classic four dollar stamp featuring Kenny Dalglish in a Mexico 86 qualifier.

In 2013 the Royal Mail did, however, issue a set of 11 stamps under the heading 'Football Heroes' which featured famous, stylish and extremely talented British footballers in order to commemorate the 150th anniversary of the establishing of the rules of Association Football. The issue also celebrates the 150th anniversary of the (English) Football Association (i.e. the first such association in the world), as well as the 140th anniversary of the Scottish Football Association (i.e. the second one).

The stamps, which were illustrated by artist and musician Andrew Kinsman, show the stars in their country's home strip and the end result is an attractive composite piece of work, so that when the 11 stamps are placed together they form a traditional team shot.

Seven Englishmen are depicted – Gordon Banks, Bobby Moore, Bryan Robson, John Barnes, Kevin Keegan, Bobby Charlton and Jimmy Greaves. However, there are also two Scots – Denis Law and Dave Mackay – plus Welshman John Charles and Northern Ireland's George Best.

A presentation pack cost £7.10, whilst a set of 12 postcards (11 players plus one team photo) was priced at £5.40. The presentation pack of mint first-class stamps includes biographical notes and statistics for each player, as well as images of associated big match programmes, ticket stubs, pin badges, stickers and trading cards. Collector heaven!

Questions remain, however, like why so many players with a Manchester United connection, and who chose Dave Mackay ahead of Billy Bremner ... or Martin Buchan or Graeme Souness?

Also in 2013, Scottish (and Liverpool) footballing legend Bill Shankly (five full and seven wartime caps) made it into a set of ten stamps depicting 'Great Britons', which also included the actor Peter Cushing and former UK Prime Minister David Lloyd George.

Similarly, in 2009 another genuine Scottish (and Manchester United) legend, Matt Busby (one full and seven wartime caps, plus manager briefly in 1958), was one in a set of ten 'Eminent Britons', with the likes of tennis player Fred Perry and writer Arthur Conan Doyle for company.

With both Scotland and England involved in co-hosting Euro 2020 the opportunity is there for the Royal Mail to redeem themselves tournament-wise, both in the run-up to the finals and afterwards when the Henri Delaunay trophy is sitting proudly in the (newly built) trophy room at Hampden Park. I wonder if my old stamp hinges are leaking hallucinatory chemicals ...

Costa Rica 1 Scotland 0
11th June 1990

POSTCARDS BEYOND THE EDGE

It has been suggested that postage stamps are the undisputed aristocrats of the collecting world and as such postcards by comparison are looked down upon and considered something of a flibbertigibbet pastime. 'Male bovine waste!' I would reply.

Bigger than stickers and trading cards but smaller than posters and leaflets – size matters when you are a compulsive collector with spatial problems. This links me to a confession – the favourite postcards in my collections are the totally non-pc, British saucy seaside postcards with well-dodgy captions (e.g. attractive female swimmer to lecherous male lifeguard: 'Ooh, will I really sink if you take your finger out, Mr Horniman?'). I also get a buzz, however, from postcards relating to international football and if Scotland are also involved then I just lose it altogether...

The UK-based Football Postcards Collectors Club (FPCC, founded in 1990) have produced a number of their own modern soccer creations, as do the likes of that esteemed football fanzine *Scotland Epistles*.

FPCC examples, by artist Stuart Avery, included specials for Euro 92, Euro 96 and France 98, with the latter comprising of rather debonair drawings of England manager Glenn Hoddle and Scotland coach/conjuror Craig Brown. Messrs Vogts, Smith, McLeish, Burley, Levein and Strachan were not similarly immortalised, but we won't go into that.

By comparison, the *Scotland Epistles* graphics guru Craig Hidell Scott has concentrated on producing his take on iconic Scotland match images, such as Wembley 67 (jubilant supporter invades pitch to give Denis Law a celebratory hug/choke), Mendoza 78 (Archie Gemmill's clenched-fist salute after he nets 'that third goal' versus the Netherlands at the World Cup finals) and Paris 07 (James McFadden celebrating his wonder goal as Scotland beat France 1–0 in a Euro qualifier).

Postcards of official tournament logos, mascots and associated match venues from those competitions which Scotland actually qualified for make for great mementoes as well. A Euro 92 postcard featuring the stadia at Stockholm, Gothenburg, Malmo and Norrkoping, with an overlay of the giant rabbit mascot, is a reminder that once upon a time Scotland reached the last eight of a major event.

It goes without saying, but postcards depicting team line-ups and match action also make for excellent collectables and a particular favourite of mine is the Scotland 2006 Kirin Cup Winners ensemble. Meanwhile, available on eBay are a whole plethora of match action postcards from the 1980s/1990s World Cup and Euro Championship finals group games, including one in which Mo Johnston looks set to score against Costa Rica at Italia 90 – if only.

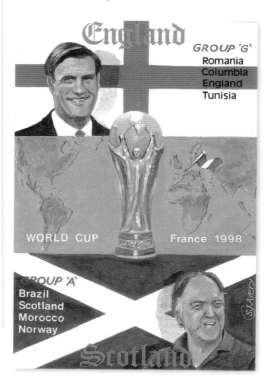

England   GROUP 'G'
Romania
Columbia
England
Tunisia

WORLD CUP   France 1998

GROUP 'A'
Brazil
Scotland
Morocco
Norway

Scotland

Mendoza '78

And finally, a quick mention for the postcards of award-winning photographer Stuart Clarke, whose *Homes of Football* series (and others) captures beautifully the passion of the game, the time and mood, both on the pitch and off it. Offbeat examples of his forays into Scottish football include the face-painting of Scotland supporters outside Villa Park, Birmingham, at Euro 96 (entitled 'And he liked what he saw') and another headed 'Allegiance to the Wall', highlighting the improvised male toilet facilities at Hampden Park in 1994! You don't get gems like these on postage stamps.

QUICK TO DISPOSE OF
— FOOTBALL EPHEMERA

Ephemera can be described as being collectable items, often made using paper or card, which were originally expected to have only short-term usefulness or popularity. Applied to football collectables, the most obvious examples are likely to be match ticket stubs. That said, many would argue that these items are now mainstream collectables, along with programmes, trading cards and stickers.

Examples of the kind of disposable tosh that I tend to hold on to include advertising and publicity material, match ticket application forms (from those halcyon pre-online days), fixed-odds coupons, menus, merchandise labels/tags (e.g. TOFFS replica retro-football jerseys), trading cards and sticker wrappers, newspaper cuttings (including a petition calling for the Scotland manager Berti Vogts to be sacked), money-off vouchers for (unwanted) football merchandise, football museum till receipts and poly bags (with football logos, of course). Okay, so I'm a seriously sad hoarder but that doesn't make me a *bad* person! And anyway, if you think I'm daft apparently there are people out there who collect ephemera such as car tax discs, luggage labels and foot and mouth disease warning notices!

Some posters and flyers worthy of a special mention include those large-sized (100cm by 65cm) adverts by the then main sponsor Safeway for match tickets for Scotland

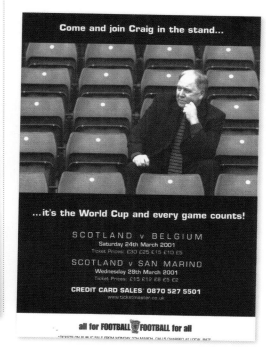

Denis Law

©mirrorpix

FIFA WORLD CUP 2006 QUALIFYING MATCH

VIP HOSPITALITY AT HAMPDEN

SCOTLAND V NORWAY
SATURDAY 9TH OCTOBER
KICK-OFF 3.00 PM

VIP PACKAGE
CHAMPAGNE RECEPTION
COMPLIMENTARY PRE MATCH BAR
SUPERIOR FOUR COURSE MEAL WITH WINE AND LIQUEURS
VIP ITINERARY WALLET
HALF TIME REFRESHMENTS
VIP SEATING IN THE BT SCOTLAND STAND
COMPLIMENTARY POST MATCH BAR FOR 1 HOUR
OFFICIAL TEAMSHEET AND SOUVENIR PROGRAMME
CORPORATE GIFT
OFFICIAL HAMPDEN CAR PARK PASS*
*One pass per four guests for the car park in front of the Stadium

£195 +VAT per person

Bookings can be made by returning the booking form overleaf or by calling... **0141 620 4040**

Hampden
SCOTLAND'S NATIONAL STADIUM
Hampden Hospitality - The **BIG** Match Experience

internationals. My own personal favourite was that for the 2004 Euro play-off match against the Netherlands, even though I had to rescue it from a skip and it smelled of sour milk and had decaying pizza as unwanted attachments.

I'm also partial to A4-sized glossy adverts for VIP corporate hospitality at Hampden Park for international matches. They serve as historical reminders that for the early part of the 21st century, around £200 would get you a VIP itinerary wallet, a champagne reception, a complimentary bar, a four-course meal with wine and liqueurs, a corporate gift, an official teamsheet and souvenir programme *and* VIP seating in the main stand. Stop it, you're spoiling us.

A couple of 'ironic' flyers are particularly appealing. One was issued in early 2001 by the SFA (not usually noted for its sense of humour) which invited supporters to 'Come and join Craig in the stand ...'

As worn by Archie Gemmill

at forthcoming Scotland World Cup qualifying matches against Belgium and San Marino. The joke being, of course, that Scotland manager Craig Brown was serving a touchline ban following an 'outburst' versus Croatia earlier in the campaign.

Then there was the upmarket, Glasgow city centre bar which invited you to their official Scotland versus Italy after-match party on 3 September 2005. An attractive, colourful souvenir in its own right, but seeing as Scotland could only manage a draw and so were all but eliminated from the 2006 World Cup, not many of us felt like partying that evening.

And finally, there was the flyer advertising the new SFA tartan kilt *featuring* two rather attractive-looking female models in mini-kilts and iconic retro Scotland away jerseys, but *starring* Archie Gemmill in an Argentina 78 shirt. A win-win – collectable and no mistake!

R RUGBY FOOTBALL

I don't have the precise figures, however, I strongly suspect that it is a relatively small number of the Tartan Army who swing both ways – by that I mean support Scotland at rugby union football as well as at association football. It will be an even smaller number of us who occasionally seek salvation supporting Scotland in other team sports such as bowls, curling or cricket!

Association football (i.e. fitba) remains the number one sport in Scotland but we can still look enviously at and maybe even learn from our 'middle-class rivals'. Scotland have appeared at the finals of ALL eight rugby union World Cups to date (Japan 2019 will

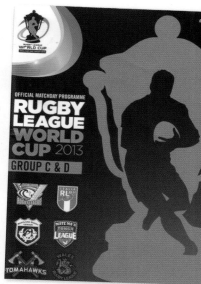

make it nine in a row) – and we reached the semi-finals in 1991. Only once have Scotland had to endure the indignity of negotiating our way through a qualifying campaign – rankings/previous tournament performances usually enabling us to remain within an 'elite' who don't have to bother with such tedious things – unlike 'non-rugby powers' such as Brazil and Germany. Tee-hee! A personal highlight from the 1999 World Cup finals was seeing Spain thrashed 48–0 at Murrayfield Stadium, Edinburgh. Tee-hee again.

In 1999 Scotland won the last ever Five Nations Championship (in effect, the European Championship). The introduction of Italy from 2000 onwards has, however, allowed for semi-regular follow-up successes to the John Greig-inspired victory over the Azzurri in 1965.

Scottish stadia (including Hampden Park on one occasion) have hosted matches at three separate World Cup finals (1991, 1999 and 2007). Furthermore, with Murrayfield Stadium's capacity of around 68,000 being about 16,000 higher than that of Hampden Park, rugby union internationals now

regularly attract larger crowds than their fitba equivalent. Galling, isn't it?

In the 2000 rugby *league* finals, the Scotland team (yes, we do have one) played two of their group matches at Firhill Stadium, Glasgow, and Tynecastle Stadium, Edinburgh – and lost to Aotearoa Maori and Samoa respectively. In 2014 Ibrox Stadium, Glasgow, hosted the Commonwealth Games rugby union sevens competition, with Scotland exiting at the quarter-final stage to South Africa, who went on to win the gold medal.

All those splendid achievements aside, there are a number of things about rugby which tend to hack off those of us who prefer the round ball game, namely:

(1) Rugby union is too feckin expensive – international match tickets and match programmes are significantly dearer than those of association football. Rugby is an inferior sport to fitba, so why pay more to watch it? Would you pay over £100 to see a Bette Midler concert when you can enjoy an Eddi Reader gig for a fraction of that cost?

(2) 'Thirsty Scottish football supporters'

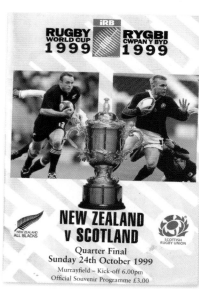

– are we the only minority group that Government legislation actively discriminates against? Either we are *all* allowed to purchase alcohol at sports stadia or none of us are. In advocating the former, however, I don't want rugby's overpriced booze or their £1 deposit on a plastic tumbler gimmick. Play fair ya shower of exploitative, money-grabbing capitalists!

(3) The custom/instruction to remain silent when opposition players are taking penalties or making attempts

Scotland v England, Murrayfield Stadium, 24 February 2018

at conversions. In the name of the wee man, if a professional rugby player can't cope with some boos and whistles then these 'sensitive, wee, lamby pies' seriously need to toughen up a bit. A season in Scottish junior football should do the trick.

(4) The 'bool-in-the-mooth' accents and the snobbery. Murrayfield badly needs a stand dedicated to the memory of Keir Hardie or Karl Marx, or even Groucho Marx. However, as the American comedy genius would perhaps have said, 'I refuse to join any club that would have me as a member'.

SOUTH AMERICAN OPPONENTS

Founded in 1916, the South American Football Confederation (CONMEBOL) is the oldest continental confederation in the world, and also the smallest, with only ten members – three of which have been crowned world champions: Brazil (five times) and Argentina and Uruguay (twice each).

Scotland have faced eight of the ten, the two exceptions being Bolivia and Venezuela. That said we have only travelled to Argentina, Brazil, Chile and Peru. Our overseas matches against Colombia were played in the USA;

against Ecuador it was in Toyama, Japan; against Paraguay it was in Norrkoping, Sweden; and against Uruguay it was in Basle, Switzerland and Nezahualcoyotl, Mexico.

Our record against the South Americans reads:

Opponent	Played	Won	Drew	Lost	Goals For	Goals Against	%
Argentina	4	1	1	2	3	5	38
Brazil	10	0	2	8	3	16	10
Chile	2	2	0	0	6	2	100
Colombia	3	0	2	1	2	3	33
Ecuador	1	1	0	0	2	1	100
Paraguay	1	0	0	1	2	3	0
Peru	4	1	1	2	4	6	38
Uruguay	4	1	1	2	4	10	38
TOTAL	**29**	**6**	**7**	**16**	**26**	**46**	**33**

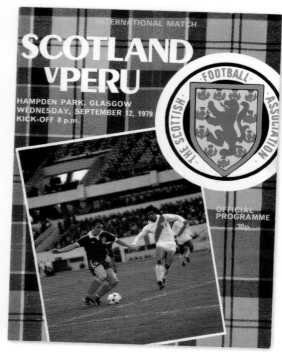

Scotland first faced South American opposition at the finals of the 1954 World Cup when we lost 7–0 to Uruguay in the St Jakob Stadium, Basle, and according to our 'wing-half eyewitness' Tommy Docherty, we were lucky to get the 'nil'.

Scotland have also lost in the World Cup finals to Paraguay (3–2 in 1958), Brazil (4–1 in 1982, 1–0 in 1990 and 2–1 in 1998) and Peru (3–1 in 1978). We managed draws at the finals in 1974 (0–0 with Brazil) and 1986 (0–0 with Uruguay).

Our first South American visitors to Hampden were Uruguay in 1962. Our guests won an ill-tempered 'friendly' match 3–2 in front of a crowd of 67,181. The Rangers duo of Jim Baxter and Ralph Brand got the Scotland goals.

Scotland's sole victory on South American soil was the infamous 4–2 win over Chile in 1977 played at the Estadio Nacional, Santiago, which had been used as a prison camp

and torture facility by the military regime following a *coup d'etat* in 1973. The Scotland scorers were Kenny Dalglish (Celtic), Asa Hartford (Manchester City) and a brace from Lou Macari (Manchester United).

The short-lived Rous Cup competition ensured South American visitors to Hampden Park in 1987 (Brazil: lost 2–0), 1988 (Colombia: drew 0–0) and 1989 (Chile: won 2–0 in front of a crowd of only 9,006 — it wasn't a boycott, it was just that a lot of supporters 'couldn't be arsed').

When Scotland defeated Argentina 1–0 (Stewart McKimmie) in March 1990 the South Americans were the reigning world champions. Maradona didn't appear at Hampden Park on that occasion; however, the line-up included Claudio Caniggia, who would later play for both Dundee and Rangers. Scotland manager Andy Roxburgh, meanwhile, gave debut caps to Craig Levein (Hearts), Stuart McCall (Everton) and Robert Fleck (Norwich City) that fine spring day.

In ten matches against the Brazilians, the Scots have managed to score on only three occasions: 1966 (Stevie Chalmers in the first minute in a friendly 1–1 draw at Hampden Park), 1982 (David Narey in a 4–1 World Cup finals defeat in Seville's Estadio Benito Villamarin) and 1998 (a John Collins penalty equaliser in the opening match of the World

Brazil v Scotland, Emirates Stadium, London, 27 March 2011

Cup finals at the Stade de France, Paris). Own goals, however, from Derek Johnstone (1973) and Tom Boyd (1998) have given the South Americans two undeserved victories in my humble, unbiased opinion.

When Craig Brown's Scotland lost 1–0 to Colombia in Miami in May 1996 and then drew 2–2 with the South Americans in New Jersey in May 1998, the games were in preparation for our appearance at the finals of Euro 96 (England) and France 98 respectively. No, I don't understand it either.

When Peru competed at Russia 2018 it was their first appearance at the World Cup finals in 36 years – so there's hope for Scotland yet.

TRAVEL AND TRANSPORT

My earliest Scotland football transport memories are of the trains, coaches and Ford Transit vans (complete with improvised toilet facilities/sleeping accommodation) which headed to London for the biennial Wembley weekends in the 1960s and 70s.

Back then, travel abroad for a football match was a luxury item. Indeed, the day after Scotland defeated Czechoslovakia in September 1973 to qualify for our first World Cup finals in 16 years, there appeared in the *Daily Record* newspaper an advert by Thistle Finance of Edinburgh offering loans (to those who owned their own house or were paying a mortgage) of £300 upwards to help get the troops to West Germany in the summer of 1974. The day after Zaire were put to the sword in our opening game at those finals, an advert by Cross Travel, Tollcross Road, Glasgow, offered a two-day trip to Frankfurt for the game against Brazil for £50, with a seven-day trip covering both the Brazil and Yugoslavia games starting at £115. Match tickets were guaranteed but extra.

As far as I can ascertain, however, the first advert to appear in a Scotland programme for supporters' travel arrangements

SCOTTISH FOOTBALL ASSOCIATION
INTERNATIONAL MATCH
SCOTLAND v. ARGENTINA
HAMPDEN PARK, GLASGOW
WEDNESDAY 28th MARCH, 1990
Kick-off 8.00 p.m.

SECURITY MARK
VISIBLE IN THIS WINDOW

Price £2·00
Turnstile **L**
NORTH ENCLOSURE UNCOVERED
04206

UNLESS PRESENTED IN FULL — SEE BACK FOR PLAN AND CONDITIONS

Scotland is just 90 minutes away from Argentina

Ninety minutes is all the time it takes for our lads to beat Czechoslovakia tonight.

And if they do, they'll qualify for the World Cup in South America next year.

In which case Thomas Cook will be running a special all-inclusive supporters' trip from Glasgow.

So follow Scotland all the way and watch out for details at your local Thomas Cook Travel Shop.

We have the widest range of travel services available and issue Thomas Cook Travellers Cheques and Foreign Currency.

Thomas Cook, 15/17 Gordon Street, Glasgow, Telephone: 221 9431.

Branches at: Clarkston, Greenock, Edinburgh, Dundee, Aberdeen, Perth and Carlisle.

Thomas Cook

The trusted name in travel. Everywhere.

to football *outwith* the UK was a bit of a false start. In the programme for the Scotland versus Czechoslovakia World Cup qualifier in September 1977 an advert by *Thomas Cook* (the trusted name in travel) proclaims that 'Scotland is just 90 minutes away from Argentina'. It adds that if Scotland beat Czechoslovakia they'll qualify for the World Cup finals in South America and in which case Thomas Cook will be running a special all-inclusive supporters' trip from Glasgow.

Scotland did manage to defeat the reigning European champions that evening, 3-1; however, qualification wasn't clinched until the following month when Wales were defeated 2–0 at Anfield!

In preparation for heading to Argentina, Scotland played Bulgaria and a crowd of 59,524 saw a 2–1 victory for the world champion wannabees. The match programme contains a hopelessly optimistic advert by the travel agent A.T. Mays for a **30**-night package to Argentina from 28 May to 29 June (the finals ran from 1 to 26 June). Furthermore, the prices started from £1,230 – which equated to about three quarters of my annual salary at the time. Needless to say, I didn't make it to the southern hemisphere that summer. Relatively inexpensive package holidays did, however, get several thousand of us to the south of Spain for the 1982 World Cup finals.

For Italia 90, Premier Travel of Ayr were offering coach travel and 13 nights in a two-star hotel for £375 and as an alternative option you could get 14 nights half board flying

from Glasgow to Genoa for £598. Although Scotland's matches were in the north-west of Italy (in Genoa and Turin), many supporters got cheaper deals by heading to the north-east and Adriatic resorts such as Rimini and Cattolica.

In the programme for the Scotland versus Finland match in March 1992 there was advertised by *Scotball*, a nine-day package at the Euro 92 finals in Sweden for £665 – and needless to say, ultimately an extension to the nine days was not required. Unfortunately *Scotball*'s package deals were never particularly competitive and the advent of budget airlines such as EasyJet, Ryanair and Wizzair, coupled with direct online booking of accommodation, hastened the demise of the SFA's very own travel agent.

West of Scotland Tartan Army spokesman Hamish Husband has reminded me of the now gone 'joys' of venturing behind the 'iron curtain' in pre-1990, cold war Europe to support Scotland. For example, a Euro qualifier versus East Germany in Halle in 1983 came complete with travel restrictions, police and military checkpoints, rigorous vehicle inspections, snarling dogs, snarling bartenders and waiters, a thriving black market and dilapidated infrastructure. A Communist Brexit-land?

Incidentally, Scotland lost 2–1, with Eamonn Bannon's only international goal being scored within the confines of the old Soviet bloc – how's that for a collector's item?

In recent years, special direct chartered flight deals to Scotland away games have all but dried up (although not so for rugby internationals). However, in the early 2000s I was able to use the services of two excellent travel agents – Hynds Travel, Glasgow, and Passport Travel, Clydebank, with the latter often offering departures from Glasgow, Edinburgh and Aberdeen, two nights in three-star hotels and as a bonus, souvenir match pin badges were thrown in! I recall former Scotland keeper turned radio pundit Alan Rough joining us on one such trip, to Milan in 2005 for a World Cup qualifier against Italy, during which time he took some friendly stick for his 'perceived shortcomings' against Peru (1978), Austria (1979), Belgium (1979) and Brazil (1982) – and all in good humour.

Coming right up to date, and where are those Star Trek teleportation machines when you need them? For the March 2019 Euro qualifier in Kazakhstan, my Surrey-based International Tartan Army comrade, Scott Kelly, had to endure the following palava – London to Moscow (four-hour flight), Moscow to Bishkek, Kyrgyzstan (five-hour flight), Bishkek to Almaty, Kazakhstan (six-hour taxi ride), and Almaty to Astana (two-hour flight) ... and all for sub-zero temperatures and a 3–0 gubbing.

Scott also recalls a group of supporters who went by the name of *The Alternative Tartan Army* and who went out of their way to create really bizarre itineraries. A simple away trip for them would often involve a round, but convoluted, trip visiting six or eight countries ... just for the hell of it.

Going off on another one of my tangents (as opposed to tandems), I once travelled to a football match by hovercraft. I was on holiday on the Isle of Wight at the time and so I utilised this mode of transport to see Leicester City play at Portsmouth in a pre-season friendly. The things I'll do just to try and get a glimpse of the likes of Scottish internationalist Matt Elliott (plus Neil Lennon, Emile Heskey and Robbie Savage). Meanwhile my colleague David Stuart now occasionally has to include Rothesay to Wemyss Bay ferry trips as part of his Hampden hike, which is fine until the weather acts up.

In conclusion I think it is worth reiterating that Scotland supporters (especially much-travelled supporters) suffer for the cause in many ways – damaged bank accounts, damaged personal relationships, damaged livers, sleep deprivation, dehydration, food poisoning, seasickness, physical and mental trauma ... and we love every minute of it.

U

UEFA OPPONENTS

As of 30 June 2019, UEFA (which was formed in 1954) had 55 member associations – five of which have won the World Cup, Germany and Italy (four times each), France (twice) with England and Spain on one apiece.

Scotland have yet to play five of our fellow Europeans – Andorra, Armenia, Azerbaijan, Kosovo and Montenegro.

Way out in front, in terms of matches played, are our three British neighbours, whom we have faced over 100 times each. After England, Northern Ireland and Wales our top ten are as undernoted:

Opponent	Played	Won	Drew	Lost	Goals For	Goals Against	%
Austria	20	6	6	8	25	33	45%
Belgium	19	4	3	12	21	37	29%
Denmark	16	10	0	6	20	12	63%
France	16	8	0	8	15	23	50%
Germany/W. Ger	17	4	5	8	23	26	38%
Netherlands	19	6	4	9	15	26	42%
Norway	18	9	6	3	34	21	67%
Portugal	15	4	3	8	14	21	37%
Spain	13	3	4	6	20	23	38%
Switzerland	16	8	3	5	26	24	59%

Scotland's first match against non-British opposition came about in 1929 when we undertook our first official overseas tour, with matches against Norway, Germany and the Netherlands.

The first 'foreign' visitors to Scotland were Austria in November 1933. 62,000 were at Hampden to see a 2–2 draw in which there was a debut cap for Middlesbrough's Robert Bruce, amongst others.

West Germany were reigning world champions when Scotland defeated them 3–1 in a friendly match in Stuttgart in 1957. Celtic's Bobby Collins bagged a double, whilst Jackie Mudie of Blackpool netted the other.

Jim Leighton's 91-cap Scotland career began against the German Democratic Republic (East Germany) at Hampden Park in 1982. East Germany were no longer in existence, however, when JL made his Scotland farewell at Tynecastle Stadium in 1998, against Estonia, who ironically were still part of the USSR at the time of his first cap.

Things were much simpler back in 1988 when UEFA had 33 member associations just prior to the dissolution of the USSR and the break-up of Yugoslavia. To the baby-boomer generation, the likes of Croatia, Estonia, Faroe Islands and San Marino will forever be 'the new kids on the block'.

Notable thrashings dished out by Scotland include: 6–0 versus Luxembourg (friendly, Luxembourg-Ville, 1947); 5–0 versus *Belgium* (friendly, Brussels, 1951); 6–2 versus Spain (friendly, Madrid, 1963); 8–0 versus Cyprus (World Cup qualifier, Hampden, 1969); 6–0 versus Finland (friendly, Hampden, 1976);

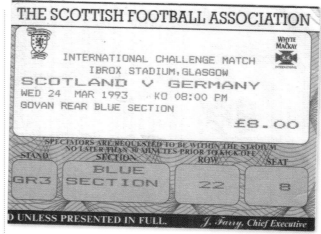

Scotland's most painful doing? Quite possibly the 6–0 stuffing we took from the Netherlands in Amsterdam in 2003. It was the second leg of the Euro 2004 play-off and our hopes were high after winning the first leg 1–0 at Hampden. Fan my brow …

6–1 versus Yugoslavia (friendly, Hampden, 1984); 5–1 versus Faroe Islands (European Championship qualifier, Hampden, 1994); 5–0 versus San Marino (European Championship qualifier, Hampden, 1995); 5–1 versus Bulgaria (Kirin Cup, Kobe, 2006); 6–0 versus Faroe Islands (European Championship qualifier, Celtic Park, 2006); 6–1 versus Gibraltar (European Championship qualifier, Hampden, 2015); 6–0 versus Gibraltar (European Championship qualifier, Faro, 2015); and 5–1 versus Malta (World Cup qualifier, Ta Qali, 2016). There were more than you thought, weren't there?

And whilst we are in masochistic mood, all of Scotland's most recent victories against Belgium, England, Germany, Italy, Portugal and Spain have taken place in the previous millennium! Scotland have lost their last five matches to Belgium (September 2001 to June 2019), have failed to score a single goal in the process and have conceded 13 – and yet in my mind, historically, we are two nations of equal standing.

Beating France 1–0 both home and away during the Euro 2008 qualifying campaign was damned enjoyable (if ultimately fruitless) but Scotland need another big scalp, a marquee humping if you will, SOON …

Norway v Scotland, Oslo, 7 September 2005

VOYAGES OF DISCOVERY
— OVERSEAS TOURS

End of season or close season tours are something of a rarity these days, due in part to fixture congestion and an ever-shortening close season. Once upon a time, however, international tours were all the rage and Scotland arranged a fair number of them – both official and unofficial. For cynical me the two key questions are: 'What were the objectives of the tour?' and 'Were the objectives achieved?'

These objectives could include showing the world how the game should really be played (once upon a time), public relations/goodwill exercises and player evaluation/experience/bonding, plus the suspicion that the tours were also 'jollies' for the blazers.

For the purposes of this exercise we'll make the definition of a stand-alone tour as being more than one match played abroad within a short time frame, with just about all of the matches being friendlies and none of them being part of our preparations for participation at an imminent World Cup or Euro Championship finals. As such, also excluded are the 1972 Brazil Independence Tournament and the Kirin Cup adventures in Japan in 1995 and 2006.

Scotland's first 143 official internationals were played against England, Wales and Ireland/Northern Ireland. The first time Scotland met 'foreign' opposition was in May/June 1929 when we embarked on a three-game overseas tour which took in Norway, Germany and the Netherlands, although an unofficial international against Canada took place in Montreal in 1921, with Scotland winning 1–0.

On 26 May 1929 Scotland fielded no less than seven debutants (including the St Johnstone duo of Alex McLaren in goal and right-half William Imrie) as they defeated Norway 7–3 in the Brann Stadion, Bergen, in front of a crowd of 4,000, with Aberdeen's Alex Cheyne hitting a hat-trick. Apparently 24 hours later, however, the Scots were victorious again, winning 4–0 at the Ulleval Stadion, Oslo, against a Norwegian XI in a match that is considered unofficial. 12,000 saw the unofficial version.

Scotland then moved on to the Deutsches Stadion, Berlin, for a 1–1 draw with Germany on 1 June in front of 40,000. William Imrie netted Scotland's equaliser three minutes from the end and this time debut caps were awarded to just two players. Apparently some people disapproved of the German leg of the tour with suggestions that Scotland should not 'fraternise with the Hun' – and this was four years *before* the Nazis came to power.

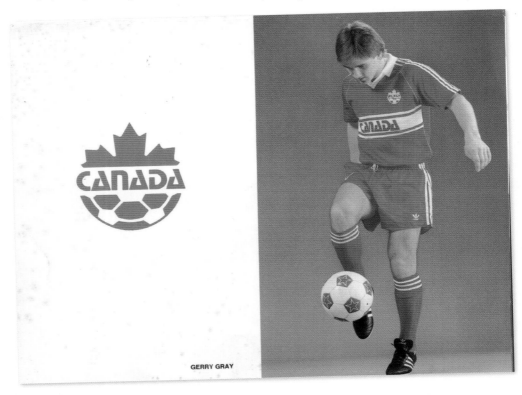

GERRY GRAY

In the third match, on 4 June, Scotland recorded a 2–0 victory over the Netherlands in the Olympic Stadium, Amsterdam. No debut caps this time but a crowd of 24,000 saw goals from Rangers's James Fleming and Robert Rankin of St Mirren.

1929 is chiefly remembered as the year that the London and New York stock markets collapsed, which led to the 'Great Depression' and economic misery of the 1930s. However, throughout the Great Depression there were subsequent European tours in 1931 (Austria, Italy and Switzerland) and 1937 (Austria and Czechoslovakia), as well as individual away friendlies.

After the Second World War the European tours resumed – 1948 (Switzerland and France), 1951 (Belgium and Austria), 1952 (Denmark and Sweden), 1955 (Austria and Hungary), 1959 (the Netherlands and Portugal), 1960 (Austria, Hungary and Turkey – with Bobby Evans as captain in his three final appearances for Scotland), 1963 (Norway – with Denis Law grabbing a hat-trick in a 4–3 defeat, Republic of Ireland – another defeat, 1–0, and Spain – an incredible victory, 6–2 at the Estadio Bernabeu, Madrid!) and 1980 (Poland and Hungary – escaping Thatcher's Britain for some light relief behind the 'iron curtain' for Jock Stein and co).

There were also tours of the USA and Canada in 1935 and 1949 (sailing across the Atlantic on the *Queen Mary* liner) during which Scotland played unofficial international matches in cities such as New York, Toronto and Regina, as well as games against the likes of the St Louis All-Stars and Belfast Celtic!

An *official* tour of North America took place in June 1983 when Jock Stein's Scotland traversed Canada, west to east, winning three out of three games, scoring seven, conceding nil and in the process awarding a debut cap to Mark McGhee of Aberdeen and a fifth and final cap to Rangers defender Ally Dawson. Leeds United defender Frank Gray also bowed out, on the 32-cap mark.

The closest Alex Ferguson got to achieving full international honours came about during the 'summer of love' (well, 16 May to 13 June 1967 to be precise), when as a Dunfermline Athletic player, he was part of a Scotland representative side which played (and won) nine matches (at least five of which could have been deemed 'full' internationals) during

a tour of Israel, Hong Kong, Australia, New Zealand and Canada. Ferguson made seven appearances (and scored ten goals) but the SFA in their infinite wisdom never awarded caps for this arduous caper, which apparently was some sort of preparation for our (ultimately unsuccessful) 1970 World Cup qualifying campaign.

In May 2002, under the stewardship of Berti Vogts, Scotland undertook a Far East tour that comprised a 4–1 defeat against the hosts South Korea in Busan, followed by participation in the Hong Kong Reunification Cup, which resulted in a 2–0 reverse against South Africa and an 'unofficial' 4–0 victory against a Hong Kong XI.

Scotland's first tour of Latin America took place in June 1977 when Ally MacLeod's Galacticos beat Chile 4–2 in the Estadio Nacional, Santiago, drew 1–1 with Argentina in the Estadio Boca Juniors, Buenos Aires, then lost 2–0 to Brazil in the Estadio Maracana, Rio de Janeiro.

The second such tour took place in May/ June 2018, when Alex McLeish's Scotland lost to two World Cup hopefuls, 2–0 versus Peru in the Estadio Nacional de Lima and 1–0 to Mexico in the Estadio Azteca, Mexico City. The statistics show that was a long way to travel just for an aggregate of two shots on target. *Loony Alba* Tartan Army stalwart Kevin Donnelly also made that tour and he advised that one of the main influences on Peruvian cuisine is choufa, a fusion of Peruvian and Chinese dishes. Much to every Scotland fan's sheer delight, essentially this meant you got a Chinese dish, such as 'lomo soltado', (beef and onions), with both rice and chips. There are over 5,000 varieties of potato in Peru apparently and out of the 4,000 varieties Kevin tasted, he confirmed that their chips were superb. In short, some useful lessons *were* learned from that tour.

WORLD CUP '82
A COMPLETE GUIDE

Nicholas Keith and
with photographs by P

World Cup 2010 Qualifier

Scotland 2
Hampde
Glasg
1st Apri

KSI

SCOT
WORL
GUI

EASY! EASY!

Words and Music by BILL MARTIN and PHIL COULTER

WORLD CUP MEXICO 1986

7th MAY 86

SCOTLAND

184

Recorded on Polydor by the

Scotland World Cup Squad

COMPLETE WORLD
PREVIEW GUI

WORLD CUP QUALIFYING CAMPAIGNS 1950 TO 2018

Year	No./names of opposition teams	No. of qualifying matches/Final position	
1950	3: England, N. Ireland & Wales	3 / 2nd / Qualified but declined to attend	[Yes, really!]
1954	3: England, N. Ireland & Wales	3 / 2nd / Qualified	
1958	2: Spain & Switzerland	4 / 1st / Qualified	
1962	2: Czechoslovakia & ROI	4+1 / Joint 1st / Scotland lost play-off match and failed to qualify	
1966	3: Italy, Finland & Poland	6 / 2nd / Failed to qualify	
1970	3: Austria, Cyprus & W. Germany	6 / 2nd / Failed to qualify	
1974	2: Czechoslovakia & Denmark	4 / 1st / Qualified	
1978	2: Czechoslovakia & Wales	4 / 1st / Qualified	
1982	4: Israel, N. Ireland, Portugal & Sweden	8 / 1st / Qualified	
1986	3: Iceland, Spain, Wales [plus Australia in two-leg play-off]	6+2 / 2nd / Scotland won play-off and Qualified	
1990	4: Cyprus, France, Norway & Yugoslavia	8 / 2nd / Qualified	
1994	5: Estonia, Italy, Malta, Portugal & Switzerland	10 / 4th / Failed to qualify	
1998	5: Austria, Belarus, Estonia, Latvia & Sweden	10 / 2nd / Qualified as Europe's best runner-up	
2002	4: Belgium, Croatia, Latvia & San Marino	8 / 3rd / Failed to qualify	
2006	5: Belarus, Italy, Moldova, Norway & Slovenia	10 / 3rd / Failed to qualify	
2010	4: Iceland, Macedonia, Netherlands & Norway	8 / 3rd / Failed to qualify	
2014	5: Belgium, Croatia, Macedonia, Serbia & Wales	10 / 4th / Failed to qualify	
2018	5: England, Lithuania, Malta, Slovakia & Slovenia	10 / 3rd / Failed to qualify	

Scotland have faced a total of 36 different nations in World Cup qualifiers – 35 from Europe, plus Australia. Notable omissions include Turkey and Hungary (for both World Cups *and* Euros) plus Greece, Russia, Bulgaria and Romania, whilst we have played Wales more than anyone else – five times (1950, 1954, 1978, 1986 and 2014).

Arguably our most impressive qualifying campaign was for Spain 82 when Jock Stein's Scotland topped a five-nation group. That said, eliminating reigning European champions Czechoslovakia en route to Argentina 78 was also pretty damned impressive. Our worst performances were reserved for the USA 94 and Brazil 2014 campaigns, when we finished fourth in groups which were composed of six teams each.

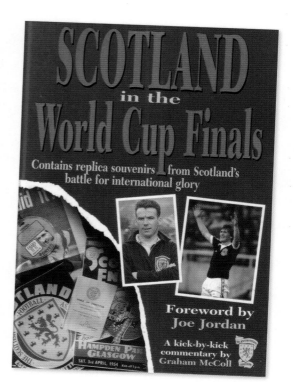

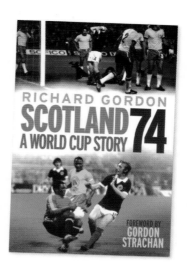

WORLD CUP FINALS
– SCOTLAND APPEARANCES 1954 TO 1998

PART 1

MATCH SUMMARY

Between 1930 and 2018 there have been 21 World Cup competitions, and between 1954 and 1998 Scotland has appeared at eight finals and on two of those occasions (1974 and 1978) we were the UK's sole representative. Scotland have yet to progress beyond the group stages but when we do, someone's going to cop it big style!

Date	Opponents	Venue	Result	Attendance
16 June 1954	Austria	Sportsplatz Hardturm, Zurich	0-1	25,000
19 June 1954	Uruguay	St Jakob Stadion, Basle	0-7	34,000
08 June 1958	Yugoslavia	Arosvallen, Vasteras, Sweden	1-1	9,591
11 June 1958	Paraguay	Idrottsparken, Norrkoping	2-3	11,665
15 June 1958	France	Eyravallen, Orebro	1-2	13,554
14 June 1974	Zaire	Westfalen Stadion, Dortmund	2-0	25,800
18 June 1974	Brazil	Wald Stadion, Frankfurt	0-0	60,000
22 June 1974	Yugoslavia	Wald Stadion, Frankfurt	1-1	54,000
03 June 1978	Peru	Estadio Chateau Carreras, Cordoba	1-3	37,792
07 June 1978	Iran	Estadio Chateau Carreras, Cordoba	1-1	7,938
11 June 1978	Netherlands	Estadio San Martin, Mendoza	3-2	35,130
15 June 1982	New Zealand	Estadio La Rosaleda, Malaga	5-2	20,000
18 June 1982	Brazil	Estadio Benito Villamarin, Seville	1-4	47,379
22 June 1982	USSR	Estadio La Rosaleda, Malaga	2-2	45,000
04 June 1986	Denmark	Estadio Neza, Nezahualcoyotl, Mexico	0-1	18,000
08 June 1986	West Germany	Estadio Corregidora, Queretaro	1-2	25,000
13 June 1986	Uruguay	Estadio Neza, Nezahualcoyotl	0-0	20,000
11 June 1990	Costa Rica	Stadio Luigi Ferraris, Genoa	0-1	30,867
16 June 1990	Sweden	Stadio Luigi Ferraris, Genoa	2-1	31,823
20 June 1990	Brazil	Stadio Delle Alpi, Turin	0-1	62,502
10 June 1998	Brazil	Stade de France, Saint-Denis	1-2	80,000
16 June 1998	Norway	Parc Lescure, Bordeaux	1-1	30,236
23 June 1998	Morocco	Stade Geoffroy-Guichard, St Etienne	0-3	35,500

In total, Scotland have played 23, won four, drawn seven and lost 12. Goals for: 25, and goals against: 41. Scotland have faced Brazil on four occasions (1974, 1982, 1990 and 1998), Uruguay twice (1954 and 1986) and Yugoslavia twice (1958 and 1974).

Scotland have won their opening match at the finals on two occasions – versus Zaire in 1974 and against New Zealand in 1982. In 1974 we returned home undefeated (one win and two draws).

Scotland have managed clean sheets on three occasions, but have failed to hit the net eight times. Scotland's first goal at the finals

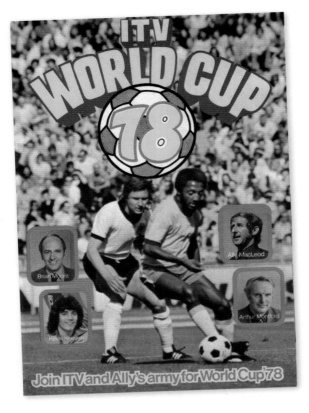

Appearing for Scotland at three World Cup finals have been Kenny Dalglish (Celtic and Liverpool), Joe Jordan (Leeds United, Manchester United and AC Milan) (1974, 1978 and 1982), Graeme Souness (Liverpool and Sampdoria) (1978, 1982 and 1986), Alex McLeish (Aberdeen) (1982, 1986 and 1990) and Jim Leighton (Aberdeen and Manchester United) (1986, 1990 and 1998). Joe Jordan also scored at each World Cup – 1974 (versus Zaire and Yugoslavia), 1978 (versus Peru) and 1982 (versus the USSR).

Dundee goalkeeper Bill Brown made his Scotland debut at the World Cup finals (versus France in 1958) and went on to win a total of 28 caps. Denis Law (then with Manchester City) won his 55th (and final) cap versus Zaire in 1974.

Craig Burley (Celtic) is the only Scotland player to have been sent off at the World Cup finals (1998 versus Morocco).

Scotland's managers at the finals were – 1954 (Andy Beattie), 1958 (No manager!), 1974 (Willie Ormond, who also played at the 1954 finals), 1978 (Ally MacLeod), 1982 (Jock Stein), 1986 (Alex Ferguson), 1990 (Andy Roxburgh) and 1998 (Craig Brown).

was scored by James Murray of Hearts versus Yugoslavia in 1958.

Three of our opponents are no longer in existence (Yugoslavia, the USSR and West Germany), whilst Zaire are now known as the Democratic Republic of Congo.

| PART 2 | **CLUB REPRESENTATION** |

Aberdeen
[7 tournaments, 10 players, 29 caps]

Fred Martin
1954: Austria & Uruguay

Graham Leggat
1958: Yugoslavia & Paraguay

Stuart Kennedy
1978: Peru & Netherlands

Joe Harper
1978: Iran (sub)

Gordon Strachan
1982: New Zealand, Brazil & USSR

Willie Miller
1982: Brazil & USSR
1986: Denmark, West Germany & Uruguay

Alex McLeish
1982: Brazil (sub)
1986: Denmark
1990: Costa Rica, Sweden & Brazil

Jim Leighton
1986: Denmark, West Germany & Uruguay
1998: Brazil, Norway & Morocco

Jim Bett
1990: Costa Rica

Stewart McKimmie
1990: Costa Rica (sub) & Brazil

Arsenal
[1 tournament, 1 player, 2 caps]

Charlie Nicholas
1986: Denmark, Uruguay (sub)

Aston Villa
[1 tournament, 1 player, 1 cap]

Allan Evans
1982: New Zealand

Barcelona
[1 tournament, 1 player, 1 cap]

Stevie Archibald
1986: West Germany

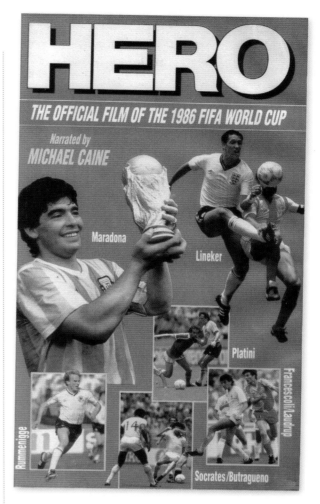

Bayern Munich
[1 tournament, 1 player, 1 cap]
Alan McInally
1990: Costa Rica

Blackburn Rovers
[1 tournament, 3 players, 7 caps]
Colin Hendry
1998: Brazil, Norway & Morocco
Kevin Gallacher
1998: Brazil, Norway & Morocco
Billy McKinlay
1998: Brazil (sub)

Blackpool
[2 tournaments, 2 players, 5 caps]
Allan Brown
1954: Austria, Uruguay
Jackie Mudie
1958: Yugoslavia, Paraguay & France

Borussia Dortmund
[2 tournaments, 2 players, 3 caps]
Murdo MacLeod
1990: Sweden & Brazil
Scott Booth
1998: Morocco (sub)

Burnley
[1 tournament, 1 player, 2 caps]
Jock Aird
1954: Austria & Uruguay

Celtic
[7 tournaments, 15 players, 44 caps]
Willie Fernie
1954: Austria & Uruguay
1958: Paraguay
Neil Mochan
1954: Austria & Uruguay
Bobby Evans
1958: Yugoslavia, Paraguay & France
Bobby Collins
1958: Yugoslavia, Paraguay & France
Kenny Dalglish
1974: Zaire, Brazil & Yugoslavia
Davie Hay
1974: Zaire, Brazil & Yugoslavia
Danny McGrain
1974: Zaire, Brazil & Yugoslavia
1982: New Zealand, USSR (sub)

Roy Aitken
1986: Denmark, West Germany & Uruguay
Paul McStay
1986: Uruguay
1990: Costa Rica, Sweden (sub) & Brazil
Craig Burley
1998: Brazil, Norway & Morocco
Tom Boyd
1998: Brazil, Norway & Morocco
Paul Lambert
1998: Brazil, Norway & Morocco
Darren Jackson
1998: Brazil & Norway
Tosh McKinlay
1998: Brazil (sub) & Morocco (sub)
Jackie McNamara
1998: Norway (sub) & Morocco

Charlton Athletic
[1 tournament, 1 player, 2 caps]
John Hewie
1958: Yugoslavia & France

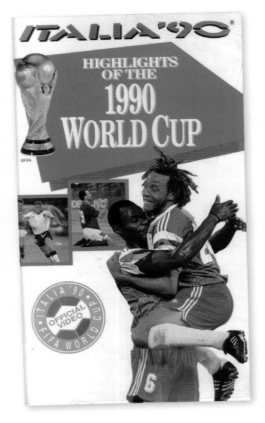

Chelsea
[1 tournament, 1 player, 1 cap]
Gordon Durie
1990: Sweden

Clyde
[1 tournament, 1 player, 1 cap]
Archie Robertson
1958: Paraguay

Coventry City
[1 tournament, 1 player, 2 caps]
Tommy Hutchison
1974: Zaire (sub) & Yugoslavia (sub)

Derby County
[2 tournaments, 3 players, 6 caps]
Don Masson
1978: Peru
Bruce Rioch
1978: Peru & Netherlands
Christian Dailly
1998: Brazil, Norway & Morocco

Dundee
[2 tournaments, 2 players, 5 caps]
Dougie Cowie
1954: Austria & Uruguay
1958: Yugoslavia & Paraguay
Bill Brown
1958: France

Dundee United
[3 tournaments, 5 players, 17 caps]
David Narey
1982: New Zealand (sub), Brazil & USSR
1986: West Germany & Uruguay
Richard Gough
1986: Denmark, West Germany & Uruguay
Maurice Malpas
1986: Denmark & West Germany
1990: Costa Rica, Sweden & Brazil
Paul Sturrock
1986: Denmark & Uruguay
Eamonn Bannon
1986: Denmark (sub) & West Germany

Everton
[3 tournaments, 3 players, 5 caps]
Alex Parker
1958: Paraguay
Graeme Sharp
1986: Uruguay
Stuart McCall
1990: Costa Rica, Sweden & Brazil

Hearts
[3 tournaments, 5 players, 9 caps]
James Murray
1958: Yugoslavia & France
Dave Mackay
1958: France
Dave McPherson
1990: Costa Rica, Sweden & Brazil
Craig Levein
1990: Sweden
Davie Weir
1998: Norway (sub) & Morocco

Hibernian
[3 tournaments, 3 players, 6 caps]
Willie Ormond
1954: Austria & Uruguay
Eddie Turnbull
1958: Yugoslavia, Paraguay & France
John Blackley
1974: Zaire

Ipswich Town
[1 tournament, 2 players, 5 caps]
Alan Brazil
1982: New Zealand & USSR (sub)
John Wark
1982: New Zealand, Brazil & USSR

Leeds United
[2 tournaments, 5 players, 15 caps]

Billy Bremner
1974: Zaire, Brazil & Yugoslavia

David Harvey
1974: Zaire, Brazil & Yugoslavia

Joe Jordan
1974: Zaire, Brazil & Yugoslavia

Peter Lorimer
1974: Zaire, Brazil & Yugoslavia

Frank Gray
1982: New Zealand, Brazil & USSR

Liverpool
[5 tournaments, 6 players, 18 caps]

Tommy Younger
1958: Yugoslavia & Paraguay

Kenny Dalglish
1978: Peru, Iran & Netherlands
1982: New Zealand & Brazil (sub)

Graeme Souness
1978: Netherlands
1982: New Zealand, Brazil & USSR

Alan Hansen
1982: New Zealand, Brazil & USSR

Steve Nicol
1986: Denmark, West Germany & Uruguay

Gary Gillespie
1990: Brazil (sub)

Manchester City
[3 tournaments, 3 players, 7 caps]

Denis Law
1974: Zaire

Willie Donachie
1978: Iran & Netherlands

Asa Hartford [
1978: Peru, Iran & Netherlands
1982: Brazil

Manchester United
[4 tournaments, 8 players, 22 caps]

Jim Holton
1974: Zaire, Brazil & Yugoslavia

Martin Buchan
1974: Brazil & Yugoslavia
1978: Peru, Iran & Netherlands

Willie Morgan
1974: Brazil & Yugoslavia

Joe Jordan
1978: Peru, Iran & Netherlands

Lou Macari
1978: Peru (sub) & Iran

Gordon Strachan
1986: Denmark, West Germany & Uruguay

Arthur Albiston
1986: Uruguay

Jim Leighton
1990: Costa Rica, Sweden & Brazil

Milan AC
[1 tournament, 1 player, 1 cap]

Joe Jordan
1982: USSR

Monaco
[1 tournament, 1 player, 3 caps]

John Collins
1998: Brazil, Norway & Morocco

Newcastle United
[1 tournament, 1 player, 3 caps]

Roy Aitken
1990: Costa Rica, Sweden & Brazil

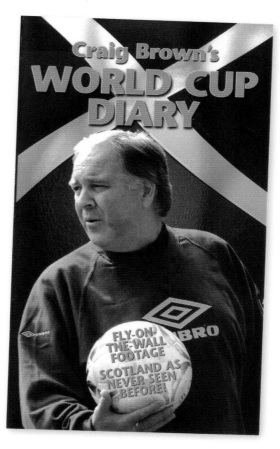

Norwich City
[1 tournament, 1 player, 2 caps]
Robert Fleck
1990: Sweden & Brazil (sub)

Nottingham Forest
[3 tournaments, 4 players, 11 caps]
Stewart Imlach
1958: Yugoslavia & France
Kenny Burns
1978: Peru & Iran
Archie Gemmill
1978: Peru (sub), Iran & Netherlands
John Robertson
1978: Iran
1982: New Zealand, Brazil & USSR

Partick Thistle
[3 tournaments, 3 players, 10 caps]
Jimmy Davidson
1954: Austria & Uruguay
John MacKenzie
1954: Austria & Uruguay
Alan Rough
1978: Peru, Iran & Netherlands
1982: New Zealand, Brazil & USSR

Preston NE
[1 tournament, 2 players, 4 caps]
Willie Cunningham
1954: Austria & Uruguay
Tommy Docherty [
1954: Austria & Uruguay

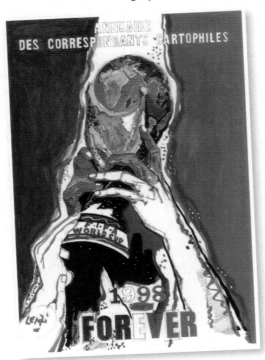

Rangers
[6 tournaments, 9 players, 23 caps]
Eric Caldow
1958: Yugoslavia, Paraguay & France
Sammy Baird
1958: France
Sandy Jardine
1974: Zaire, Brazil & Yugoslavia
1978: Iran
Tom Forsyth
1978: Peru, Iran (sub) & Netherlands
Davie Cooper
1986: West Germany (sub) & Uruguay (sub)
Richard Gough
1990: Costa Rica
Mo Johnston
1990: Costa Rica, Sweden & Brazil
Ally McCoist
1990: Costa Rica (sub), Sweden (sub) & Brazil
Gordon Durie
1998: Brazil, Norway & Morocco

Sampdoria
[1 tournament, 1 player, 2 caps]
Graeme Souness
1986: Denmark, West Germany

Tottenham Hotspur
[2 tournaments, 2 players, 5 caps]
Stevie Archibald
1982: New Zealand (sub), Brazil & USSR
Colin Calderwood
1998: Brazil & Norway

West Bromwich Albion
[1 tournament, 1 player, 1 cap]
Willie Johnston
1978: Peru

West Ham United
[1 tournament, 1 player, 2 caps]
Frank McAvennie
1986: Denmark (sub) & West Germany (sub)

Summary of no of clubs represented
English Clubs: 22
Scottish Clubs: 9
German Clubs: 2
Italian Clubs: 2
French Clubs: 1
Spanish Clubs: 1
TOTAL: 37

WORLD CUP FINALS
OTHER SCOTS WHO MADE AN IMPACT

Of course, it is not just the Scotland football team which have, ahem, lit up past World Cup (as well as European Championship) finals – Scottish match officials, Scots managing other countries and indeed Scottish footballer emigrants have also contributed to the spectacle.

At the inaugural World Cup finals in Uruguay in 1930 the USA team contained no less than five Scots-born players – Andy Auld, Jim Brown, Jimmy Gallagher, Bart McGhee, as well as a Scottish trainer in Jack Coll. Those 'Damned Yankees' reached the semi-finals.

Bill Jeffrey, who was originally from Edinburgh, managed the USA at the 1950 finals in Brazil which included the shock 1–0 defeat of England (Billy Wright, Tom Finney, Stan Mortensen et al.). It was a relatively small crowd of around 10,000 that witnessed England's humiliation by their former colonials at the appropriately named, though now demolished, Estadio Independencia. (I suspect that the English FA helped pay for its demolition.) The match took place on 29 June, just in case you want to mark that date in your diaries for BBQs or parties, etc.

At the same tournament George Mitchell of Bainsford, near Falkirk, refereed the Group 3 game between Sweden and Paraguay in Curtiba that ended in a 2–2 draw. He also ran the line at three other matches in Rio de Janeiro, including the opening game of the tournament (Brazil 4 Mexico 0) and two final pool matches – Brazil 6 Spain 1 and the trophy-winning Uruguay 2 Brazil 1. Prior to the World Cup, however, Mitchell's one match of note had been the 1949 Scottish Cup semi-final between Rangers and East Fife.

Doug Livingstone from Alexandria, West Dunbartonshire, managed Belgium at the 1954 World Cup finals in Switzerland. Belgium opened their campaign with a 4–4 draw with England in Basle before losing 4–1 to Italy in Lugano, in a lopsided format in which teams only played against two of their three group rivals!?!?

Prior to 1954, the bold Dougie (who had played for Celtic and Aberdeen amongst others) managed Sparta Rotterdam and the Republic of Ireland. Post-1954 he was in charge at Newcastle United, Fulham and Chesterfield.

Our referee at the 1954 finals was literally faultless – Charles Edward Faultless. Mr Faultless from Giffnock refereed the 1–1 draw

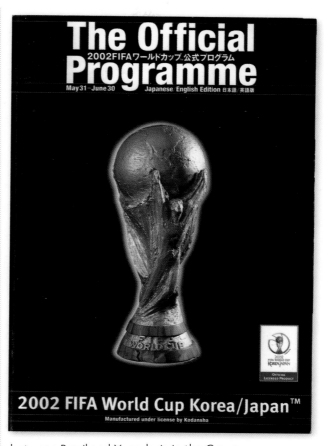

between Brazil and Yugoslavia in the Group A match in Lausanne, as well as an incredible quarter-final match in the same city, which finished Austria 5 Switzerland 7.

Faultless would go on to referee the 1955 Scottish Cup Final between Celtic and Clyde. Furthermore, the Glasgow Referees Association chose his name for its annual trophy, partly to honour him but also to provide a marvellous name for the award.

At Sweden 1958, Jack Mowatt of Rutherglen was our man in the middle in Stockholm when Sweden triumphed 2–1 against Hungary in a group match, whilst Motherwell whistler Hugh Phillips ended his career at the 1966 World Cup where he oversaw West Germany's 5–0 group match demolition of Switzerland at Hillsborough, Sheffield.

Robert Holley 'Bobby' Davidson is the 'main man' having represented Scotland at *three* World Cup finals – 1962, 1970 and 1974. He refereed four matches in total – two group matches in Santiago, Chile, in 1962 (Italy 0 West Germany 0 and West Germany 2 Chile 0), one group match in Puebla, Mexico, eight years later (Uruguay 2 Israel 0), plus the second phase group match in Gelsenkirchen in 1974

in which the Netherlands thrashed Argentina 4–0, with two of the goals coming from none other than Cruyff himself.

Davidson also ran the line at a further six matches across these three tournaments, including the 1962 final in which Brazil (featuring Garrincha, Didi and Zagalo but minus the injured Pele) defeated Czechoslovakia (Scotland's conquerors at the play-off stage) by three goals to one. Returning to Germany 74 and there was much speculation by the Scottish press at the time that our Bobby would referee the final as some sort of 'consolation' for Willie Ormond's Scotland team being eliminated from that tournament undefeated. The honour, however, went to Englishman Jack Taylor.

When Australia made their first ever appearance at the World Cup finals – in 1974 – three Scots-born footballers played in all three games against East and West Germany plus Chile. The trio were goalkeeper Jack Reilly (formerly of Inverurie Loco Works and Hibernian), midfielder Jimmy Mackay (Bonnyrigg Rose and Airdrie) and left-winger Jimmy Rooney (Lochee United and Montrose).

And so to Argentina 78 where John Gordon of Inverness succeeded in reaching the second group phase of the competition,

where he refereed the Netherlands' 5–1 stuffing of Austria in Cordoba. Earlier he had been in charge of Tunisia's 3–1 group victory over Mexico in Rosario.

Dundee's Bob Valentine had a memorable 1982 World Cup. Whilst Jock Stein's Scotland team were battling it out in the south of the country around the Costa del Sol, Bob was up north to take charge of the infamous 'Great Gijon Swindle', in which West Germany and Austria contrived to play out a 1–0 victory for the Germans, which allowed both teams to progress at the expense of Algeria. Shame! Shame!

FIFA recognised, however, that it wasn't Mr Valentine who had spread the Teutonic love and so he was given a second phase group match to oversee in Barcelona between old 'friends' Poland and the USSR, which ended 0–0. *Solidarity* would win the replay, so to speak.

By way of a 'bonus' Dundee Bob also ran the line in Seville at that brilliant game of football that was the semi-final between France and West Germany. Brilliant, of course, except for German keeper Harald Schumacher's attempt to decapitate the on-running Patrick Battiston, which somehow went unpunished, and ultimately the Germans won 5–4 on penalties following a 3–3 draw. Shame! Shame! (again).

Similar to Australia in 1974, the New Zealand team which appeared at *their* first World Cup finals, in 1982, included Scots-born players. Defender Adrian Elrick, who hailed from Aberdeen, and midfielder Alan Boath, a Dundee man who had played for Forfar Athletic, both played in the group matches against Scotland, USSR and Brazil.

There were no Scottish match officials at the 1986 finals so it's just as well the *team* made it. Brian McGinlay, the Bard of Balfron, was due to officiate in Mexico that year but apparently withdrew for personal reasons. That was a pity because if he had travelled to Central America, that would have been ten World Cup finals in a row for Scotland; indeed, ultimately it would have been part of 14 in a row.

At Italia 90 we sent George Smith from Edinburgh to Florence to referee the group game between Czechoslovakia and Austria. By way of a thank you he handed out seven yellow cards as the Czechoslovakians won 1–0.

The Scotland team failed to make it to USA 94; however, we were ably represented by comic book hero and former Airdrie footballer Les

'Stanchion Man' Mottram, who flew to Boston to supervise two group games (South Korea 0 Bolivia 0 and Nigeria 2 Greece 0).

To many Americans the word *Dallas* will forever be associated with the assassination of their President John F. Kennedy. For many Scots, however, the word *Dallas* will forever be associated with Hugh, a controversial referee from that grassy knoll known as North Lanarkshire, who was our man in the middle at France 98.

Monsieur Dallas reffed the group match in Bordeaux between Belgium and Mexico that finished 2–2, sending off Gert Verheyen and Pavel Pardo in the process, and so incurred the wrath of pundits Alan Hansen and Martin O'Neill in BBC-land. Good on you, Shuggie. Dallas was also in charge of the quarter-final tie in Saint-Denis in which the host nation overcame Italy 4–3 on penalties after a goalless 120 minutes. No red cards, just the five bookings this time, which included one for Didier Deschamps and one for Alessandro Del Piero. Hughie baby was never one to be star-struck.

Four years later and the Shugmeister is working his magic in South Korea and Japan. In Korea he got two gigs (Portugal 4 Poland 0 – a group game in Jeonju, and a quarter-final tie in Ulsan which ended Germany 1 USA 0). In the latter game he declined a legitimate penalty claim by the Americans and also booked Oliver Neuville for a foul committed by teammate Jens Jeremies – ach, these Germans all look the same don't they?

As a 'punishment' for these two 'oversights' our man was the fourth official when Brazil beat Germany 2–0 in the final in Yokohama. Just think, another two cock-ups and it might have been him instead of Pierluigi Collina that got the big gold medal.

Sadly, we have had no match officials representing Scotland at the last four World Cup finals (2006 to 2018 inclusive), which hurts a little. Sure it is ok for football supporters in Scotland to shout at our referees and their assistants and to tell them that they are visually challenged, next to useless or just plain crap but I don't like the idea of FIFA agreeing with us. Scots referees have, however, played a supporting role at the ultimate match at three World Cup finals and I think we should derive some pleasure from that.

I should also mention Allan John Russell, the Scot who has worked for the English cause at Russia 2018. Allan won particular praise for his work on set pieces, with England scoring the most goals in the tournament from dead-ball situations. He was only a journeyman footballer (with the likes of Hamilton Accies, St Mirren, Partick Thistle, Airdrie United and Kilmarnock) but he obviously knows his stuff, doing his bit to help England to fourth place in the competition.

Looking ahead, however, let's hope for a double celebration at Qatar 2022 – with Scotland's players and officials both putting in an appearance – and just for good measure, let's make it beyond the initial stages as well.

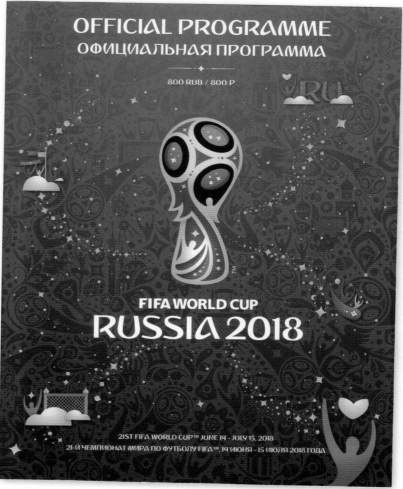

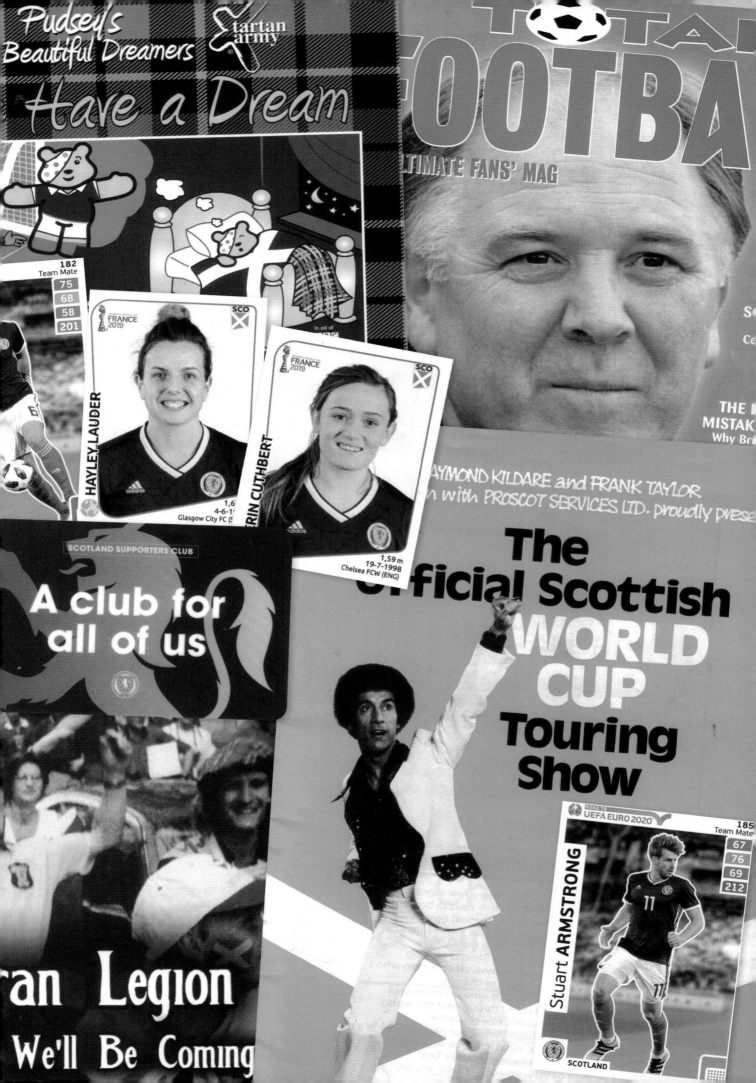

X-CERTIFICATE ATTIRE
SARTORIAL ELEGANCE AND THE TARTAN ARMY

It's now a long time — probably about 50 years or so — since a considerable proportion of the Scotland support would turn up at Hampden Park wearing a suit, shirt and tie, with perhaps only rosettes and tartan scarves/bunnets to enhance the monochrome look. The Tartan Army have, of course, had a few 'Gok Wan' makeovers since then and whilst the multi-coloured gathering of the clans and fancy dans look is mostly pleasing to the eye (as well as to the cameras) I still have a few bugbears that I have to get off my chest, if you will indulge me please.

First things first — I don't like the kilt. It's *highland* dresswear and I'm a lowlander. They say it is great for attracting the ladies but to me it will always be a pleated skirt. Now I know that statement is probably enough to elicit a whole series of death threats from Hoorah Hamishes and the like but that is my humble opinion, so it's 'Callard and Bowsers' for me (denim or black watch tartan) and a wallet in my pocket as opposed to fumbling about in a sporran right in front of my dangly bits when it's my turn to buy a round.

If truth be told I still find it a somewhat disconcerting experience when someone stands next to me at the urinals at a football stadium, then proceeds to lift their skirt (sorry kilt) to reveal a distant (sometimes *very* distant) cousin of the Loch Ness monster. Equally disconcerting is the array of 'meat and two veg' that tends to be on display in whiffy-smelling airport departure lounges the morning after a Scotland away game. And whilst I'm in Victor Meldrew mode, I don't like the Jacobean shirt either — the character Nelly Pledge (played by Hylda Baker in the 1960s TV sitcom *Nearest and Dearest*) had a phrase for it — ***A big girl's blouse***.

As for the Tartan Army 'Babes', well, that's a different matter altogether. They tend to look great in kilts — mini ones especially — irrespective of age, shape or size. Then again, I loved Fran and Anna (a 'mature' Tartan-kitsch singing duo from Coatbridge famed for their rouged cheeks and fishnet stockings).

Oh yes, almost forgot — See you Jimmy hats — the ultimate self-loathing Scottish piss-take, as someone on the *Scotland Epistles* Facebook once said. Anyway, if you've left school but want to reinforce the stereotype whilst looking like a complete eejit, then go ahead and wear one — and yes, I have been that eejit.

Time now to clamber down from my soapbox and own up to some more fashion faux pas of my own. Going to Scotland games in the mid-1970s often involved me tying a tartan scarf round my wrist like a Bay City Roller wannabe. The end result, however, was that I looked more of a Diddy than a Woody.

Talking of scarves and for some daft reason my younger brother Allan and I thought it would be a good idea to wear them at the Spain 82 World Cup finals. In the stifling heat of Malaga and Seville, those neck-appendages helped us stay cool (not), whilst under pressure from New Zealand, Brazil and the USSR. Perhaps it was a case of choosing to be at the opposite end of the numptie spectrum from those supporters who like to go topless when it's around minus five degrees centigrade.

I wised up, however, by the time I went to Genoa for Italia 90 — a time when shorts were short ... and tight. Scotland keeper Jim Leighton might not have appeared too clever when Juan Cayasso struck the winner for

Costa Rica in the 49th minute, but boy did *I* look (and feel) good!

Er, em, moving along and being a bit of a hoarder, I still have all my replica Scotland jerseys in my possession with the medium-sized (i.e. redundant) versions now pinned to the ceiling of my spare room/mini-museum. Of the extra-large versions (let's call them XL, it sounds better), I regularly squeeze into the dark-blue retro top with the white crew-neck from the 1960s. In my dreams I'm either John Greig or Colin Stein but when I'm wearing a jacket and only the white crew neck (dog collar) is visible I'm like a hybrid of *The Vicar of Dibley* and the *Reverend I.M. Jolly*.

My criticisms and misgivings notwithstanding there's no denying that we Scotland supporters do add a bit of colour as well as carnival atmosphere to the proceedings (Qatar will love us – hopefully). It's not just our apparel, though – I don't think there is anything to beat the visual spectacular that is a sea of red and yellow lion rampant flags – in spite of their royal connections. To conclude then on a positive note, in a Scotland that is all too often grey, dreich and miserable, sometimes – just sometimes, we are our own best medicine.

YOU'LL NEVER SWAP ALONE
MISCELLANEOUS MEMORABILIA

When it comes to collecting football memorabilia, the biggies (i.e. programmes, ticket stubs, trading cards, stickers, etc.) all merit chapters of their own. Also worthy of a mention, though, are some of the more unusual Scotland mementoes – however, for obvious reasons we shall exclude some of the more 'dodgy' souvenirs picked up on away trips!

CRAIG BROWN'S TIE

I was delighted when a former member of the London Tartan Army (Lunnain Albannaich) donated to my collection a bright, yellow and blue tie which had been presented to him by the former Scotland manager Craig Brown. The design was the official SFA manager's pattern cum tartan, and when I tried it on I swear I could feel the power surge through me like Thor's hammer! With trembling hands I quickly placed the garment within my display cabinet and have yet to work up the courage to wear it in public.

WEMBLEY '77 VINYL RECORD

This is a naff record with a capital N. One of those productions that falls into the category of 'it's so bad, it's good', if you know what I mean. Sung by Ben Gunn (Scottish folk singer/comedian) with backing from The New Elastic Band, it commemorates Scotland's 2–1 victory over England at Wembley in 1977, as well as the exuberant post-match celebrations (or acts of wanton vandalism, dependent on your point of view). The fact that the record sleeve proudly proclaims that the song was recorded 'Live at Gartcosh Social Club' – rural North Lanarkshire's answer to the Hollywood Bowl – serves only to add to the appealing absurdity of it all.

Back in 1977 my musical favourites were Disco Diva Donna Summer and punk outfit The Stranglers, but I could always make time for a melodic dedication to the oldest international football fixture in the world.

TRIVIAL PURSUIT BOARD GAME – FRANCE 98 WORLD CUP EDITION

I've never broken the seals on the contents of this game – maybe I'll do so if and when Scotland qualify for the finals again. Until then it remains locked safely away like Indiana

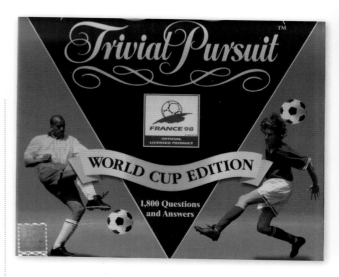

Jones's Ark of the Covenant. Just for the record this board game, which features the Brazilian Ronaldo on the box front cover, was a present from my wife from the days before we were engaged. She was trying to woo me at the time but it's a matter of record that since I met Marion (in 1999) Scotland have failed to qualify for ten successive tournaments. I'm just saying, that's all ...

MODEL STADIA

For a while I had 'Lilliput Lane syndrome' whereby I collected miniature models of stadia at which I had seen Scotland perform/underperform/fail to turn up. The collection included the usual suspects, such as Hampden Park, Ibrox Stadium (the 1–0 mugging of Sweden in November 1996 was my favourite) and Celtic Park (clinching World Cup qualification with a 2–0 win over Latvia in October 1997 stands out).

There was also room, however, for the old Wembley Stadium (where David Seaman broke my heart in the November 1999 Euro play-off second leg), the Emirates Stadium, London (Brazil versus Scotland – a friendly in March 2011) and the Parc des Princes, which I purchased from the Paris Saint-Germain store on the Champs Elysees on a flying visit to the French capital. Later that evening, on 12 September 2007, a James McFadden wonder goal gave Scotland a 1–0 victory in a Euro Championship qualifying match against France. Ultimately we failed to make it to the finals (again) but as Humphrey Bogart said to Alex McLeish, 'We will always have Paris' – and I'll always have the model stadium, the programme, the ticket stub, the photographs, the fixed-odds coupon ... and the poly-bag from the PSG shop.

Now I know you should always try to retain the packaging of your collectables, however, when it comes to stadia models I have to confess to committing a cardinal sin by using the box, which contained Celtic Park, to encase the last remains of my son's pet hamster when we buried him in the back garden. It was a short life but at least he made it to Paradise in the end! I'm beyond therapy ...

PANINI KEYCHAINS/FOBS

Metallic gems from Panini's 2018 heritage collection are the £4.99 keychains featuring historic World Cup album cover fobs (5cm by 4.5cm) which make for wonderful campaign badges/medals – and so Espana 82, Italia 90 and France 98 now dangle proudly from wherever takes my fancy! These historic album covers are also featured on T-shirts which some trendy online shops flogged for around £30, although Sainsbury's did the Italian job for £12, which became a Fathers' Day present to myself. I even held on to the associated tag, which depicts the 12 album cover images available – you can keep your designer labels.

REPLICA TROPHIES

I've got a couple of 'Holy Grails' in the spare room in the shape of official, six inch, metallic replicas of the FIFA World Cup trophy and the Henri Delaunay European Championships trophy. Not only are they attractive to look at but they also serve as a reminder that I've spent a considerable amount of time, energy and money supporting Scotland in pursuit of the real versions – and I wouldn't change a minute of it.

WOODEN SEAT FROM OLD SOUTH STAND AT HAMPDEN PARK, GLASGOW

In 1996, as part of the redevelopment/ rebuilding of Hampden Park, the SFA flogged off the old, black-coloured, wooden tip-up seats from the South Stand. For £10 (or was it £20?) I managed to acquire seat number 54 which came complete with a protective coating of bird droppings. Until that redevelopment, my preferred vantage point at Hampden was the old North Enclosure, but unfortunately the SFA didn't release any of the crush barriers, railway sleepers or urine-infused black ash which comprised that section of the stadium.

Anyway, I still like to think that my South Stand souvenir has been graced by some famous Scottish buttocks – Billy Connolly's, Sean Connery's or even Rod Stewart's? Surely to God, though, I didn't purchase the seat on which Margaret Hilda Thatcher parked her de-industrialised arse at the 1988 Scottish Cup Final? Holy Conservative nightmare, Batman.

ROY AITKEN

JIM BETT

GARY GILLESPIE

ANDY GORAM

RICHARD GOUGH

MAURICE JOHNSTON

JIM LEIGHTON

MURDO MacLEOD

MAURICE MALPAS

BRIAN McCLAIR

ALLY McCOIST

ALEX McLEISH

1990

PAUL McSTAY

WILLIE MILLER

STEVE NICOL

ITALIA 90 ESSO COINS

As a card-collecting child of the 70s one of the biggest disappointments growing up in the north of Glasgow was seeing the ads everywhere for the Esso FA Cup coin collection of 1971/72. The coins depicted the club crest of each of the FA Cup winners up until that season. It was a set of 31 coins with a large coin for the then current holders of the cup – Billy Bremner's Leeds United.

The problem was that I didn't know anyone who owned a car back then, so collecting the set was a non-starter. I did once buy some coins off of a dodgy guy in the school playground but the thumping I got for misuse of my lunch money meant that I was never destined to complete the collection until later in life.

For the Italia 90 World Cup, Esso released a set of cheaper-made coins consisting of players from England and Scotland, with 15 from each. Interestingly, there are included a couple of Anglo favourites who never made the actual squad, i.e. Brian McClair and Steve Nicol. Sadly, Willie Miller never made it to Italy either due to injury.

SFA WRISTWATCH

It might only be a basic, 21st century stainless steel wristwatch complete with SFA lion rampant/saltire two-part crest, but we've been through a lot of hard times together, not least Harry Kane's late, late, late equaliser for England in that June 2017 Hampden World Cup qualifier/ heartbreaker. It was also a gift from the missus so I really wouldn't swap it for a TAG Heuer or a Rolex – more fool you, I hear you say.

Anyways, is it a good timekeeper? Well in Malaga, it will always be five past New Zealand...

By the way, if you think I'm daft, my colleague David Stuart also has the following gems and memories within his collection.

The Esso World Cup Coin Collection

SNICKERS EURO 96 POGS

So who remembers that caps/pogs collecting/ gaming craze that swept the country for about a fortnight way back in the mid-90s? Fortunately for those who don't recall, I can tell you that Pogs were small, circular, cardboard milk caps with a collectable image on the front, and Panini and the Snickers bar people got together to commemorate football coming home with a nice set for the 1996 Euro finals. There were 96 pogs in total to collect, with a smattering of Scots in there too. Eight Scots in fact, including the likes of Colin Hendry, John Collins and Stewart McKimmie. Many are the nights in which I sit and look at my eight pogs and wonder what the hell I am supposed to do with these? Cherish them, of course.

ACTION TRANSFERS

For someone growing up in the early 70s, the occasional Letraset Action Transfer was a must, whether they depicted a favourite TV programme, wild animals or even a football game. Letraset brought out a few footie sets, one of leading players in England and others of actual games, such as England versus Scotland, Rangers versus Moscow Dynamo and Celtic versus Inter Milan – where apparently you can see Dixie Dean hitting his penalty over the bar to enable the Italians to reach the 1972 European Cup Final. Sorry about that, Dixie.

The trick of the transfers was not to rub too hard with a pencil or too lightly, as sometimes as you lifted the transfer sheet up, an arm or a leg would come away from it and your veritable masterpiece was gubbed.

Recently I broke the collectors' golden rule of never buying unseen and so my depiction of the Scotland and Peru match from 1972 (which Tommy Docherty's Scotland won 2–0) has a few things wrong with it, but still somewhere in my heart I love it all the more because of its shortcomings.

International Match 1972

Scotland 2 Peru 0

There was plenty of skill from both sides in the first half but very little push. Asa Hartford went close in the 14th minute and Scottish claims for a penalty were turned down when Law was brought down in the area 10 minutes from half time. There was more bite to Scotland in the second half and O'Hare put them one up after 47 minutes following a free kick from Morgan. Cubillas and Munante played well for Peru but it was Scotland who scored again in the 65th minute when Hartford and O'Hare worked well to give Law the chance to crash home a spectacular shot which went in just under the bar. This was Scotland's first victory over a South American side at International level.

ZZ TOPS
FOREIGN SUPERSTARS AT HAMPDEN

Some of the world's greatest footballers have 'crossed swords' with Scotland at the National Football Stadium and as a football fan I consider myself privileged to have seen a small number of them in action. My 'Magnificent Seven' listed below are but a taster, with the first two named being legends that I didn't actually get to see – being too young or not even born yet was a bit of a hindrance in this respect.

Ferenc Puskas [Hungary]
8th December 1954
Friendly match

Six months after Hungary slipped up in the World Cup Final against West Germany in Berne, an incredible 113,146 came along to Hampden Park on a Wednesday afternoon (!) to see the mighty Magyars defeat Scotland 4–2.

The 'Galloping Major' (to give Ferenc his nickname) didn't manage to score that day and I like to think that was due in part to the performance of Clyde defender Harry Haddock, who was making his Scotland debut.

Puskas would, of course, return to Hampden in 1960 and score four goals for Real Madrid in a 7–3 victory over Eintracht Frankfurt in the European Champions Clubs Cup Final – the second of three European Cup winners' medals collected. Puskas also helped Hungary to the Football gold medal at the 1952 Olympics and scored 84 goals in 85 matches for his country between 1945 and 1956. In addition, he played for Spain on four occasions.

THE ILLUSTRATED BIOGRAPHY OF PERHAPS THE GREATEST FOOTBALLER OF ALL TIME

WITH PREVIOUSLY UNSEEN PHOTOGRAPHS FROM THE PUSKAS INSTITUTE ARCHIVES!

FERENC PUSKAS
'THE MOST FAMOUS HUNGARIAN'

Rézbong Kiadó 2015

MATCH WORLD CUP WONDERS

No. 1 Pele (Brazil)

Pele [Brazil]
25th June 1966
Friendly match

Brazil, winners of the World Cup in 1958 and 1962, stopped off at Glasgow en route to England and an ill-fated attempt at making it three titles in a row. Scotland manager John Prentice awarded debut caps to Peter Cormack of Hibs plus Celtic's John Clark, and the latter's clubmate Stevie Chalmers gave the home side the perfect start with a goal in the first minute.

The game, which was watched by a crowd of 74,933, ended 1–1, however, with Servilio equalising for the visitors after 16 minutes. At the final whistle Pele refused to give his shirt to Billy Bremner as apparently 'The Black Pearl' had taken umbrage at some of the Leeds United man's 'meaty' challenges and so Chalmers was the lucky recipient of the much-coveted Brazilian jersey.

Incidentally, Pelé and co prepared for that match by training at the ground of Troon Juniors FC – it proved as famous a sighting as Elvis Presley at nearby Prestwick Airport six years previous.

Pelé would, of course, get his third World Cup winners' medal at Mexico in 1970 and would retire from international football the following year, having scored 77 goals in 92 appearances for Brazil.

EUSÉBIO (PORT)

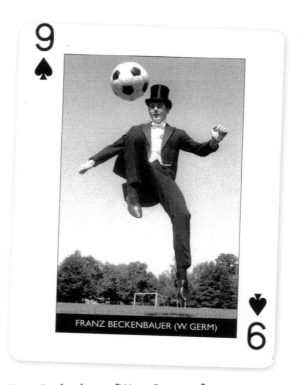

FRANZ BECKENBAUER (W. GERM)

Eusebio [Portugal]
13th October 1971
Euro Championship qualifier

My first ever Scotland match was also Tommy Docherty's first game as Scotland manager and the total attendance was 58,612. The opposition were Portugal, who had finished third at the World Cup five years previous having lost in the semi-finals to the eventual winners. Portugal's Eusebio won the Golden Boot award at that 1966 World Cup thanks to his nine goals, and the former European Footballer of the Year would lead the attack against Scotland. Scotland were victorious, however, as Rangers's Sandy Jardine somehow helped snuff out the threat of Eusebio, and headed goals from John O'Hare and his Derby County teammate Archie Gemmill either side of a Rui Rodrigues free kick made it 2–1 for the boys in dark blue.

Eusebio was a class act, however, on and off the park, and so it was great to have seen the striker nicknamed 'The Black Panther' before he retired from international football in 1973, having scored 41 goals in 64 appearances for his country.

Franz Beckenbauer [West Germany]
14th November 1973
SFA Centenary celebration match

In between winning the 1972 European Championship and the 1974 World Cup, West Germany's elegant sweeper (he created the concept) and skipper (aka Der Kaiser) strutted his stuff at Mount Florida. 58,235 of us were at Hampden that night to see our captain, Billy Bremner, go toe to toe with the Bayern Munich man in a game that Scotland should have won but had to make do with a 1–1 draw. Bremner missed a penalty would you believe?

Beckenbauer won three consecutive European Cup winners' medals (the third was collected at Hampden in 1976), was European Footballer of the Year in 1972 and 1976, and would win a total of 103 caps for the Federal Republic of Germany (to give them their Sunday name) between 1965 and 1977. Just prior to German reunification in 1990 Der Kaiser also managed his country to World Cup glory at Italia 90.

DIEGO MARADONA (ARG)

Diego Maradona [Argentina]
2nd June 1979
Friendly match

Diego Armando Maradona (Scotland's 'Player of the Year' in 1986) was an advanced playmaker in the number 10 position, who was well-nigh unstoppable the day he scored his first senior international goal for Argentina in front of 61,918 at Hampden Park in a 3–1 victory for the then reigning world champions. The scorer of the Scotland goal was Leeds United's Arthur Graham, who, like Maradona was a surprising omission from his country's 1978 World Cup squad. Diego would, of course, collect his World Cup winners' medal at Mexico 86 on his way to 91 caps and 34 goals for his country.

Hampden was again a happy hunting ground for the man from Buenos Aires when in November 2008 he managed Argentina for the first time and 32,492 saw the visitors win another friendly match, 1–0. In 2000 he won the FIFA Player of the Century award.

Andrea Pirlo [Italy]
3rd September 2005 – World Cup qualifier

Peerless Pirlo was a deep-lying playmaker in midfield who appeared 116 times and scored 13 goals for Italy between 2002 and 2015, and who was instrumental in the Azzurri's 2006 World Cup triumph in Germany. Indeed, he was named Man of the Match in the final itself. He also picked up six Serie A and two Champions League winners' medals, amongst a whole raft of honours.

In the qualifiers for the 2006 World Cup, Italy came up against Scotland and in the fixture at Hampden, with 50,185 looking on, Pirlo appeared effortless in dealing with the likes of Barry Ferguson, Nigel Quashie and Darren Fletcher to help ensure that his team, who trailed 1–0 at half-time thanks to a Kenny Miller goal, fought back to earn a 1–1 draw. Six months earlier in Milan, Andrea (let's call him Andrew) had put two superb 25-yard free kicks past the Scotland keeper Rab Douglas (yes, just the two) to give Italy a 2–0 victory.

Andres Iniesta [Spain]
12th October 2010
Euro qualifier

The central midfielder is the most decorated Spanish footballer of all time (including four Champions League winners' medals and 131 caps between 2006 and 2018), and he was key to Spain's unprecedented three consecutive major titles – Euro 2008, World Cup 2010 (scoring the winning goal in the final) and Euro 2012.

On their way to qualifying for Euro 2012, Spain had to overcome Scotland – Phil Bardsley, Davie Weir, Graham Dorrans et al. At Hampden Park, and in front of a crowd of 51,322, Iniesta ran the show and scored a goal as the then reigning world champions won 3–2.

A lack of space prevents proper mentions to other great players, such as Lev Yashin (goalkeeper for USSR – friendly, May 1967); Carlos Valderrama (Colombia, creative playmaker – Rous Cup, May 1988); Gheorghe Hagi (Romania, attacking midfielder – Euro qualifier, September 1990); Andriy Shevchenko (Ukraine, striker – Euro qualifier, October 2007); Luka Modric (Croatia, playmaker – World Cup qualifier, October 2013); and Robert Lewandowski (Poland, striker – Euro qualifier, October 2015), to name but a few.

Notable exceptions, however, to a list of the greats who have faced Scotland at Hampden include Johan Cruyff, Lionel Messi and Cristiano Ronaldo, with possible reasons for their absence from Mount Florida on international duty being injury, loss of form or just plain crapping themselves. Aye, right! Real Madrid's French genius Zinedine Zidane did, of course, grace the national stadium when he orchestrated the 2002 Champions League Final.

Flipping the coin, I can't help but wonder if opposition supporters still recall fondly the day Lee Wilkie graced the playing fields of Hong Kong, Braga and Amsterdam.

BIBLIOGRAPHY AND ACKNOWLEDGEMENTS

Ward, A. – *Scotland The Team* (Derby: Breedon Books, 1987)

Lamming, D. – *A Scottish Internationalists' Who's Who 1872–1986*
(Bridlington, Hutton Press, 1987)

Cairney, J. – *A Scottish Football Hall of Fame* (Edinburgh, Mainstream Publishing, 1998)

Keir, R. – *Scotland – The Complete International Football Record* (Derby: Breedon Books, 2001)

Scott, A. – *Fitba Gallimaufry* (Cheltenham: SportsBooks Limited, 2006)

Hayes, D.P. – *Scotland! Scotland! The Complete Who's Who of Scotland Players Since 1946*
(Edinburgh: Mercat Press, 2006)

Davies, H. – *Confessions of a Collector* (London: Quercus, 2009)

Devlin, J. – *International Football Kits – The Illustrated Guide*
(London: Bloomsbury Publishing plc, 2018)

MacPherson, A. – *Adventures in the Golden Age – Scotland in the World Cup Finals 1974–1998*
(Edinburgh: Black & White Publishing, 2018)

Daily Record newspaper archives.

Thanks also to the websites: www.londonhearts.com and www.fitbastats.com

And thank you to the Scottish Football Museum for kindly allowing the inclusion of photographs taken within the confines of that must-see visitor attraction.

Also available at all good book stores

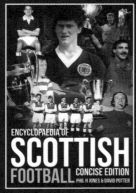

9781909626294

9781848182004

9781905411832

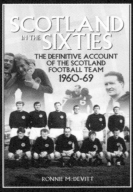

9781785311802

9781785314391

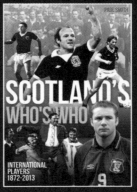

9781909178847

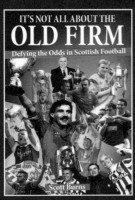

9781785313172

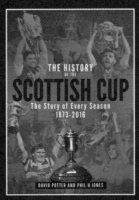

9781785312144

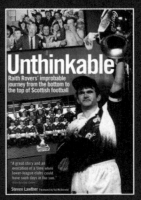

9781909626645